Instructor's Manual to Accompany

The Critical

Reader, Thinker,

and Writer

W. ROSS WINTEROWD
University of Southern California

GEOFFREY R. WINTEROWD
University of Southern California

Mayfield Publishing Company
Mountain View, California
London • Toronto

International Standard Book Number: 0–87484–929–2

Manufactured in the United States of America

Mayfield Publishing Company
1240 Villa Street
Mountain View, CA 94041

Preface

Teachers who use <u>The Critical Reader, Thinker, and Writer</u> will find that this Instructor's Manual reflects the book in an important way: like the book, the manual results from the collaboration of an old pro (Ross) with an informed layperson (Geoff). The Old Pro has explained the technical and scholarly background for the chapters; most of the answers to discussion questions are by the Informed Layperson. Thus, those responses to discussion questions can serve as models against which students' responses can be judged.

A word about the discussion questions throughout <u>The Critical Reader, Thinker, and Writer</u>: The first questions of the group following a selection (usually about the first five) relate directly to the concepts developed in the present chapter and, in the case of Chapters 3 and 4, the concepts developed in preceding chapters. Thus the questions are cumulative, demonstrating that even though each chapter focuses on a given set of concepts, those concepts apply generally, not merely to certain types of texts. The rest of the questions relate to the structure of the essay and to the ideas and values it expresses.

All of the exercises and questions in the book have been reprinted in this manual so that the the instructor need not continually flip back and forth between book and manual. Occasionally a question is expected to elicit responses so varied or so subjective that we have not attempted to suggest a response; nevertheless, we have reprinted the question itself.

We felt that exercises for Chapter 5, "Researched Writing," were unnecessary and might even be an encumbrance. Thus there is no "apparatus" for that chapter here.

We would welcome suggestions for improvement of both the book and this manual. Please write to us in care of Mayfield Publishing Company, 1240 Villa Street, Mountain View, CA 94041.

W. Ross Winterowd
Geoffrey R. Winterowd

Contents

3. Thinking Critically about Exposition   77

4. Thinking Critically about Argument and Persuasion   155

5. Researched Writing

[No material included in Instructor's Manual]

1. Critical Reading, Thinking, and Writing

The purpose of the chapter is to show students that meaning is not somehow buried in the text, as the Comstock Lode was buried in the mountains around Virginia City; on the other hand, readers are not free to claim that the text means whatever they want it to mean. Readers construct meaning on the basis of information supplied by the text and the knowledge that they bring to it. Reading, like writing, is transactional.

Background and Sources

Goodman, Kenneth. "Reading: A Psycholinguistic Guessing Game." Journal of the Reading Specialist 6 (1967): 126-35. In this classic essay, Goodman explains reading as a process of sampling a text, predicting meaning, testing that prediction, and then either confirming or re-predicting. Goodman conceived of the text as a series of cues that enable readers to derive meaning.

Smith, Frank. Understanding Reading. 4th ed. Hillsdale, NJ: Erlbaum, 1988. This is an excellent layperson's introduction to the psychology and pedagogy of reading.

Taylor, Insup, and M. Martin Taylor. The Psychology of Reading. San Diego: Academic, 1983. Taylor and Taylor give a synoptic treatment of psychological and psycholinguistic work in reading. The book is technical but well worth the effort for readers who are interested in the scientific background of reading theory.

Winterowd, W. Ross. "To Read" and "To Learn to Read." The Culture and Politics of Literacy. New York: Oxford UP, 1989. 57-102.

Page 2. How We Read

Which analogy works best: the reader is like a miner, digging the buried meaning out of the text, or the reader is like a detective, constructing meaning on the basis of "clues" that the text provides? Neither analogy is perfect, but the reader-detective correlation helps students understand that they take an active part in making the text mean. The danger of the reader-detective analogy is that students might conclude that all texts have a "solution," a definitive meaning that can be proved beyond reasonable doubt. You might point out to students that the Supreme Court of the United States provides ongoing "readings" of the Constitution and that in Western civilization the Bible is perhaps the richest source of discussions about meaning.

Pages 2-3. Exercise: Miner or Detective?

In your opinion at this point, is the reader more like a miner, digging meaning out, or like a detective, constructing meaning? Explain your opinion. The following questions might help you.

1. If you pronounce the words in a text but don't und2erstand the information or ideas, can you say that you have read the text? (What if someone asks you to summarize what you have read?)

Discussion should lead students to understand that we read for meaning, not for sound. For example, suppose that I (silently) read the following sentence: "We took the lift to the seventh floor." Suppose further that someone asks me what I have just read, and I respond, "We took the elevator to the seventh floor." Obviously, I have derived the meaning of "lift" and have repeated that meaning in terms of my own vocabulary. I have not _mis_read. (Perhaps, however, I have given inaccurate information to the person who asked the question, since the term "lift" implies that the action took place in Great Britain, whereas "elevator" places the action in the United States.)

2. No machine--even the most sophisticated computer--can "read" a text and then summarize the meaning. Do you think that at some time in the future machines will be able to read, in the full sense of that word? Why or why not?

Computers can "read" in the limited sense that they can scan a text, "translate" it into computer language, and store it; they can also play it back word for word. They cannot, however, derive the gist of the text and then repeat it. If computers could do this, we would be in the age of artificial intelligence. Communicating long-distance with a computer, one would be unable to determine whether or not a human was intervening. In other words, HAL of 2001: A Space Odyssey would be a reality.

3. If someone asks you to summarize a text that you have read, do you simply repeat the words and sentences of the text, or do you express the meaning in your own words? What does your answer imply about your reading process?

The question reinforces the idea that we read for meaning, not for sound and not for the surface form of the text: words, sentences, or passages. The question should also lead students to realize that they remember ideas, gists, and even details of information, but not the exact language that appears in the text.

Page 4. Exercise: Filling Gaps in Texts

What are the most important gap fillers you supply when you read the following text? To get you started, some of the gaps at the beginning have been filled in.

You might, at this point, want to introduce students to the semantics of textual coherence. The "gaps" are _implicatures_: _presupposition_, which is knowledge taken as given, and _inference_, knowledge derived from the text but not directly stated. Take the following sentence as an example:

The twenty-five-year-old man will marry the octogenarian millionairess.

Among presuppositions that understanding the text entails: both the man and the woman are now single; both have consented to the marriage. One inference, of course, is this: the man is marrying the woman for her money. If asked to explain the sentence, a reader would be quite likely to say, "A young man is going to marry an old woman for her money." Another likely inference is that the speaker or writer of the sentence has passed an unfavorable moral judgment on the young man.

Page 7. Exercise: Your Knowledge of the Language System

Paradoxically, we know very little about what we know about language. We learn the "rules" of language without realizing that we are doing so and without being able to explain these rules. For instance, we are able to use adjectives correctly without being able to explain why or how: the beefy wrestler; the wrestler, beefy and odoriferous; Beefy, the wrestler. . . . This exercise will demonstrate to students that they do have a significant knowledge of the English language.

One member of each of the following pairs is "correct," or idiomatic English--that is, what a person whose native language is English would say or write. Which ones are idiomatic? Try to explain the "rule" or principle that governs the correct usage (but do not be at all discouraged if you cannot give an explanation, for in most cases only a trained linguist could do so).

1a. Bertrand no have enough money to buy a Rolls Royce.
1b. Bertrand does not have enough money to buy a Rolls Royce.

In 1a, the faulty use of the negative ("no have enough money" as opposed to "does not have enough money") marks the user as non-native. No native speaker would make this particular error.

2a. Alexander Pushkin is author of novel Dead Souls.
2b. Alexander Pushkin is the author of the novel Dead Souls.

In Russian, definiteness and nondefiniteness are unmarked; hence, the absence of the definite article in 2a makes us suspect that the speaker is Russian.

3a. The document official gives custody of the estate to a trustee.
3b. The official document gives custody of the estate to a trustee.

In English (unlike French), attributive adjectives precede their nouns; thus, we suspect that 3a was spoken or written by a non-native.

4a. There is no doubt that Jacqueline must lose weight.
4b. There is no doubt that Jacqueline lose weight must.

In German the modal auxiliary comes at the end of subordinate clauses: "Es gibt keinen Zweifel, dass Jacqueline Gewicht abnehmen muss." Sentence 4b was clearly not generated by a native speaker.

5a. Dabney bringed his computer to class with him.
5b. Dabney brought his computer to class with him.

The verb form <u>bringed</u> might well have been used by a child who is a native speaker of English. In standard English, the past and past participle of <u>bring</u> are <u>brought</u> and <u>brought</u> (<u>brought</u> the computer yesterday, has <u>brought</u> the computer many times). However, the forms <u>brang</u> and <u>brung</u> are common among children and some adult speakers (<u>brang</u> the computer, has <u>brung</u> the computer many times).

Page 8. World Knowledge

In <u>The Culture and Politics of Literacy</u>, W. Ross Winterowd discusses cultural literacy thus:

> During the summer of 1987, <u>Cultural Literacy</u>, by E. D. Hirsch, Jr., remained high on the national list of best sellers for several weeks, a fact that gives evidence of widespread concern about <u>both</u> literacy <u>and</u> culture. (A book very much akin to <u>Cultural Literacy</u>, Allan Bloom's <u>The Closing of the American Mind</u>, was higher on the lists and remained longer.)
>
> Now then, the crux of the issue regarding cultural literacy--which Hirsch defines as "that knowledge that enables a writer or reader to know what other writers and readers know within the literate culture" ("Reading" 146) is not "whether," but "what?" How could literacy be other than cultural? Might one conceive of a disembodied literacy, an abstraction, independent of scene and a tradition of texts? How could reading specialists teach students the "skill" of understanding "the patience of Job" or "sour grapes"?
>
> Hirsch is one of many who present evidence that literacy is critically declining in the United States and that the need for literacy is ever more compelling. (For example, regarding the Scholastic Aptitude Tests: " . . . out of a constant pool of about a million test takers each year, 56 percent more students scored above 600 in 1972 than did so in 1984. More startling yet, the percentage drop was even greater for those scoring above 650--73 percent") (Hirsch, <u>Cultural</u> 5). Which brings us to the subtitle of Hirsch's book: <u>What Every American Needs to Know</u>, to which we might add the sub-subtitle <u>in Order to Be Literate</u>. The answer is crucial. One needs some specialized knowledge and a great deal of general knowledge, <u>intensive</u> and <u>extensive</u> learning (Hirsch, <u>Cultural</u> 127-33).
>
> In order to understand this morning's newspaper, I need an enormous reservoir of general knowledge concerning Kurt Weill, HMOs, the American Kennel Club, the Persian Gulf, the Supreme Court, and on and on, but in order to function in my profession I need to know about and understand in depth such matters as "illocution" and "perlocution" (from speech act theory). (By the way, in order to understand the letters I receive from friends, I need equally specialized knowledge.) And the reasoning leads to the inevitable question: In what does cultural knowledge--and hence cultural literacy--consist? Hirsch and his colleagues Joseph Kett, a historian, and James Trefil, a physicist, all of the

University of Virginia, answer the question with a list of some 4,500 or 5,000 items, developed primarily by the three principals.

I must now forestall objections to what Hirsch and his colleagues did. First, they do not set themselves up as cultural dictators. Second, they view their list as provisional and invite the dialectic of response and critique. "The authors see the list as a changing entity, partly because core knowledge changes, partly because inappropriate omissions and inclusions are bound to occur in a first attempt" (Hirsch, Cultural 146). I find it impossible to understand how anyone could object to the project of cultural literacy so far. Of course, one might argue for a radical individualism, with each person inhabiting his or her own cultural universe; however, Hirsch is merely saying, "If we want to communicate, we must have a body of shared knowledge."

Hirsch repudiates formalism (drills, dry-run exercises)--in theories of literacy, in educational practice, and in his own earlier work--yet clearly his cultural literacy project implies a kind of formalism. By this I mean that one does not become culturally literate merely by absorbing a body of information. Or the point can be made another way: one will not absorb a body of cultural information until one is attitudinally prepared to do so. The fundamental cause of the literacy crisis is not lack of skills _or_ lack of information, but unwillingness or inability to change cultures.

Case studies of the development of reading and writing ability in individual homes (e.g., Taylor and Bissex) or among social groups (e.g., Scribner and Cole, Heath, Schieffelin and Cochran-Smith, and Scollon and Scollon) convey what is almost a truism: children in homes where reading and writing are highly valued unconsciously _acquire_ cultural literacy almost inevitably, and those homes are part of societies or social groups in which literacy has value.

The "uses" of literacy within a society--the advantages that it bestows--determine not only the "level" but the consequences.

No one, I think, would argue with the premise that a higher level of national literacy will come only through a higher level of nationally shared information. The question is how to bring about that sharing--and, I suppose, in a discussion of cultural literacy, the usefulness of a list for the goal.

The distinction between _acquiring_ language subconsciously and _learning_ it consciously is important here. Acquisition takes place as a natural consequence of using language to communicate. For example, in the process of trying to get meaning from language and to make meaning with it, a child discovers the rules of grammar and uses them with more and more accuracy, which is to say that the child acquires the language system without consciously attempting to master rules, and, in fact, the number of rules that can be consciously mastered is extremely small, considering the complexity of language. In spite of the long school tradition, people do not learn language through studying "grammar."

The question I am leading up to, of course, is whether or not people can gain cultural literacy by studying lists or, indeed, by studying canons. Suppose the four or five thousand items in the Cultural Literacy list do, indeed, roughly map out the territory of our culture. How are students meaningfully to learn those items? I would argue that the key is <u>acquisition</u>, not conscious learning, acquisition taking place only when the focus is on semantic intention, on purpose, not on items.

In fact, I think that the <u>deconstructionist</u> educational theories of Paulo Freire hold the answer to the question of cultural literacy. Freire would argue that we can achieve cultural literacy only through what he calls "problem-posing education," in effect, a productive redefinition of "acquisition" that means "learning" involves gaining information through attempting to deal with existential problems (<u>Pedagogy</u> 67).

Hirsch advances telling arguments against the content-neutral ideas of Rousseau and Dewey (<u>Cultural</u> 19). However, Freire would counter that culture has no hard-and-fast parameters, but is continually created by creators who reinterpret what is and was and who contribute their own works to the immediate future. Thus, the problem of cultural literacy is not so much one of compiling lists as demonstrating through a dialogic and loving pedagogy that every human is part of the culture-making process.

> Thus the educator's role is fundamentally to enter into dialogue with the illiterate about concrete situations and simply offer him the instruments with which he can teach himself to read and write. This teaching cannot be done from the top down, but only from the inside out, by the illiterate himself, with the collaboration of the educator. (Freire, <u>Education</u> 48)

Hence, Freire and his colleagues were skeptical of "primers" (<u>Education</u> 49). From one point of view, cultural literacy, as developed to this point by Hirsch, is primer-bound.

In fact, the real problem in cultural literacy is not one of canons or lists, but of creating the dialogue whereby culture is made.

Page 8. The following is a glossary for the list of terms on the page:

<u>acid rain</u>: pollution caused when sulfur and nitrogen dioxides combine with atmospheric moisture to produce rain or snow containing sulfuric and nitric acids.

<u>Bangkok</u>: capital of Thailand.

<u>cartel</u>: an international organization of manufacturers, united to fix prices and control supplies of goods.

<u>Degas</u>: French painter and sculptor (1834-1917), famous for his studies of ballerinas.

<u>Ellington, Duke</u>: American jazz musician and composer (1899-1974).

<u>fascism</u>: theory of government that glorifies the state and gives the state control of every aspect of life. The term was first used by the party that Benito Mussolini founded in 1922.

<u>gamma rays</u>: one of three types of rays emitted by an element that has an unstable nucleus. The other two types of rays are alpha and beta.

<u>holding company</u>: a corporation organized to buy interests in other corporations.

Irish Republican Army: known as the IRA, organized by Michael Collins in 1916. The goal of the IRA is unification of Ireland and independence from Great Britain.

Jazz Age: the 1920s; the Prohibition Era.

King Lear: Shakespeare's tragedy set in pre-Roman Britain; first performed in 1606.

malignancy: a cancerous tumor.

NATO: North Atlantic Treaty Organization, a defense pact among Belgium, Canada, Denmark, France, Great Britain, Greece, Iceland, Italy, Luxembourg, the Netherlands, Norway, Portugal, Turkey, the United States, and West Germany. The first nations joined the pact in 1949.

orbit: the path in space of one body (such as the moon or a satellite) revolving about a larger body (such as the earth).

Paine, Thomas: American writer and patriot (1737-1809); author of Common Sense, an argument for the separation of the American colonies from English rule.

quasars: a shortening of "quasi-stellar radio source." When they were discovered, quasars were believed to be the most distant objects in the universe.

realpolitik: politics based on current situations as they develop, not on theories or ideologies.

Scopes trial: In 1925, John Scopes was charged with illegally teaching the theory of evolution in Tennessee. He was defended by Clarence Darrow and prosecuted by William Jennings Bryan. Scopes was found guilty. The case is known as "the monkey trial."

Tarzan: the fictional character (of novels, funny papers, and films) who was adopted by apes and grew up in the jungle. Edgar Rice Burroughs invented Tarzan.

United Nations: international organization established after World War II for the purpose of maintaining international peace.

Van Allen Belt: two belts of radiation extending from about 400 to about 40,000 miles above the earth.

WASP: white Anglo-Saxon Protestant.

x-ray: electromagnetic radiation, used in medicine as a diagnostic tool.

Yom Kippur: day of atonement, the most sacred Hebrew holy day, falling at the end of September or the beginning of October.

Zapata: Emiliano Zapata (c. 1879-1919), a Mexican revolutionary.

Page 9. Exercise: Your World Knowledge

For a computer to be able to read, it would need an enormous bank of "world knowledge." For example, to understand the following passage, a computer would need to "know" that crane has two meanings: (1) a device for hoisting and (2) a bird. If the machine were to read the following sentences, it would need to "know," among other things, that devices for lifting do not stand on one leg in the swamp, but that some birds do, and that birds are incapable of lifting twenty tons.

1. The crane was standing on one leg in the swamp.
2. The crane could lift twenty tons.

Here is your problem. What "knowledge" would the computer need in order to understand the meaning of it in the following sentences?

1. The cat fell off the roof because it was slanted.

2. The cat fell off the roof because it was sick.

Among other knowledge the computer would need in order to determine the antecedent of it is the following: First of all, it would need to know what cats and roofs are and that cats are not slanted, but roofs sometimes are. It would need to know that cats can be sick, but roofs can't--except metaphorically. And it would need the ability to distinguish metaphor from literal statement. (As a metaphor, "sick roof" makes perfectly good sense: "We had to have our sick roof replaced before the rainy season started.")

Page 12

"The Achievement of Desire"
Richard Rodriguez

1. What sorts of readers do you think Rodriguez has in mind? (For example, is he writing for specialists in some field? For Mexican Americans? For teenagers?) On what evidence in the text do you base your opinion?

One of the most striking images in Rodriguez's essay is that of the scholars who patronize the British Museum, sitting next to each other on a daily basis without acknowledging each other's presence, and revealing precious little emotion. The author presents view of academic life that is almost a cliche, a view that people with diverse educational backgrounds, from the high school dropout to the doctoral candidate, also share. In addition, Rodriguez's description of elementary and high school should be familiar to all regardless of whether or not the reader is a "scholarship boy or girl."

Nonetheless, there is also a part of the autobiography that is addressed to a more limited audience. The selection's major theme, that of alienation, arises both from Rodriguez's drift from the working class culture of his Mexican American family and its attendant home life towards the culture embodied by public schooling and from Rodriguez's drift away from the world of public interaction to the seclusion of the scholarly life. Thus, the book's theme would probably best be understood either by people with a college education who belong to minorities or by those who come from working class backgrounds, or both.

2. Explain "scholarship boy." What sort of person and student is a "scholarship boy"? Cite evidence from the text to back your opinion. Is the "scholarship boy" a critical thinker? Explain.

Among the traits of the "scholarship boy": a working class background which doesn't emphasize education; a degree of intelligence; guilt feelings as a result of choosing school over family; ambition; the desire to achieve intellectual success by following a preordained curriculum or course of study even if it does not suit his or her talent; having less intellectual curiosity than desire to achieve; "He is the great mimic; a collector of thoughts, not a thinker."

On some level, of course, the scholarship boy is a critical thinker. For example, Rodriguez read many classic novels in order to obtain a moral from the story. Even his simplistic analysis of Wuthering Heights ("the danger of 'letting emotions get out of control'") at least questioned the reason that the novel was written even if he tended to overlook the obvious point that the book can also be read for pleasure.

The scholarship boy, however, is more eager to please his teachers than to think critically. Rodriguez and Hoggart portray the scholarship boy as reciting back what the teachers wish to hear and diligently trying to find the "right answer" as if more than one opinion on any one subject could not exist. This tendency to rely on and memorize the opinions of others rather than formulate one's own ideas, this acceptance of the entire school curriculum, is the scholarship boy's downfall as a critical thinker because the critical thinker should naturally self-generate questions as he or she encounters opinions, arguments, or written texts.

3. Rodriguez tells of the consequences his mother suffered when she misspelled a word.

> **One morning there was a letter to be sent to a Washington cabinet officer. On the dictating tape, a voice referred to urban guerrillas. My mother typed (the wrong word, correctly): 'gorillas.' The mistake horrified the anti-poverty bureaucrats who shortly after arranged to have her returned to her previous position. She would go no further.**

Why would such an apparently unimportant mistake have such grave consequences? What does it say about the typist's world knowledge?

The letter being written was addressed to a sophisticated audience with a wide command of the English language. The letter's misspelling implies that the writer (or the writer's typist) doesn't have a sure grasp of the language. Even though most people would realize that the letter was typed by another, still the mistake would reflect on the author of the letter, making it a less than trivial matter of concern.

4. Explain why Rodriguez was upset by his parents' failure to read for pleasure. What did pleasure reading mean to him? Do you share the same idea of pleasure reading? Why or why not?

Rodriguez prized reading as the sign of an education and learning. His mother's failure to read Willa Cather's My Antonia showed Rodriguez how little education his mother had actually received. In addition, it made pointedly clear the distance between Rodriguez and his parents as the boy became more and more educated. The paragraph that contains the reference to My Antonia begins, "It mattered that education was changing me. It never ceased to matter." Finally, the mother's lack of interest in reading Cather's book for pleasure revealed her inability to understand her son and his own motivations and pleasures. ("But at home I would hear my mother wondering, 'What do you see in your books?'. . . Always, 'What do you see . . . ?'")

5. Rodriguez says, "In the sixth grade I simply concluded that what gave a book its value was some major idea or theme it contained. If that core essence could be mined and memorized, I would become learned like my teachers." Clearly, the value of a book comes from other factors as well as the major idea. In your opinion, what are some of those factors?

Rodriguez begins to answer this question almost immediately after writing that statement: "In spite of my earnestness, I found reading a pleasurable activity." "Reading [Dickens'] fat novels, I loved the feeling I got--after the first hundred pages--of being at home in a fictional world where I knew the names of the characters and cared about what was going to happen to them." "My habit of reading made me a confident speaker and writer of English." "Reading also enabled me to sense something of the shape, the concerns, of Western thought." That is to say, reading helped Rodriguez with his ability to empathize with other people, gave him confidence, and helped him to understand the culture in which he lived.

6. Explain why Rodriguez did not actually read the Republic.

Reading is not only comprehending the written word but also understanding how words fit together in a unified whole to create meaningful text. Rodriguez admits, "Most books, of course, I barely understood. While reading Plato's Republic, for instance, I needed to keep looking at the book jacket comments to remind myself what the text was about."

7. What other aspects of reading do you think Rodriguez overlooked when he read the important books of world literature? Explain what the author means when he says, "I was not a good reader. Merely bookish. . . . "

Rodriguez did not read as much for pleasure as he did in order to obtain "epigrams, scraps of information, ideas, themes. . . ." In one sentence he admits, first, to having been merely bookish and, next, that he lacked a point of view. In other words, he did not critically compare the ideas and opinions expressed in a book with those opinions and ideas which he himself possessed. Instead, he absorbed the book's point of view unquestioningly.

8. "How, after all, could one read a book more than once?" asks Rodriguez. In what ways can one reread a book and truly call it reading?

What Rodriguez seems to be implying by his question is that he viewed reading as if he were a miner, digging out tne core meaning of the book. Once he felt that he had extracted this core meaning, the scholarship boy saw no reason to reread the book.

9. In your own words, state the main point of this selection.

Rodriguez emphasizes his main point with italics: "<u>A primary reason for my success in the classroom was that I couldn't forget that schooling was changing me and separating me from the life I enjoyed before becoming a student</u>."

The opening part of the selection leading up to this thesis statement emphasizes the point. Rodriguez writes that he was ashamed of the grammatical errors made by his parents when they spoke (they rarely wrote) and his father's inability to understand second-grade arithmetic instructions. Rodriguez then flashes forward to his graduate work at the British Museum and his discovery of <u>The Uses of Literacy</u>, in which Richard Hoggart vividly portrays the schism between the scholarship boy's life at home and at school. After this, Rodriguez details the myriad small instances that revealed the increasing separation from his parents as he grew toward manhood. A telling incident occurs when a nun asks Rodriguez why he is reluctant to read by himself. The reason, unstated by Rodriguez, is that the act of reading is a solitary activity that creates, to some degree, feelings of loneliness and isolation. In the final section of the piece, Rodriguez is at the height of his educational career, studying in the British Museum, never talking or saying hello to the many other scholars whom he sits next to on a daily basis.

10. When asked by the nun why he was so reluctant to read by himself, what reason does Rodriguez give? Compare this with his mother's complaint about how their family was changing. Do you believe that there is some correlation between the two? Explain.

As explained in the answer to question 9, reading is a solitary pursuit, and as a scholarship boy, Rodriguez felt isolated in any case. At the same time, Rodriguez was becoming more distant from his parents as a result of his increasing educational sophistication and because of the great amount of time that he devoted to his studies. At the same time, his mother regretted the loss of closeness which the family had had before Rodriguez entered school. ("Why weren't we close [Rodriguez writes, paraphrasing his mother], 'more in the Mexican style'?") As a sign of this increasing distance, Mrs. Rodriguez asked that her children retain their ability to speak Spanish. As Rodriguez studied at the kitchen table, his mother would read his lessons over his shoulder. Writes Rodriguez, "Instead of the flood of intimate sounds that had once flowed smoothly between us, there was this silence."

11. According to Rodriguez, what is the goal of education? Do you agree? If not, what do you think it is?

The selection concludes with some thoughts on what education has meant to the author. In essence, Rodriguez states that education allowed him to think and reason in the abstract. This had both a negative and positive aspect. It removed the author from the life of immediacy; he could not simply, unquestioningly encounter experiences without first thinking about their meaning. On the other hand, abstraction allowed him to deal with issues that he would not otherwise have been able to contemplate.

Such a goal has ancillary results, which Rodriguez discusses throughout the chapter. For the child whose second language is English, education gives the child the self-confidence to succeed in the larger culture from which his or her parents are alienated. No matter what problems of his own education Rodriguez might admit, it certainly gave him the assurance with which to travel to different countries and mingle with educated people.

Rodriguez also gained satisfaction from academic achievement. Although the education might have been more superficial than he wished it to have been, nonetheless it gave him the rewards that a person in a minority culture needs to have when confronting the larger society around him.

12. Why do you think this chapter of Hunger of Memory was titled "The Achievement of Desire" rather than "The Desire for Achievement"?

The desire for achievement is the mark of the scholarship boy. He follows the instructions of the teachers and writes down their comments unquestioningly. His motivation is not so much the desire to learn as the desire to achieve. Rodriguez regrets that his motivations were such because they created a rather joyless, dispassionate life. What he wishes to achieve is the ability to relish his existence without the alienating effect of rationalization and intellectualization as filters on his experiences.

Page 33

"I Developed the Ability to Read Closely"
Mike Rose

1. Explain what Mike Rose learned about close reading from Don Johnson.

"Mr. Johnson was helping me develop an ability to read difficult texts--I was learning how to reread critically, how to tease out definitions and basic arguments. And I was also gaining confidence that if I stayed with material long enough and kept asking questions, I would get it." Rose explains how Johnson directed his students back to the text and to carry on a dialogue with the text in order to derive its meaning.

2. The chapter from which this selection comes is entitled "Entering the Conversation," which means the acquisition or cultivation of the knowledge, intellectual abilities, and language skills a person needs to participate fully in the educated community. In what ways did Dr. Carothers help Mike Rose enter the conversation? (What did Rose learn from Dr. Carothers?)

Within the classroom, Dr. Carothers provided a history of English literature and a historical context for individual works.   But as Mike Rose writes, "he started his best work once class was over." Dr. Carothers helped Rose enter the dialogue by showing how academic life can fuse with social and personal life. Carothers did so by keeping long office hours during which students could drop in to talk and by creating the English Society. The English Society held poetry readings, became a recognized organization on Loyola's campus, and sponsored social events such as card games or the barbecues which Dr. Carothers had at his home.

3. What did Rose learn from Dr. Erlandson? Explain why you think it was or was not an important lesson.

Dr. Erlandson taught Rose that good writing can be regarded as a craft; that is, it is a skill which can be learned and is not simply the result of a "gift" which some people have and others don't. Erlandson helped Rose develop an ear for writing, the ability to spot awkward phrases by reading the sentences out loud to see how they sound. But Erlandson did not simply show Rose which sentences required changes; he showed the student how to revise so that the sentences were simpler and more intelligible.

4. Rose tells us that Erlandson "rarely used grammatical terms, and he never got technical." In your opinion, would grammar lessons have helped Rose? Explain.

Traditional grammar ("a noun is the name of a person, place, or thing; a verb names an action or state of being"), with its fill-in-the-blanks and identify-by-underlining exercises, does not help students use language more accurately or effectively. However, grammar as usage ("in formal writing, one uses the term 'person' rather than 'guy'") can be effective. Massive evidence leads to the conclusion that teaching formal grammar of any variety--traditional, structural, transformational-generative--does not help students improve their writing abilities. See

> Elley, W. B., and others. "The Role of Grammar in a Secondary School Curriculum." Research in the Teaching of English 10 (1976): 5-21.
> Hartwell, Patrick. "Grammar, Grammars, and the Teaching of Grammar." College English 47 (1985): 105-27.
> Williams, Joseph M. "The Phenomenology of Error." College Composition and Communication 32 (1981): 152-68.

5. Father Albertson asked three kinds of questions. Explain those types, and discuss how such questions would help students become critical readers.

The first type of questions, those which are broad and speculative, help the reader see the "forest" rather than the "trees." They were designed to get the students thinking about the work as a whole. The second set concerned themselves with specifics within the text, pertaining to the author's techniques, and they help the readers pay close attention to details. The third set were designed to set the work within a historical context by asking the reader questions which related the text to a critical or historical study. The three sets of questions are complementary. The questions relating to details show how the overall effect, the concern of the first set, is achieved. The third set help explain which of the techniques and ideas within the text are unique to the author and which are conventional for the times. Taken together, they show the student various ways in which to approach and to understand literature.

6. The section on Don Johnson ends with these sentences:

> **I rang the bell and heard steps on a hardwood floor. Mr. Johnson opened the door and stepped out. He was smiling and his eyes were attentive in the light . . . present . . . there. They said, "Come, let's talk."**

What is the meaning of these sentences? What do they tell you about Mike Rose's educational experiences? What do they tell you about his concept of teaching?

Teaching for Don Johnson was a dialogue conducted with his students: "'Come, let's talk.'" And the anecdote about teaching The Metaphysical Foundations of Modern Science reads almost like a Socratic dialogue. Rose believes that the best teaching is done at the personal level, that it is an activity which the professor conducts with students, each of whom he is aware of as an individual. Each of the other teachers helped Rose on an individual basis and discussed his problems with him rather than simply dictating the correct answers.

7. As Mike Rose characterizes it, "Nothing is more exclusive than the academic club: its language is highbrow, it has fancy badges, and it worships tradition. It limits itself to a few participants who prefer to talk to each other." How do you feel about this club? Are its effects on society positive or negative? Explain why you would or would not want to belong.

The point of Rose's essay is that the professors he most remembers and is most indebted to would not generally be considered typical members of the academic club (with the possible exception of Father Clint Albertson). An interesting contrast to Rose's undergraduate experience is that of Richard Rodriguez's graduate studies as described in "The Achievement of Desire."

Page 43

"From Outside, In"
Barbara Mellix

1. In contemporary American society, what might have been some possible consequences if Mellix had not mastered standard English?

Mellix certainly wouldn't have been able to become an academician without mastering standard English. In fact, virtually every white collar job in America requires that employees use standard English. As a result, without such mastery Mellix probably wouldn't have been able to advance professionally or economically in today's society. (An interesting variation on this question: Should society force people to abandon their native dialects, or should social attitudes toward dialect change?)

2. Do you have two "languages"--one that you use at home and with friends and one that you use in other situations (such as your classes in college)? How do the two languages differ? Why are the two languages necessary? Does everyone have several "languages" for use in different situations?

Most people have two languages. The stockbroker, for example, employs not only standard English in the workplace but also the argot of his calling (e.g. "leveraged buyout," "selling short," "selling long"). Even people whose work doesn't require special terminology change the way in which they speak when they are outside of the workplace. At home, for instance, when one is around family members speech is oftentimes abbreviated. Answers of simply a "yes" or "no", "yeah" or "nah" to questions are given where a more formal and expansive response would be required in other situations. A great deal of humor has been derived from a person's use of a "second" language in a public place which normally would require standard English. Much of Groucho and Chico Marx's humor derived not just from turning the English language inside out but doing it while attending high society functions.

3. What are your reactions to the following passage? What are its implications? Do you agree or disagree with Mellix's point?

"To speak," says Frantz Fanon, "means to be in a position to use a certain syntax, to grasp the morphology of this or that language, but it means above all to assume a culture, to support the weight of a civilization." To write means to do the same, but in a more profound sense.

The authors agree with this statement in one respect but disagree with it in another. Because speech is generally more spontaneous and less reflective than writing, it tends to assume a culture more readily than the written word. For example, Mellix's "second" language says much about the black culture within which she was raised while her essay communicates only the fact that she has quite a good deal of education. The writing style would not indicate to the reader that the author is black. Standard English also assumes a culture.

4. Do you think the title "From Outside, In" would be appropriate for the selections by Richard Rodriguez and Mike Rose? Why, or why not?

None of the three authors was born into a family which used standard English. Rodriguez's parents spoke primarily in Spanish, Mellix's family used black American dialect, and Mike Rose's family was part of the lower middle class which didn't require the use of standard English. In their selections, all three discuss the difficulties of learning to speak and write in standard English while attempting retain the feeling and emotion of their "first" language. First they simply imitated the form and style of standard English. Only later did they learn how to express themselves easily and naturally in standard English. All recognized, and Rodriguez writes movingly of this, that one of the keys to their future success in the American mainstream is the mastery of standard English.

5. Why do you think it was easier for Mellix to write about other people's thoughts and feelings than about her own?

The greatest writing problem faced by Mellix as she began her college career was self-consciousness. Her need to express herself in proper English stymied her natural expressiveness so that she was more concerned with rules of grammar than with conveying her ideas in a lively, interesting manner. When she was writing about others, some of her self-consciousness fell away. She was not required to reveal her own feelings directly. In addition, Mellix was ambivalent about her use of the public voice when writing because she felt that it was not part of her own culture and heritage. Writing about others allowed her to use the language of "others" without this sense of betrayal or guilt.

Page 53

"The Invisible Discourse of the Law"
James Boyd White

1. Explain the "invisible discourse" of the law.

White defines invisible discourse as "the unstated conventions by which the language operates." These conventions are the shift from a language of description to a language of judgment (the necessity of applying a rule to a situation), the false appearance of deductive rationality (the inability oftentimes to eliminate ambiguity by simply reasoning logically), the necessity of arriving at a definitive decision when the issue might actually be more complex than the decision implies, and the necessity of remaining consistent in diverse situations.

2. What is "the plain English movement"? Why would its objectives have limited effect on legal literacy?

From White's perspective, the plain English movement "aims at a translation of legal language into comprehensible English." However, because of the problems inherent in the invisible discourse of the law--which are independent of the complexity of the language used, problems which require the reader to use legal reasoning regardless of the phrasing or style of the text-- there will always be difficulties in achieving legal literacy.

3. Explain the shift from a language of description to a language of judgment.

The shift from a language of description to a language of judgment occurs when an interpreter attempts to fit the "if, then" clauses of the law to a particular situation. The "if" clause describes the conditions which must be met, and the "then" clause determines the penalties that will result should those conditions be met. The shift occurs in determining whether the particular situation fits the description in the "if" clause.

4. **In what ways does the following summary apply to the discourse of other groups with which you are familiar? Reread the summary, substituting for** legal **such terms as** fraternity, sorority, family, baseball, and CB.

> [W]hat characterizes legal discourse is that it is in a double sense (both substantively and procedurally) constitutive in nature: it creates a set of questions that define a world of thought and action, a set of roles and voices by which experience will be ordered and meanings established and shared, a set of occasions and methods for public speech that constitute us as a community and as a polity. In all of this, legal discourse has its own ways of working, which are to be found not in the rules that are at its center of the structure but in the culture that determines how these rules are to be read and talked about.

5. **Does the process of discerning the meaning of legal writing seem more like discovering meaning (mining) or recovering meaning (detecting) to you?**

White's article emphasizes the major role of the reader in understanding the law; the whole discussion reinforces the concept of reading as a constructive process of detection rather than reading as discovering a meaning buried in the text. The reader must resolve ambiguities in the definitions and must determine for himself or herself that a particular situation fits the description contained in the law.

6. **Technical terms such as** felony, writ, **and** mandamus **are very common when lawyers are writing for the general public. Do you feel that they should substitute everyday language for such terminology? Explain.**

There is a fine line between the appropriate use of plain English and the attempt to "dummy down" to the reader. The use of these technical terms is certainly common within the legal domain, and any dictionary contains their definitions. "Felony" is in the general vocabulary, although "writ" and "mandamus" are not. The answer to this question is a value judgment that each person must make.

7. **White's notion of literacy is more involved and extensive than most people's notions. How would White determine whether a person is completely literate in legal discourse?**

White believes legal literacy includes the ability not only to understand the literal meaning of the law but also to reason from these general, abstract principles and apply them to particular situations. Legal literacy is almost equated with the ability to reason legally.

8. **Does White present a convincing case for the need to increase legal literacy? Explain.**

In the second paragraph of his essay, White convincingly sets forth the need for legal literacy. He notes that our society is increasingly "legalistic and litigious," that citizens need to know how to protect their own self-interest in matters such as drafting wills, dealing with landlords or tenants, dealing with the police, or coping with the Social Security Administration. Within the first and second paragraphs, White makes clear that the average citizen can learn to be legally literate without comprehensive instruction in the law and that such a skill is useful.

9. Explain "the false appearance of deductive rationality."

The false appearance occurs when there is the slightest ambiguity in the use of words. The person using the law must decide whether the general rule fits the specific situation. By necessity, the general rule must be more vague than the specific situation. The problem occurs when one uses logic to limit the ambiguity. As White notes, oftentimes strict logic is of no help in reducing the ambiguity.

Page 65

"The Language of the Bureaucracy"
Janice C. Redish

1. What sorts of readers do you think Redish has in mind? (What are their levels of education? Their socioeconomic status? Their interests?) Explain your opinion.

2. Which details in the selection did you find particularly interesting or useful? In what ways do these details contribute to the meaning and effect of the piece?

3. Why is Example 1 so difficult to read? Does it consist of words or concepts that you are not familiar with? Is its grammar unduly complex?

The intent of the regulation is comprehensible only after several careful readings. The words and concepts are ones that the layperson understands (with the exception of a grade of papaya designated as Hawaii No. 1), but the syntax is extremely complex. The regulation consists of two exceptions and three provisions to the second exception, all of which are explained in a run-on sentence.

The regulation could be more clearly expressed as follows:

Between January 1 and April 15, 1980, the only papayas which can be shipped to the production area are either immature papayas which conform to paragraph 928.152 of these regulations or those which receive a grade of at least Hawaii No. 1. The grading of the papayas allows for no more than 5% of the fruit to have serious damage, no more than 1% to be immature, and no more than 1% to suffer decay. In addition, the total percentage of defects shall not total 10%. Finally, each papaya must weigh at least 11 ounces.

4. The author states that regulations that are difficult to read are often the result of a conflict between the writer's intention and the purported reason for publishing the regulations. Explain.

It is Redish's contention that many regulations are written by people who are protecting themselves. As writers, they try to cram in every detail that their supervisors might consider important. The clarity of the writing is not as much of an issue when the supervisor reads the text since he or she is so familiar with the information that it is comprehensible even if it is written in a convoluted style. In addition, these writers are concerned that every fine point be laid out in the regulation so that anyone who violates the regulations can be said to have been warned.

5. Did you have to look up the definition of <u>nominal</u> in order to understand the point made about nominal writing? Why, or why not? Would you classify the term <u>nominal writing</u> as jargon? Why, or why not?

The author gives sufficient context for the reader to deduce the meaning of <u>nominal</u>. Even if the reader did not know the exact definition, the point of the section on the style of writing has so many examples that the author's point about use of the nominal form is understandable. The term <u>nominal writing</u> is jargon. It is a term used by composition instructors, English professors, linguists, and the like to denote a particular style of writing. <u>Nominal writing</u> is not jargon in the pejorative sense of pretentious, inflated use of language where simpler terms would do just as well. The term <u>nominal writing</u> is simpler than, for example, "the use of nouns rather than verbs."

6. How does the organization of this article assist you in understanding its main points? Can you use these techniques in your own writings for school?

Redish uses headings, subheadings, and a great number of examples to highlight the points she is making. In addition, the article introduces bureaucratic writing, allowing the reader to understand the general nature of the problem before Redish starts to define that problematic style and prescribe remedies. Even in the subsections, Redish uses an introductory statement and outlines to orient the reader. For example, Redish very simply introduces her section on style: "Bureaucratic writing that is difficult to understand has three major stylistic problems. It is nominal, full of jargon, and legalistic." In addition, because the author introduces many key points in her essay, she uses bullets in her summary toward the end of the essay. She also uses bullets to highlight the major points of the discussion to follow. All of the organizational and stylistic techniques employed by Redish could be directly applied to any college student's writing.

7. What organizational characteristics of a bureaucracy contribute to bad writing?

Since a bureaucracy has distinct, clearly defined areas of responsibility (within the larger organization), it is only natural that the workers within its structure would begin to use words which they fit to their own particular working circumstances. That is, they develop a jargon which often creeps into their writing inappropriately. People who wish to advance or move around in the organization (by definition a bureaucracy consists of many smaller, interlocking offices which comprise the complete organization) tend to play it safe and write in the same style as has been used in the past, what Redish terms institutional inertia. The fact that a bureaucracy is required by another part of the government to produce a written regulation quickly (time pressures) and that the document must be approved by other levels of the organization (review process) are both additional structural impediments to clear writing. Redish points out several other factors which contribute to bureaucratic writing (legal tradition, the government as impersonal guardian of the public welfare, traditional models, social prestige, lack of training), but these deal less with the bureaucratic structure per se. The class, however, might very well disagree. For example, because a good number of the important workers who comprise the bureaucracy are lawyers, one might argue that the legal tradition is indeed one of the structural impediments to clear writing.

8. Explain the distinction made between the words simplify and decomplexify. How does this relate to document writing?

Ideas or instructions can often be simplified with no loss of information. Complex writing does not necessarily mean that the ideas or instructions contained within are themselves complex. Decomplexify means to make less complex or less convoluted; simplify means to make a difficult idea or instruction less hard to understand by omitting some of the nuances or concepts so that the overall intent or meaning can be understood. Redish would support the concept of decomplexified writing and would argue that such writing would not necessarily mean that the concepts would be simplified, as well.

9. What, according to the author, is the intention of the public passive style? What is the intention of plain English?

The public passive style is used to imply an impartial and fair institution, such as the federal government. Plain English is simply the attempt to write in a clear, comprehensible style for the intended readers, who might well come from diverse backgrounds. Redish provides the example of the instructions for applying for a Basic Educational Opportunity Grant as an example from a "small but growing body of well-written, direct, personal, and understandable bureaucratic documents," although such a style is not identified as plain English until later in the essay. Such instructions are made for one of the largest, most diverse populations and must be comprehensible to all. The CB regulations are another set which go out to a large pool of readers, many of whom have not attended college.

10. The 1970s saw the rise in the plain English movement. What events during that decade affected the movement's development?

Deregulation, dissatisfaction with the size of the bureaucracy in general and the amount of paperwork which it required, and the rise of consumerism all influenced the plain English movement, at least within the bureaucracy.

11. Do you feel that college instruction in bureaucratic writing is appropriate? Why, or why not? Why do you think that so few colleges offer such courses?

The authors believe that higher education has a twofold purpose: to prepare the student to succeed in the work force and to become a productive citizen within the larger world around him or her: in other words, professional training and what is often called "liberal education" in the sciences, the social sciences, and the humanities. Bureaucratic writing fits in well with the first goal. However, we also feel that the business major should not simply take a course in business writing but should also be well versed in the other forms of composition traditionally taught in the first year of college. The instructor might find it interesting to determine from the class which majors hold to which opinion. Do prelaw students think bureaucratic writing is appropriate training? Do English majors find it appropriate?

Page 92

"Of Studies"
Francis Bacon

1. As a critical reader, what is your opinion of Bacon's views of the uses of learning in the essay? For example, do you believe, as Bacon says, that "histories make men wise"?

2. Explain why Bacon's characterization of books--those that are "tasted," those that are "swallowed," and those that are "chewed and digested"--does or does not fit your own reading patterns. If these categories do fit your own reading patterns, provide specific examples of books for each category.

This question is designed to point out that different texts demand different reading strategies. Two major variables that influence the manner in which the reader approaches the reading task are the complexity of the writing and thoughts contained within and the amount of interest the reader brings to the subject. An unauthorized biography written by Kitty Kelley, for example, is not difficult for anyone who can read a newspaper and could certainly be skimmed through quickly without a significant loss of understanding. A busy politician, for example, might wish to read Kelley's biography of Nancy Reagan in order to learn what is written in that book but probably would not wish to wade laboriously through the entire tome. On the other hand, an enemy of Nancy Reagan might wish to savor every spiteful sentence, consuming the book with relish and delight. Most people reading the Reagan biography lie somewhere between these extremes. That is, they read the book thoroughly but quickly without much pause for reflection. On the other hand, one could not simply browse through <u>Ulysses</u> by James Joyce because the writing and ideas are so complex that they cannot be "digested" quickly. The Bible, to cite another example, is a work whose writing is clear but whose ideas are deep. A speed reader would lose both the "message" and the manner of the book.

3. Some essays analyze their subjects (for example, "The Invisible Discourse of the Law," by James Boyd White). Other essays are speculative, discussing what might have been or what might be (for example, the one by Lewis Thomas). Still other essays are interpretive, explaining a problem, an experience, or a belief (for example, "The Achievement of Desire," by Richard Rodriguez). Is this essay analytic, speculative, or interpretive? Given the subject matter, what topics might the author cover if he were to slant the essay toward one of the other two possibilities?

The essay is extremely analytic. Bacon divides books into the categories mentioned in question 1 (those to be merely sampled, those to be read quickly, and those to be read slowly and carefully). In addition, he prescribes a particular course of study in order to complement or to improve various personality traits. Insofar as an interpretive essay is subject to debate or to the consideration of alternatives, "Of Studies" precludes interpretation. Likewise, if the essay were speculative, the author's pronouncements would not be so adamant or peremptory.

4. Do you think that the essay is meant to persuade the reader? Why, or why not?

Given the dogmatic tone of the essay, it would be justifiable to conclude that Bacon is pronouncing, not persuading. However, the thesis of Bacon's essay (the last sentence, "So every defect of the mind may have a special receipt") is a call to action. Bacon wants the reader to take specific actions to remedy particular intellectual weaknesses (study the Schoolmen if one cannot easily make distinctions; study mathematics if one's mind wanders).

5. The following sentence is, in important ways, like some other sentences in the essay: "Reading maketh a full man; conference a ready man; and writing an exact man." What characteristic of this sentence stands out prominently? What is the effect of this characteristic on you, the reader? In your opinion, is this sentence effective or ineffective?

In style, the sentence is perfectly balanced, as are other sentences in the essay:

> Studies serve for delight, for ornament, and for ability.
> Their chief use
>   for delight
>   is in privateness and retiring;
>   for ornament
>   is in discourse;
>   and for ability
>   is in the judgment of disposition of business.

6. What type of studies do you think the author might prescribe for someone who was attempting to become learned? Cite parts of the text that support your opinion.

The essay is, of course, a characterization of Renaissance education. A student commenting on the essay might remark that the study of Latin is highly regarded by Bacon for there are two Latin phrases in his essay. In addition, one of the phrases is from Ovid's Heroides. A study of the classic Greek and Roman authors must also have been highly regarded by Bacon. He seems to see history as a miracle cure-all for the educationally impaired because that area of study makes people wise, witty/ingenious, subtle, deep, and able to contend or debate. The author mentions other areas of study which also are highly regarded by him: mathematics, rhetoric, natural philosophy, logic, and the law. The essay itself is predisposed towards philosophy and logic, and surely Bacon prized these two areas of study highly. Nonetheless, because the point of the essay is to explain and persuade the reader how he or she can become a well-rounded and educated citizen, Bacon values each of these areas of learning as important in a person's educational growth.

7. If you had written "Of Studies" for your composition class, would your instructor have remarked that your discussion was too general, that you needed to supply more detail and examples? Why, or why not?

Students should note the generality of the essay. The points are not illustrated or supported. What books are to be tasted, which ones chewed, and what others swallowed? Why should this be the case. "Of Studies" is not a five-paragraph expository essay, with an opening paragraph that contains the thesis statement, two paragraphs that provide support or evidence for the thesis, and the fifth paragraph summing up.

8. Explain your reaction to the following "Poetical Essay" by Bacon. Is it in your opinion a good poem? Why, or why not? Is it a good essay? Why, or why not? Besides having meter and rhyme, in what other ways does the "Poetical Essay" differ from "Of Studies"? Which of the two is easier to read? Which is easier to understand? Why?

The world's a bubble, and the life of man less than a span;
In his conception wretched, from the womb so to the tomb:
Curst from the cradle, and brought up to years with cares and fears.
Who then to frail mortality shall trust,
But limns the water, or but writes in dust.

Domestic cares afflict the husband's bed, or pains his head.
Those that live single take it for a curse, or do things worse.
Some would have children; those that have them moan, or wish them gone.
But is it then to have or have no wife,
But single thraldom, or a double strife?

Yet since with sorrow here we live opprest, what life is best?
Courts are but only superficial schools to dandle fools.
The rural parts are turned into a den of savage men.
And where's the city from all vice so free,
But may be term'd the worst of all the three?

Our own affections still at home to please is a disease:
To cross the seas to any foreign soil perils and toil.
Wars with their noise affright us: when they cease, we are worse in peace.
What then remains, but that we still should cry
Not to be born, or being born to die.

Page 96

"The Literature of Knowledge and the Literature of Power"
Thomas DeQuincey

1. According to DeQuincey, what is the essential characteristic of literature? What qualities or characteristics must a text have for <u>you</u> to view it as literature?

The characteristic that sets literature off from other writings is universality: "some relation to a general and common interest of man, so that what applies only to a local, or professional, or merely personal interest, even though presenting itself in the shape of a book, will not belong to literature."

2. "What do you learn from <u>Paradise Lost</u>?" asks DeQuincey. And his answer: "Nothing at all.   What do you learn from a cookery book?   Something new, something that you did not know before, in every paragraph." Why does DeQuincey claim that we learn nothing from <u>Paradise Lost</u>? What seems to be his conception of knowledge?

The "literature of knowledge" provides information, "Something new, something that you did not know before." The "literature of power" gives "exercise and expansion to your own latent capacity of sympathy with the infinite." It makes you a more sensitive and more elated person. "All the steps of knowledge, from first to last, carry you further on the same plane but could never raise you one foot above your ancient level of earth, whereas the very first step in power is a flight--is an ascending movement into another element where earth is forgotten."

3. What does one gain from the literature of power?

See question 2.

4. Is it possible for one reader to view Paradise Lost **as literature of knowledge and another reader to take it as literature of power? Explain.**

Most works of literature reflect the times in which they were written, the moral beliefs, the people's conception of their place in the universe, and so on. Paradise Lost richly captures ideas and beliefs and for a historian could be a valuable source of information about the times in which it was written. Such a reader would be viewing the work as a literature of knowledge rather than power.

5. Can a piece of literature be both powerful and informative? How does the distinction between knowledge and power relate to your own reading preferences?

Most literature is both powerful and informative. The great realistic novel of the nineteenth century and modern nonfiction novels are examples. Charles Dickens is not only a great teller of stories but also a significant social historian and critic. Norman Mailer (in, for example, The Executioner's Song) is not only a significant social historian and critic, but also a great teller of stories. It is inconceivable that a person could read Paradise Lost without understanding its knowledge base (i.e., Milton's theology). Knowledge and power are at opposite ends of a spectrum. In our analysis, Stephen Hawking's A Brief History of Time is far to the left, toward the "knowledge" pole of the spectrum; Annie Dillard's Pilgrim at Tinker Creek is well toward "power," on the right; and Peter Matthiessen's magnificent work The Snow Leopard is in the middle since it is both exceptionally informative and lyrically powerful.

Page 102

"The Library of Babel"
Jorge Luis Borges

1. Here is the biblical account of the Tower of Babel. Explain how Borges's story relates to it.

Now the whole world had one language and a common speech. As men moved eastward, they found a plain in Shinar and settled there.

They said to each other, "Come, let's make bricks and bake them thoroughly." They used brick instead of stone, and tar instead of mortar. Then they said, "Come, let us build ourselves a city, with a tower that reaches to the heavens, so that we may make a name for ourselves and not be scattered over the face of the whole earth."

But the Lord came down to see the city and the tower that the men were building. The Lord said, "If as one people speaking the same language they have begun to do this, then nothing they plan to do will be impossible for them. Come, let us go down and confuse their language so they will not understand each other."

So the Lord scattered them from there all over the earth, and they stopped building the city.
                                        --11 Genesis, New International Version

Babel has become a symbol of any organization which has grown so large and cumbersome that effective communication among the members is impossible. The library in Borges's story is likened to Babel because it is so large that its inhabitants rarely meet each other and the vast number of variant texts make absolutely no sense.

2.   If we are in the Library of Babel and the library is infinite, what consequences might we suffer in regard to our search for understanding?

The implication of Borges's story is that the search for meaning is ultimately a hopeless endeavor because not only is the "library" infinite, but it is also random. The story is very effective in presenting this viewpoint. However, this argument ignores a very real fact: the universe is not random. There is order in its structures: subatomic particles ordered in particular ways compose the atom, atoms are arranged in particular ways to create molecules, many types of molecules are arranged in particular order, and so on. Human life is one of the greatest counters against randomness. Not only is the human intelligence ordered, but it also has the ability to reconstitute itself continually into higher levels of order that did not exist previously. That is, human intelligence is a form of order that is self-generating.

3. Is there some order, some system, in the library?   Explain.   (For example, can there be order when possibilities are infinite?)

The narrator contends (in the last paragraph) that although the library is infinite, the texts in the volumes of the library are finite.   Therefore, the narrator concludes that the volumes in any given direction repeat themselves, and it is in this repetition, which does not vary, that order can be found.   The narrator states, "My solitude rejoices in this elegant hope."   Borges implies that the human condition cannot live with disorder and that it strives to find order in the external universe.   As mentioned previously, it is the human species itself which contains order, but it is the sad and lonely pursuit of the narrator to look for this order in the external world.

4. Give the literal meaning of the following allegorical passage:

> **Other men, inversely, thought that the primary task was to eliminate useless works.   They would invade the hexagons, exhibiting credentials which were not always false, skim through a volume with annoyance, and then condemn entire bookshelves to destruction: their ascetic, hygienic fury is responsible for the senseless loss of millions of books.   Their name is execrated; but those who mourn the "treasures" destroyed by this frenzy, overlook two notorious facts. One: the Library is so enormous that any reduction undertaken by humans is infinitesimal.   Two: each book is unique, irreplaceable, but (inasmuch as the Library is total) there are always several hundreds of thousands of imperfect facsimiles--of works that differ only by one letter or one comma.**

The library represents, of course, the repository of all knowledge.   At its most literal, the allegory points out that knowledge is not held by any one person or contained in any one book and so cannot be eliminated by destroying a particular volume or silencing a particular individual. The allegory has resonance with particular episodes in history during which censorship and, in particular, book burning was rampant, such as Germany in the 1930s.

5. What is "the total book"?

The total book would be the equivalent of God: that which is omniscient and would justify our existence. The link between the total book and God is made clearer when Borges relates heaven to the discovery of the tome. "May heaven exist, though my place be in hell. Let me be outraged and annihilated, but may Thy enormous Library be justified, for one instant, in one being."

6. Borges warns, "You who read me, are you sure you understand my language?" In light of this warning, do you think Borges views readers as miners or detectives?

This question refers the student back to the discussion of reading in the first chapter.

7. The light in the Library is "insufficient, incessant." Allegorically, what does the light stand for?

Conventionally, light stands for understanding or knowledge.

8. Why are the library rooms hexagonal? (What other common structure is made up of hexagonal cells?)

Honeycombs are made up of hexagonal cells. Is Borges implying that the "librarians" are drones without a concept of totality? Furthermore, the hexagon implies more structuring than does a square, as if there were an order to the universe.

9. Does Borges believe in God? Explain. Since he is forever confined to the Library, could he learn the ultimate truth about God?

Borges seems to be an uneasy theist. For example:

(a) Man, the imperfect librarian, may be the work of chance or of malevolent demiurges; the universe, with its elegant endowment of shelves, of enigmatic volumes, of indefatigable ladders for the voyager, and of privies for the seated librarian, can only be the work of a god. (103)

(b) To me, it does not seem unlikely that on some shelf of the universe there lies a total book. I pray the unknown gods that some man--even if only one man, and though it have been thousands of years ago!--may have examined and read it. If honor and wisdom and happiness are not for me, let them be for others. May heaven exist, though my place be in hell. Let me be outraged and annihilated, but may Thy enormous Library be justified, for one instant, in one being. (106-7)

10. What is Borges's opinion of most books? How do you know?

They are formless and chaotic. (See page 104.)

11. What are the "Vindications" in the following quotation: "Thousands of covetous persons abandoned their dear natal hexagons and crowded up the stairs, urged on by the vain aim of finding their Vindication."

They are "books of apology and prophecy, which vindicated for all time the actions of every man in the world and established a store of prodigious arcana for the future" (page 105). These can only be holy books: the Bible, the Koran, and so on.

12. Did you find "The Library of Babel" interesting? Intriguing? Enjoyable? Uninteresting? Overly difficult? Obscure? Explain your answer.

2. Thinking Critically about Narratives

The purposes of the chapter are (1) to give students an understanding of narrative and a method of analyzing it critically and (2) to demonstrate the uses of narrative to explain, argue, and persuade.

Background and Sources

Your students might find it interesting and useful to think about the nature of stories. In Tropics of Discourse, the historian Hayden White distinguishes between chronicle and story. A chronicle is a list of events, one after another in their time sequence; it has no logical beginning, middle, or end. Here, from The World Almanac 1988, is a chronicle of some of the important dates in the exploration of the South Pole:

> 1911--Roald Amundsen (Norway) with 4 men and dog teams reach the pole Dec. 14.
>
> 1912--Capt. Scott reached the pole from Ross Island Jan. 18, with 4 companions. They found Amundsen tent. None of Scott's party survived. They were found Nov. 12.
>
> 1928--First man to use an airplane over Antarctica was Hubert Wilkins (Britain).
>
> 1929--Richard E. Byrd (U.S.) established Little America on Bay of Whales. On 1,600 mi. airplane flight begun Nov. 28 he crossed South Pole Nov. 29 with 3 others.

To make this chronicle into a story (that is, a history), a writer would supply a logical beginning, explaining the importance of the subject and discussing the reasons for the effort to reach the South Pole. And the story, of course, would have a logical ending--even though exploration of Antarctica is ongoing. In other words, (1) a story has a structure that consists of a beginning, a middle, and an end; (2) the writer or story teller--whether a historian or a novelist--explains the reasons or motives behind the actions in the tale.

It will be obvious to many that Kenneth Burke is the guiding spirit of this chapter. He is one of those unique American geniuses, like Ben Franklin, Thomas Edison, and Buckminster Fuller, who fits into no categories. He has influenced philosophers, social scientists, literary critics, and historians. One of his most important contributions to the analysis of both history and texts--that is, to critical thinking--is what he calls the Pentad, which in A Grammar of Motives he explains in this way:

> What is involved when we say what people are doing and why they are doing it? An answer to that question is the subject of this book. The book is concerned with the basic forms of thought which, in accordance with the nature of the world as all men [and women] necessarily experience it, are exemplified in the

attributing of motives. These forms of thought can be embodied profoundly or trivially, truthfully or falsely.   They are equally present in systematically elaborated metaphysical structures, in legal judgments, in poetry and fiction, in political and scientific works, in news and bits of gossip offered at random.

We shall use five terms as generating principles of our investigation. They are: Act, Scene, Agent, Agency, Purpose. In a rounded statement about motives, you must have some word that names the act (names what took place, in thought or deed), and another that names the scene (the background of the act, the situation in which it occurred); also, you must indicate what person or kind of person (agent) performed the act, what means or instruments he used (agency), and the purpose. Men [and women] may violently disagree about the purposes behind a given act, or about the character of the person who did it, or how he did it, or in what kind of situation he acted; or they may even insist upon totally different words to name the act itself. But be that as it may, any complete statement about motives will offer some kind of answer to these five questions: what was done (act), when or where it was done (scene), who did it (agent), how he did it (agency), and why (purpose). (xv)

This, in brief, is Burke's explanation of dramatism and its five key terms. This Pentad is both powerful and portable, an extraordinarily useful tool in critical reading and thinking.

The Pentad is obviously powerful in analyzing narratives--stories, whether factual (as in history or the newspaper) or fictional (as in novels and films). To understand Hamlet, we need to know about the characters (agents), what they do (acts), where and when the actions take place (scene), what means were used to carry out the action (agencies), and the reasons for the actions (purpose). What sort of person was Hamlet (agent)? What exactly did he do (act)? Where and when did he perform the act or actions (scene)? What means did he use to perform them (agency)? Why did he perform them (purpose)?

However, we can view any text as an act performed by an agent (the author) at a given time and in a certain place (scene), with the help of some agency (or several agencies such as a computer on which the author composes the text and the college literary magazine that publishes it), and for some purpose.

This double nature of the Pentad makes it an extremely useful tool in critical reading, for it allows us to ask the important questions about all kinds of texts. For example, when we analyze an argument in behalf of some position, we want to know as much as we can about the arguer (agent): his or her background, philosophy, politics, and so on; the scene in which the argument arose: the time and place, the political and social conditions of the scene, and much more; the agency or agencies whereby the argument is conveyed: for example, television, newspaper, radio.

From this point of view, the act is what the author did. In other words, the act is the text itself. If your students can summarize the plot of a novel or short story or outline the development of an expository text or argument and state the gist, they have demonstrated that they comprehend what I. A. Richards in his classic book Practical Criticism called "the plain sense." (Such comprehension, however, is often difficult to achieve. Reading even just to grasp the "plain sense" of the text is frequently hard work.)

The gist, or thesis, of a text is not necessarily the same as the purpose of the text. For example, the gist of an editorial might be the argument that taxes are too high. The purpose of the text, however, would be to effect change in the tax code by persuading readers to support the author's point of view.

One maxim regarding the attempt to get the plain sense of the "act" (or text) is this: be objective. No reader is a "blank slate" upon which the opinions and arguments of the text can be written. Everyone brings his or her own world knowledge to the text, the prior experience that forms the basis for the reader's own attitudes and opinions.

Page 114. Exercise: Narrative as Persuasion

Students will undoubtedly discover that the Lands' End ad is an attempt somehow to "talk" its intended readers' language. It is not aimed at childless couples of whatever age, but it is, obviously, aimed at middle Americans. It tries to achieve identification with potential customers. Whereas Aristotle stressed persuasion, Kenneth Burke took identification as the basis of rhetoric. Aristotle said, "So let Rhetoric be defined as the faculty [power] of discovering in the particular case what are the available means of persuasion" (7). The image is that of a rhetor working his or her will upon the reader or hearer. Kenneth Burke said, "You persuade a man only insofar as you can talk his language by speech, gesture, tonality, order, image, attitude, idea, identifying your ways with his. . . . True, the rhetorician may have to change an audience's opinions in one respect; but he can succeed only insofar as he yields to that audience's opinions in other respects" (Rhetoric 55-56). The image is that of a dialogue, the participants cooperating to achieve understanding and knowledge.

With this view, the terms associated with rhetoric shift:

persuasion	becomes	understanding
convincing		agreeing
logic		dialectic
argument (debate)		discussion
speaker		participant
hearer or reader		participant

Clearly, Burke is setting forth not merely a new "technical" rhetoric, but a view of how language brings about (or might bring about) unity rather than division, peace rather than war.

1. Specifically, what action does the Lands' End ad persuade readers to take?

The ad attempts to persuade readers to call or write for a Lands' End catalog.

2. In your opinion, what are the advantages of using the story "Tim Falls in Love" to persuade readers? What are the disadvantages?

Answers to this question will be as diverse as the people who read the ad. The story is definitely soft-sell, and it is relatively charming, conveying the message in a mildly humorous way. Millions of people like comic strips and therefore a large number of readers would probably spend time with the ad. On the negative side: the ad is just a bit coy. The "cuteness" undoubtedly puts some readers off.

3. To persuade a person to take action, the writer must give reasons. What reasons for action does the advertisement give readers?

(a) The Lands' End catalog contains great stuff: polo shirts, Roveralls, and rugbys. (b) The people at Lands' End are "nice." (c) Orders are sent within twenty-four hours. (d) Merchandise is completely guaranteed. (e) The catalog is free. (f) The call is toll free.

More subtly, the Lands' End catalog presents not just merchandise, but a new collection of children's wear.

4. Do you think the advertisement purposely relates itself to the "Peanuts" strip? Explain. What advantages does such a relationship confer?

The advertisement echoes "Peanuts" in the simple art work, which conveys the impression that anybody could do the drawing. The humor is very much like that in "Peanuts": low-key, good-natured play on the attempts of children to be adult and on the child in adult readers. In Burke's terms, the ad is a definite attempt to persuade through identification.

Page 114. Exercise: Questions about Narratives

Survey the stories for one day in your local newspaper or in a national newspaper such as the New York Times. As you examine each story, consider what it emphasizes. Do any stories simply chronicle an event without analyzing it? Do some focus on the reasons for acts or events? Do others emphasize the people involved? Are some stories especially interesting because of the time or place in which the action occurred? Be prepared to suggest the possible reasons for each writer's choice of focus and to discuss what you have learned about narratives from this investigation.

Here are some brief examples of the kinds of analyses students might do. Stories on the front page of the October 30, 1991, issue of the Orange County Edition of the Los Angeles Times emphasize:

People: Presidents Bush and Gorbachev vow not to interfere in Arab-Israeli peace talks, "But both Bush and Gorbachev hold out the possibility of taking a hand in the second phase." The article quotes Bush and Gorbachev extensively, thus letting them speak for themselves. The two presidents are symbols of their nations' relationship to the Middle East. Thus, in narratives actual characters can serve as symbols. Another story--"Wofford Victory Would Give Democrats New Life"--is a character sketch of a Pennsylvania candidate for the U.S. Senate. This article explains Wofford's political philosophy, and we see that a story can inform us about concepts as well as events.

Place: an article discusses "The Growing Contempt for Orange County [California]." "Ever more urbanized, the area has become a model of what not to do--particularly in Ventura. With the area's image as a haven from L.A., it's an ironic twist." The article uses a given place--Orange County, California--to explain the problem of suburban overdevelopment. Ironically, people flee to the suburbs to escape the problems of the city, but then the suburbs become urbanized. A story about one place can serve as an analysis of a general problem.

Page 115. Exercise: Agent

In **The Pine Barrens**, John McPhee writes about a sparsely populated, primitive area located, surprisingly, almost within sight of New York City and equidistant from Richmond, Virginia, and Boston, Massachusetts. One of the inhabitants of the Pine Barrens is Fred Brown. As you read the selection, think about the following questions.

1. Before McPhee introduces the character, he sets the scene. In what ways does this scene help us to understand Fred Brown?

Students should be encouraged to use specific details as "evidence" for an opinion about Brown. For example, from the scene that McPhee sets, we learn that Brown acquires junk and apparently never disposes of it. His house is surrounded by a great variety of useless items such as the gas pump and the engine heads, suggesting that Brown has no single direction or ambition in life. Since he lives on the edge of a cranberry bog, we know that he is fairly isolated from civilization. Brown is obviously not prosperous, since the tarpaper is peeling from his house.

2. What would be the effect if the specific details were removed from the passage? For instance, McPhee writes, "I walked through a vestibule that had a dirt floor, stepped up into a kitchen, and went on into another room that had several overstuffed chairs in it and a porcelain-topped table, where Fred Brown was seated, eating a pork chop." Here is that same passage with the specific details removed: "I walked through a vestibule, stepped up into a kitchen, and went on into another room that had several overstuffed chairs in it and a table, where Fred Brown was seated, eating."

In a word, the selection would lose its interest. The details enable us to understand Brown and his life style. In The New Journalism, Tom Wolfe explained status details: details that enable us to determine the social status and values of a character in literature. It is these status details that make Brown an interesting and archetypical character.

3. What sort of person is Fred Brown? For instance, what social class does he apparently belong to? Which details help you begin to understand him?

For example: Brown is affable and easygoing, as his reception of McPhee indicates. Since he is in his underwear, we can assume that he is not self-conscious, and everything about him (his house, his meal) suggests that he is not conscious of status. In fact, we get the impression that he is satisfied with life. He is also healthy, for, as McPhee tells us, he looks much younger than his age.

Page 116. Exercise: Scene

Here is the scene that Truman Capote sets in <u>In Cold Blood</u>, his account of a particularly senseless and grisly murder of a Kansas family by two ex-convict drifters. As you read this vivid descriptive prose, think about the following questions.

1. Capote gives us both a panoramic and a closeup view of the scene. Why does he give us two perspectives?

The panorama sets the geographical scene, with its loneliness and vastness, its purity and remoteness. The closeup begins to characterize the town itself. The details--muddy streets, the abandoned dance hall--portray the status of the town itself: an out-of-the-way community in which not very much is going on. Note, however, that the scene has its beauty and dignity: the grain elevators rise as gracefully as Greek temples.

2. What does Capote do to characterize the people who inhabit the scene?

He gives two details: the people talk with a prairie, nasal twang, and the men wear "narrow frontier trousers, Stetsons, and high-heeled boots with pointed toes." These two details, carefully chosen, show the place of Holcomb's residents in American society. They are ranchers and farmers who probably enjoy country and western music, go to the county fair, drive pickup trucks, and send their children off to the state university rather than Harvard or Yale.

3. What use does Capote make of the details of sound?

We hear the nasal twang of the people's speech, the pronunciation of Arkansas (Ar-kan-sas), "the keening hysteria of coyotes, the dry scrape of tumbleweed, the racing, receding wail of locomotive whistles"--and four shotgun blasts. The shotgun blasts, of course, foreshadow the story that the book tells.

Page 117. Exercise: Agency

1. Give an example of a story--factual or fictional--in which money is the most important agency.

For example: any aspect of the savings and loan debacle; Senate debates over the budget.

2. Has anyone ever "used" you? That is, has anyone ever treated you as if you were an agency, not an agent? Explain.

3. In what sense is a computer language or mathematics an agency? Explain how ordinary language can be viewed as an agency.

A computer language is the "tool" through which you gain access to the machine. Mathematics is a "tool" used to solve problems. When we focus on style as persuasion, we are viewing language as an agency or tool. For instance, we use laudatory terms as tools for persuading people to do what we want them to.

Page 117. Exercise: Purpose

In the great American classic <u>Walden</u>, Henry David Thoreau directly explains his purpose for going to live alone by Walden Pond. What is that purpose? How would you paraphrase Thoreau's explanation?

Excerpts from <u>Henry David Thoreau</u>, by Joseph Wood Krutch, bear on this question:

> He was determined to "move away from public opinion, from government, from religion, from education, from society." "There are certain current expressions and blasphemous moods of viewing things, as when we say 'he is doing a good business' more profane than cursing and swearing. There is death in such words. Let not the children hear them." And he was willing to go even further. "No true and brave person will be content to live on such a foot with his fellows and with himself as the laws of every household require. The house is the very haunt and lair of our vice. I am impatient to withdraw myself from under its roof as an unclean spot. There is no circulation there; it is full of stagnant and mephitic vapors."

Thoreau feels that civilization is artificial; only nature is real. He wants to experience nature--and hence life--directly. With Wordsworth, Thoreau might have said,

> The world is too much with us; late and soon,
> Getting and spending, we lay waste our powers:
> Little we see in Nature that is ours;
> We have given our hearts away, sordid boon!
> The Sea that bares her bosom to the moon;
> The winds that will be howling at all hours,

And are up-gathered now like sleeping flowers;
For this, for everything, we are out of tune;
It moves us not.--Great God! I'd rather be
A Pagan suckled in a creed outworn;
So might I, standing on this pleasant lea,
Have glimpses that would make me less forlorn;
Have sight of Proteus rising from the sea;
Or hear old Triton blow his wreathed horn.

Page 120. Exercise: Applying the Questions

"Barbara Allan," which appears below, is an anonymous Scottish ballad (a ballad is a kind of poem that tells a story). The story of Barbara and her lover, however, is puzzling.

Using <u>act</u> as the key term, develop a theory about unexplained events in the story. What actually happened? What were the causes or motives? The questions following the ballad may help you develop your theory.

It was in and about the Martinmas time,
    When the green leaves were a-falling,
That Sir John Graeme, in the West Country,
    Fell in love with Barbara Allan.

He sent his men down through the town
    To the place where she was dwelling:
"O haste and come to my master dear,
    If ye be Barbara Allan."

O slowly, slowly rose she up,
    To the place where he was lying,
And when she drew the curtain by,
    "Young man, I think you're dying."

"O it's I'm sick, and very sick,
    And 'tis all for Barbara Allan."
"O the better for me you'll never be
    Though your heart's blood were a-spilling.

"O dinna ye mind, young man," said she,
    When ye was in the tavern a-drinking,
That ye made the healths go round and round,
    And slighted Barbara Allan?"

And slowly, slowly rose she up,
    And slowly, slowly left him,
And sighing said, she could not stay,
    Since death of life had reft him.

She had not gone a mile but two
    When she heard the dead-bell ringing,
And every stroke the dead-bell gave
    It cried Woe to Barbara Allan!

"O Mother, Mother, make my bed!
    O make it soft and narrow!
Since my love died for me today,
    I'll die for him tomorrow."

    1. Questions concerning <u>act</u> (what happened): Outline the story, the events in their chronological sequence. Are there are any aspects of the story that are not stated directly, forcing you to guess what happened? Explain.

    A student might give the following synopsis: Sir John Graeme, who had fallen in love with Barbara Allan, is ill, so he sends his men to fetch Barbara. She comes to him, draws the curtain, and tells him that he appears to be dying. He replies that he is very sick, all because of Barbara. She responds, enigmatically, "O the better for me you'll never be / Though your heart's blood were a-spilling." Then she explains her anger: in a tavern when he had been drinking the healths of others, he slighted Barbara Allan. She leaves, and before she gets very far, she hears the death bell ringing. At home, she tells her mother that since Sir John had died for her today, she will die for him tomorrow.

    Several aspects of the story need to be explained. What was the cause of Sir John's death? (Did Barbara have anything to do with it?) Why was Barbara so deeply offended over Sir John's failure to drink her health? Did Barbara intend to commit suicide? Did she believe that she would die of a broken heart?

    2. Questions concerning <u>agents</u> (the characters in the story): What sort of people do Sir John Graeme and Barbara Allan seem to be? What evidence do you have for your characterization? Does your characterization of the agents help you reconstruct that act? Explain.

    Some possibilities: Sir John Graeme is a member of the nobility, and Barbara seems not to be; thus, the class difference may have kept them apart. (The failed toast would be the evidence of the separation brought about by class difference. Sir John, among his friends in the tavern, could hardly toast a village maiden.) Clearly, Barbara felt the bitterness of a woman scorned, but she also was in love with Sir John. She was, then, torn. She is also very proud.

    3. Questions concerning <u>agency</u> (the means used to accomplish the act): What did Sir John Graeme die of? What did Barbara Allan die of? (A broken heart? Smallpox?)

    Our favorite hypothesis--based, certainly, on slim evidence--is that Barbara poisoned Sir John and then resolved to take poison herself. Finally, one cannot determine the cause of either death.

4.   Questions concerning <u>scene</u> (the time and place of the act): In what geographical location did the act take place?   At what time in history did the act take place?   (The Classical age before the Christian era?   The Middle Ages?   The Twentieth Century?)   What is Martinmas time?   Does it have any symbolic significance?

The setting is the Scottish Highlands--the same as the scene for <u>Macbeth</u>. The people are rough and clannish.   The date of the ballad is around the thirteenth century, the Medieval Period.   More importantly, the time of year in which the action takes place is Martinmas, late fall.   It is the season of dying--the prelude to winter.

Saint Martin (c. 316-397) was born a heathen but converted to Christianity.   In 371 he was proclaimed bishop, but he continued to live as a monk in a monastery near Tours.   He was greatly loved, and his cloak symbolizes Christian charity.   St. Martin's summer is the British equivalent of Indian Summer in the United States.

Students might be encouraged to investigate the Medieval Scotland.

5.   Questions concerning <u>purpose</u> (why the acts took place, motivation): Does what you know about the agents help you understand purpose?   Does scene help you understand purpose?   Can you be really sure about purpose, or will your conclusions always be tentative and speculative?   Explain.

We have already suggested that a nobleman could not marry a common village maiden in Medieval Scotland.   However, we think that one interesting factor of the ballad is its enigmatic nature.   There is not just one interpretation, even of the acts that take place, let alone the purposes.

Works Cited

Burke, Kenneth. <u>A Grammar of Motives</u>. Berkeley and Los Angeles: U of California P, 1969.

Richards, I. A. <u>Practical Criticism: A Study of Literary Judgment</u>. 1929. New York: Harcourt, 1956.

White, Hayden. <u>Tropics of Discourse: Essays in Cultural Criticism</u>. Baltimore: Johns Hopkins UP, 1978.

Page 123

"The Interior Life"
Annie Dillard

1. Explain why agent could be considered the most important element in this selection.

This question could be broadened to consider why the main element of most autobiographies is the agent.   It is so basic that an answer is almost tautological: the subject of the autobiography, by definition, is the author's life.   In autobiography the actions, observations, and opinions contained in the work either involve the author or are expressed by the author as a reflection of his or her beliefs. Therefore, act, purpose, scene, and agency are considered in relation to the key term, agent.

2. What does the scene in this autobiographical sketch tell us about the agent (Annie Dillard)? Which aspects of the scene are most important? Why?

Dillard's bedroom is the most important scene because it best exemplifies the author's main point ("A mind risks real ignorance for the sometimes paltry prize of an imagination enriched."). It is in that setting, during nighttime, that Dillard is truly able to understand how the runaway imagination deprives a person of other information (the phantom is merely a reflection of light from a car) which would assure her that all was well and that she could go to sleep in safety. The larger scene of the selection is Pittsburgh in the year 1950. This is a fairly unimportant aspect of the scene since Dillard does not explain what influence the city of that time had on her. The story could just as easily have taken place in any other city or town and at any time from 1950 (or earlier) to the present. The only item that would let the reader know that the events took place some time ago, aside from the mention of the date, is the fact that the car windows are in two halves and held in place by a sash, which presumably runs down the middle of the front windshield.

The scene reveals something, although not a great deal, about the author and her life. The fact that she shares a room with her sister, the only sibling mentioned, implies that the family was not very wealthy since they did not live in a house or apartment with enough space for each girl to have her separate room. The author also mentions the curious fact that the room is painted pale blue even though two little girls use it. (Remember that gender roles in the 1950s were not as pronounced then as they are now.) The author never explains why the color is blue rather than pink, but certain hypotheses are intriguing. (Were the parents expecting a boy rather than a girl? Was the color simply there when they moved in? Why didn't the parents repaint the house or apartment if that was the case?)

3. What do the agent's acts tell us about her?

Dillard's relevant acts are the mental processes that she undergoes. The author showed that as a child she had the ability to use deduction during times of terror and that she had the ability to use her imagination during the most mundane of times. Little imagination was required to transform the light from the street which danced over her room into the image of a spirit and that of a Chinese dragon. However, it took a large degree of rationalization in order to determine the source of the spirit. This same rationalization came in handy at later times when the reflection would reappear, because the author was able to control her fears through her own thought processes.

On the other hand, the author's use of her imagination in mentally charting the course required to walk from her bedroom out to the street where the roadbed was being torn apart by construction and, more importantly, relating that mental exercise to the interior/exterior worlds which she inhabits, is impressive. Many children would not be able to make that intuitive leap from concrete thought to mental abstractions of that thought.

The author apparently has a great yearning for order in her life. For example, she is envious of the way her younger sister can easily fall asleep in such a poised pose. In addition, she had absolutely no interest in experiencing the thrills provided by the "spirit" until she had the ability to thoroughly control her thoughts during its appearance as she alternated between viewing it as an apparition and as simply the reflection of light from a car.

4. Is the purpose of the narrative to explain, to argue, to persuade, or something else? How do you know?

The primary purpose of the narrative is to persuade the reader that the "trick of reason is to get the imagination to seize the actual world" rather than allow the interior life solipsistically to blind oneself to actuality.

Dillard's intention, we think, is to persuade almost by the process of elimination. The selection is too adamant in its declaration that the imagination must be ruled by reason to be merely an explanation of an event in her childhood. The selection is compact and does not digress from the thesis statement.

While both arguments and persuasive writings have theses, successful arguments convince readers but do not necessarily bring about actions. (We might convince you that being grossly overweight is unhealthy without persuading you to diet.) The success of an argument is in its internal consistency and sound reasoning, not in its call to action. The authors believe that Dillard wishes to persuade the reader as to the truth of her thesis rather than to argue.

The authors have an advantage over the students in answering this question for they have also read Dillard's Pilgrim at Tinker Creek. In this book, Dillard repeatedly provides surprising glimpses of nature removed from sentimental views which often cloud an author's perception. She portrays a chaotic animal world that is predatory and parasitic. Pilgrim at Tinker Creek, like "The Interior Life," is a statement of the theme that the imagination must seize reality; thus, it appears that Dillard wants to persuade the reader of the truth of this idea.

5. As a reader, do you need any specialized background information to understand the selection? Explain.

6. In your own words, state the main point of the selection.

As noted previously, the main point is contained in the first paragraph of the selection: "A mind risks real ignorance for the sometimes paltry prize of an imagination enriched."

7. Why doesn't the author immediately explain what the apparition was?

The author is able to achieve a highly dramatic effect by not revealing the nature of the apparition. The reader's interest is immediately engaged because it is obvious that the apparition is not simply a figment of the child's imagination. In addition, ignorance of the cause allows the reader to empathize more fully with the child's fear and reinforces Dillard's point about the problems that occur when the imagination is given free reign.

8. Explain what Dillard means when she says that "the trick of reason is to get the imagination to seize the actual world."   Explain how the following metaphors help clarify the statement: (a) "a long and forced ascent to the very rim of being, to the membrane of skin that both separates and connects the inner life and the outer world"; (b) "like a diver who releases the monster in his arms and hauls himself hand over hand up an anchor chain till he meets the ocean's sparkling membrane and bursts through it"; (c) "'Outside,' then, was conceivably just beyond my windows."

Dillard is a philosophical idealist. Since the time of the German Idealists (Kant, Fichte, and Schelling) in the eighteenth century, we have been troubled by the question of the world "out there," beyond our own beings. If there is something out there, how can we know it, for knowledge is filtered through our own senses and prior experiences. When you and I look at a tree, do we see the same thing? When we speak of love, do we mean the same thing? As Dillard says (quoting Donald E. Carr) in Pilgrim at Tinker Creek, "[O]nly the simplest animals perceive the universe as it is" (20). Once we have language, we can never see das Ding an sich ("the thing in itself"), for all experience, all cognition, is filtered through language. In Tristes Tropiques, Levi-Strauss remarks that he wishes he could visit the tribes of the Amazon rain forest without having any prior knowledge of anthropology, so that he might see them as they are, not as they are filtered through his European culture; yet he realizes that without his culture, he could not see them at all, that they would be meaningless. By calling attention to the separation between the interior and exterior worlds, Dillard also calls attention to the way in which the outside world is perceived by the imagination.

9. Dillard says, "A mind risks real ignorance for the sometimes paltry prize of an imagination enriched." Explain her view of the relationship between imagination and reason. (Think about the last two paragraphs of the selection.)

Dillard believes that without the leavening of rationality, the imagination is given too much control. With too much control, the misperceptions of the imagination can become destructive. The example in the selection portrays the author as a little girl who is terrorized by such a misperception.   The author doesn't provide any redeeming, positive results of this terror. However, once the apparition is understood to be the reflection of passing cars, Dillard enjoys both the thrill in reimagining the light as an apparition and the power of her rationality which she is able to use to control the terror and convert the apparition into a passing car.

10. Dillard contrasts her tormented nights of apparitions with the untroubled sleep of her younger sister. What was her attitude then? What do you think it would be now?

As a young girl, Dillard was envious of her younger sister's untroubled sleep. It was an escape from the terrors of the night.

11. This and the next two selections, Frank Conroy's "White Days and Red Nights" and Katherine Anne Porter's "St. Augustine and the Bullfight," are autobiographical. The two selections that follow--from Scott Berg's <u>Goldwyn</u> and Elizabeth Salter's <u>Daisy Bates</u>--are biographical.   As sources for reliable information--facts--about a person's life, what are the advantages and disadvantages of autobiography over biography and of biography over autobiography?

Autobiography has at least one obvious advantage: the author knows the "interior life" of the subject: the feelings, emotions, and opinions of the author. The biographer, on the other hand, often has the advantage of objectivity. The interior life of the subject, with the possibility that it is ruled by the tyranny of the imagination, might not be an accurate portrait, whereas the biographer, who must inevitably rely more on facts than the autobiographer, has his or her own opinions and evaluations tempered by the objective facts at hand. The biographer also has the ability to see more clearly his or her subject in proper perspective against the backdrop of history or the times in which the subject lived. The autobiographer doesn't have the ability to step outside him- or herself and gain such a perspective. Inevitably, there is also a greater self-consciousness in the autobiographer, which can distort the perceptions and the style in which they are expressed.

Page 127

"White Days and Red Nights"
Frank Conroy

1. Explain why <u>agent</u> could be considered the most important element in this selection.

By definition, the single most important element of any autobiography is the author as an agent. Other types of first-person writing have different emphases. Memoirs are very much like autobiography but are more concerned with the historical events the author has witnessed first-hand or a straightforward recording of the events of an author's life within a particular period of time. The emphasis in memoirs would be on scene (a historical period) or acts (the events of the historical period or of the author's life).

2. Which author--Dillard or Conroy--gives us the more fully developed scene? Provide specific examples to back up your choice.

The first sentence of the Dillard piece ("The interior life is often stupid") implies that the exterior scene will not be emphasized. Conroy's piece, however, vividly describes the scenes of white days and red nights and the people who are part of those scenes. Among the more memorable instances:

> The low sky was empty, uniformly leaden.   Stands of trees spread pools of darkness, as if night came up from their sunken roots.

> I wake up in the dark, a giant hand squeezing my heart.   All around me a tremendous noise is splitting the air, exploding like a continuous chain of fireworks.   The alarm clock!

> Rising before me over the foot of the bed is a bright, glowing, cherry-red circle in the darkness, a floating globe pulsating with energy, wavering in the air like the incandescent heart of some dissected monster, dripping sparks and blood.

> First of all it was hot, really hot, like a furnace room.   I began to sweat immediately.   The smell was overpowering.   It was useless to breath carefully as I'd done outside; here the smell was so pungent and thick it seemed to have taken the place of air--a hot substitute filling my lungs, seeping into my blood, and making me its own creature.   With the first deep breath I was no longer an air breather.   I'd changed to another species.   It was noisy.   A noise that raised the hair on the back of my neck.   Far-out throats, tongues, and lips forming sounds that wound their independent way up and down the scale with no relation to anything.   Whispering, mumbling, fake laughter and true laughter, bubbling sounds, short screams, bored humming, weeping, long roller-coaster yells--all of it in random dynamic waves like some futuristic orchestra.

> He was all eyes, immense white eyes impossibly out of his head, rushing at me. No, he was wearing his eyes like glasses.   Two bulbous eyes in steel frames.   He turned his head and the illusion disappeared.   Thick lenses, that was all.   His bald head gleamed with sweat.   His arm was as big as my leg.

> The creature lifted one leg and touched his toes to the surface of the wall as if it was a ladder he was about to climb.   Below the tangle of black hair in his crotch, his veined penis and scrotum hung limply almost halfway to the knee, against the inside of his thigh. It was as if they'd been grabbed and stretched like soft taffy.

> Zooming into the room was a flash of chrome-man, a monstrous human machine blurred with speed, bearing down on me like a homicidal hot-rodder. A man in a wheelchair, but what kind of man?   His body was tiny, like a child's, his head impossibly huge, the size of a watermelon.

> The days were emptiness, a vast spacious emptiness in which the fact of being alive became almost meaningless.   The first fragile beginnings of a personality starting to collect in my twelve-year-old soul were immediately sucked up into

the silence and the featureless winter sky. The overbearing, undeniable reality of those empty days!

3. Explain how the title of the selection denotes scenes.

4. What do the scenes in this selection tell us about the agent?

There are only two scenes in the selection, the cabin and Southbury Training School and its dormitories. The white days in the cabin tell the reader about the child's need for human contact and relationship. The red nights help explain the normal fears that children have and the imaginations that fuel such fears. Finally, the Southbury Training School revealed to the author that his difference, his intelligence, was a positive quality when set against the misery of the feeble-minded people who lived at the school.

5. What are significant acts in the narrative? What are the purposes behind those acts? (For example, what was the purpose of ordering Frank to go for a dozen eggs?)

Act: Frank remaining at the cabin while his mother and Jean worked their night shifts. Purpose: Besides the general nuisance of having Frank accompany them to work, Frank was required to stay behind so that he could keep the cabin warm for his mother's and Jean's return.

Act: Frank's reluctance to read during the day even though the days were dreary and uneventful. Purpose: Frank wished to save his reading for the nighttime so that he could be preoccupied and dispel momentarily the fears he suffered from.

Act: Taking Frank along to the night shift. Purpose: "She [Frank's mother] was tired of dealing with me, tired of my complaints and my silences. (Alternative unconscious motivations for her change of heart: one, she felt guilty about me; two, she decided to show me something that was worth being afraid of. . . .)"

6. In what sense is Frank merely an agency, something to be used (particularly by Jean), not an agent?

Frank is used by his parents as domestic help. He is required to keep the cabin warm for the return of his mother and Jean and is sent out on errands and to draw water from the well; he was required to dry and put away the dinner dishes.

7. Young Frank, like other children, struggles to establish his own identity. What acts and purposes characterize this struggle?

Conroy states that, given the loneliness he felt as a boy, the Southbury Training School had a positive effect on him because it established his uniqueness among the boys: his intelligence. Conroy implies in the latter section of "White Days and Red Nights" that one reason for visiting the school, aside from the obvious motivation of establishing human contact, was to reinforce this sense of positive uniqueness. In addition, Frank almost admits to a bit of half-conscious fantasizing during his nights in the cabin in order to enforce his individuality. He writes:

> At night I materialized. The outlines of my body were hot, flushed, sharply defined. My senses were heightened. I knew I was real as I animated the darkness with extensions of myself. If the sky was more real than I was, then I was more real than my phantoms.

8.   Since "White Days and Red Nights" is a chapter from Conroy's autobiography, we can assume that the rest of the book supplies information that appears to be lacking in the selection. Can you point to instances where the reader lacks sufficient information to understand the selection completely and easily?

The selection makes it clear that Jean is Frank's stepfather, but the chapter doesn't explain how long his mother has been married to Jean. The length of time that Jean has been a member of the household would help to explain his apparent indifference to Frank. In addition, it is never explained why Frank is not allowed to stay in the city during the weekends. No mention is made of the other father or of other relatives who could help take care of Frank. As a result, it is difficult to determine whether the fact that he is dragged to the cabin each weekend is cruel or simply a necessity. In addition, it is not quite clear why Jean and his mother work at Southbury. Probably it is out of economic necessity. However, the reader would have a different impression of them if the reason were simply the fact that it was an easy job for which they were fairly well compensated. In the latter case, their motivations would be less admirable.

9. State the main point of the selection.

In our opinion, the main point is to explain the fragile identity of children. Conroy discusses this fragility several times, stating that the child has no confidence in his ability to distinguish between a command that is just or unjust (when he is sent out to buy eggs at the farm down the road). The conclusion of the chapter discusses this fragility in even greater detail in its evaluation of the red nights as an assertion of individuality and Southbury as a valuable lesson in the value of his own uniqueness.

10. The first paragraph states that Frank, his mother, and Jean spent only the weekends at the cabin and the Southbury Training School. Why doesn't Conroy mention ordinary weekdays, when, like other children, he went to school and had a room of his own at home?

The terrible effect of unrelenting bleakness which Conroy wishes to achieve would be diluted if he were to include scenes in which he associates with other boys and enjoys and participates normally in the larger world.

11. Explain why, at the end, Conroy preferred the "red nights" to the "white days."

As noted previously, the red nights at least allowed Frank to assume an identity as an individual who had to oppose imagined terrors. The white days, on the other hand, sucked all of the life out of Frank because they were so desolate, "so cosmically threatening." As a result, Conroy writes that of the two he thinks that "in some ways the nights were better than the days."

12. The selection has a nightmare quality, particularly with the red, glowing stove and the residents of Cottage Eight. How does Conroy achieve this effect? What specific images does he present? What sort of language does he use?

The sudden transitions to horrific images that are dissociated from their origins contribute to the nightmare. Some examples of these effects have been noted previously in the examples of scenes which have been successfully developed, scenes such as the alarm clock going off or Frank's first look at Olsen or the hydrocephalic. The images are described in almost supernatural terms (e.g., "a giant hand squeezing my heart"; "immense white eyes impossibly out of his head, rushing at me"; "a flash of chrome-man, a monstrous human machine blurred with speed"). The language is graphic. It is not measured, but frantic.

13. If you were writing the autobiography of your first five years, what sources would give you the details, the "facts" you need? (People? Legal documents? Books? Would you visit important places to get the "feel" of them?)

This question anticipates the discussion of sources in Chapter 5.

Page 144

"St. Augustine and the Bullfight"
Katherine Anne Porter

1. Explain why agent could be considered the most important element in this selection.

The principal dramatistic element of autobiographical (and biographical) writing is the agent. Certain passages of the autobiography might digress from the author as the focus of attention, however, and it is the student's obligation, when answering this question, to decide whether such a digression occurs in this selection. For example, the selection concerns, in large part, a consideration of bullfights. Would the student consider the act of bullfighting the most important element of the selection? Is the exotic scene, populated with dashing expatriates from around the world, the most important? The reason agent supersedes scene and act in importance is the fact that each is filtered through the perceptions and opinions of the author, and her reactions to the events and to the scene at hand are given as much importance as the events to which she reacts.

2. Which author--Porter or Conroy--gives us the more fully developed scene? Give specific examples to substantiate your choice. Why is scene important in the selection by Porter?

Conroy provides the most completely developed scene. In detail, he describes the one-room cabin, the winter landscape outside this cabin, and the Southbury dormitory which he visits with Jean.   Porter, on the other hand, provides no description of the cafes at which the aficionados endlessly discuss the art of bullfighting nor much about the bullfight which she attends and which is the central event of her selection. She writes, "I shan't describe a bullfight. By now surely there is no excuse for anyone who can read or even hear or see not to know pretty well what goes on in a bullring."

Within the broader definition of scene, it is Porter who provides the greatest detail. She points out that the events surrounding the bullfight took place in Mexico as the revolution was being waged.   In addition, she provides a very exacting thumbnail sketch of the group of internationalists that she falls in with and who provide an important aspect of the scene:

> They all had titles and good names: a duke, a count, a marquess, a baron, and they were all in some flashy money-getting enterprise like importing cognac wholesale, or selling sports cars to newly rich politicians; and they all drank like fish and played fast games like polo or tennis or jai alai; they haunted the wings of theaters, drove slick cars like maniacs, but expert maniacs, never missed a bullfight or a boxing match; all were reasonably young and they had ladies to match, mostly imported and all speaking French. These persons stalked pleasure as if it were big game--they took their fun exactly where they found it, and the way they liked it, and they worked themselves to exhaustion at it.

Conroy, on the other hand, never provides any insight into the socioeconomic background of his parents although it can be guessed that they had very little money.

Scene is important to Porter because the bullfight, which plays a central role in the essay, is specific to Spain, Portugal, and Latin American countries and is not, therefore, a universal part of culture. Porter begins the selection with a discussion of how hollow an experience adventure really is. This sets the remainder of the selection into relief when she relates the tale of her encounters with a group of what could be called international adventurers. It is important to know that this group had settled in Mexico. They had come to a country which was in turmoil from revolution at the time of Porter's visit and which was relatively undeveloped and foreign to them, lending it an exotic aura. It is through her association with this international set that she learns a very deep lesson from what at first glance would appear to be mere adventure, for the bullfight, instead of providing a temporary thrill, reveals a great deal to the author about her own basic character.

4. What do the scenes in this selection tell us about the agent?

Porter is probably a person who wants a variety of experiences and goes out of her way in order to obtain them. This trait is evident in her remark that she mingled with both the fashionable international set and the poor artists and revolutionaries of Mexico in the early 1900s.

5. What are significant acts in the narrative? What are the purposes behind those acts? (For example, why did Porter attend the bullfight?)

Act: Porter's ascent of the Colorado cliff is illustrative of adventure, in which a daring or physically challenging feat yields no further self-knowledge than before the adventure was undertaken.

Act: The author attempts to write her autobiography but finds that she wants to fill the book neither with small gossip or trivial details nor with the major events in her life. Porter believes these events are so personal that they should be kept secret even though they have greater meaning than simply recounting adventures encountered in one's life.

What the two acts above reveal is, in essence, an apology from the author for the essay which she is writing. Porter is obviously very reluctant to reveal her innermost self and wants to make sure that the reader is prepared for a recounting of events which are not gossipy but also not of great scope or sweep. The third major act, that of relating the story of the bullfight, provides the reader with some insight into the human condition, in this case the latent bloodlust that seems to lurk in even the most pacifist of people.

Act: Porter goes to Mexico "for the express purpose of attending a Revolution, and studying Mayan people's art. . . . "

Act: Porter "ran with this crowd of shady characters [the international set] and liked their company and ways very much. [She doesn't] like gloomy sinners but the merry ones charm [her]."

Act: As an act of will, Shelley insists that Porter attend a bullfight in order to reveal to her something about human nature.

Act: Porter attends a bullfight in order to placate Shelley. The importance of the act is the revelation provided to Porter at the bullfight.

Act: Porter rereads St. Augustine and realizes that the bloodlust which she experienced at the bullfight appears to be a universal part of human nature.

6. In what sense is Porter merely an agency, something to be used (particularly by Shelley), not an agent?

Shelley's personal philosophy placed great importance on the strength of one's will. In particular, he took great pains to avoid letting emotions get in the way of what he wanted to achieve or to do. For example, he had absolutely no liking for the horses that he bred and at least claimed that the best way to work a vice out of a particular breed was either to shoot it or send it to the bullring which, according to Porter, was also to doom the animal. On one occasion, Shelley told Porter that she should not have ridden the stallion that Porter's host had provided her even though the host had been insistent. Shelley's concern was not about Porter's safety but rather her failure to override the insistence of the host. Shelley's insistence that Porter attend a bullfight was another test of his will against that of another. In essence,

Porter was another agency to be used by his will. Parenthetically, Porter could easily be viewed as an agency used by the publisher to produce an autobiography.

7. Porter suggests a reason for a writer's interest in writing fiction. What is it?

Porter writes, "My own habit of writing fiction has provided a wholesome exercise to my natural, incurable tendency to try to wangle the sprawling mess of our existence in this bloody world into some kind of shape: almost any shape will do, just so it is recognizably made with human hands, one small proof the more of the validity and reality of the human imagination." The natural tendency to find meaning in the world is given an outlet in Porter's fiction although she goes on to imply that the pursuit of true meaning within the world is an elusive goal. The meaning more often resides in the storyteller and not in the world from which the storyteller draws his or her inspiration.

8. Explain Porter's distinction between adventure and experience.

"The difference then between mere adventure and a real experience might be this: That adventure is something you seek for pleasure, or even profit, like a gold rush or invading a country; for the illusion of being more alive than ordinarily, the thing you will to occur; but experience is what really happens to you in the long run; the truth that finally overtakes you." Adventure is planned for whereas experience is unplanned; it is an unnatural heightening of the sensation of being alive by placing oneself in situations which one is not otherwise likely to find oneself in, but experience is the sensation and knowledge gained from situations in which one typically finds oneself. Finally, and most importantly, adventure has no lesson to teach. Experience, on the other hand, is nothing if not a lesson on life. To paraphrase Porter, experience is the truth which overtakes you.

9. Why did Porter finally stop writing her autobiography? Is the reason at all related to her distinction between adventure and experience?

Porter notes that an autobiography can contain trivial or monotonous details, entertaining asides, gossip, and accounts of life crises. Porter regards each of these elements as being unworthy to include in an autobiography because of its failure to illuminate or as too personal to reveal to the public at large regardless of how revelatory the material. There can be analogy between her disdain for adventure and her refusal to include the minutiae of her life since neither, in Porter's opinion, can offer insight.

10. What do the similarities between the following two passages suggest about Porter's view of the relationship between art and life?

> Literary art, at least, is the business of setting human events to rights and giving them meanings that, in fact, they do not possess, or not obviously, or not the meanings the artist feels they should have--we do understand so little of what is really happening to us in any given moment.

We struck up a hands-off, quaint, farfetched, tetchy kind of friendship which consisted largely of good advice about worldly things from him, mingled with critical marginal notes on my character--a character of which I could not recognize a single trait: and if I said, helplessly, "But I am not in the least like that," he would answer, "Well, you should be!" or "Yes, you are, but you don't know it."

Porter believes that there is a failure to arrive at the truth both in the writer's attempt to interpret the world and in Shelley's evaluation of Porter's own character. Instead, Porter notes that one's own personality (one's desires, biases, and beliefs) is the filter through which the world is perceived and it is this filter which distorts reality. The comparison between an author and Shelley is particularly apt because both exert a great deal of their own willpower in shaping their perception of the world.

11. Was Porter's attendance at a bullfight an adventure, in the special way in which she defines adventure? Why, or why not?

Prior to going to the bullfight, Porter certainly believed the event would be a hollow experience which would only confirm that which she knew beforehand. Her decision to go was the result of personal pressure applied by Shelley and was thus an act antithetical to her nature. In this respect also, her attendance resembled adventure since adventure is the result of forced or contrived situations. However, Porter was surprised to learn that the experience of the bullfight revealed a basic truth about human nature and so her attendance could not, finally, be defined as an adventure.

12. Explain the importance of the St. Augustine episode to Porter.

The Confessions of St. Augustine confirmed for Porter that her own bloodlust was not an aberration but, instead, a deep-seated part of human nature. In addition, the realization that she was not alone in having such feelings relieved her, in part, of the guilt which she was experiencing: "I longed to be free of my uniqueness, to be a fellow-sinner at least with someone: I could not bear my guilt alone--and here was this student, this boy at Rome in the fourth century, somebody I felt I knew well on sight, who had been weak enough to be led into adventure but strong enough to turn it into experience."

13. Does Porter ever explain what she learned from her experience at the bullring? In your own words, explain what she learned.

Porter does explain what she learned from her experience. She writes, "I loved the spectacle of the bullfights, I was drunk on it, I was in a strange, wild dream from which I did not want to be awakened. I was now drawn irresistibly to the bullring as before I had been drawn to the race tracks and the polo fields at home. But this had death in it, and it was the death in it that I loved. . . ." This forthright explanation occurs a good deal later in text than her cryptic remark that "we [Porter and Shelley] shared an evil secret, a hateful revelation." It also precedes her elliptical conclusion:

"When the time came to kill the splendid black and white bull, I who had pitied him when he first came into the ring stood straining on tiptoe to see everything, yet almost blinded with excitement, and crying out when the crowd roared, and kissing Shelley on the cheekbone when he shook my elbow and shouted in the voice of one justified: 'Didn't I tell you? Didn't I?'" Because the explanation is sandwiched between the two passages which have dramatic impact, the reader could easily overlook the fact that the author is extremely blunt in stating the self-knowledge gained as a result of the experience.

14. Porter's description of her climb in Boulder, Colorado, has the potential to be either a very exciting or a comic story. How would you describe the narrative tone? How does Porter achieve the effect, and for what reason?

The narrative tone is purposefully flat and monotone because Porter wishes to emphasize the hollowness of experience. A comic or exciting tone would give the tale an interesting aspect which Porter takes great pains to avoid.

15. Porter writes, "Yet I intend to write something about my life, here and now, and so far as I am able without one touch of fiction, and I hope to keep it as shapeless and unforeseen as the events of life itself from day to day." Does she fulfill this intention? Point out passages in which Porter does not simply set forth the facts but evaluates them as well. Even if the author gave only the facts without background or interpretation, would it be as "shapeless and unforeseen" as life itself? Why, or why not?

Porter's essay is not, of course, shapeless and unforeseen, but it does ramble to some extent. Her essay begins with a discussion of adventure and of her basic dislike for adventuring. It then mentions briefly her foray into autobiography before settling down to recount the story of the bullfight and the events leading up to it.

Porter foreshadows her discussion of St. Augustine and calls attention to that very act: "I have already betrayed by occupation, and dropped a clue in what would be the right place if this were fiction, by mentioning St. Augustine when I hadn't meant to until it came in its right place in life, not in art." This enticement to the reader is disingenuous because Porter is indeed shaping the narrative as if it were fiction.

Her description of Shelley is culled from many events and distilled into a character sketch which is highly ordered. She relates, for example, Shelley's disgust at Porter for having ridden a stallion which was not a good horse as a way of revealing his emphasis on personal will after she has offered a sketch of Shelley as being "rich and willful."

Porter interrupts her discussion of the bullfight and its attendant ceremonies with a discourse which deals with her reluctance in attending and with the more general issue of her inability to reconcile her taste for meat with her basic abhorrence towards all forms of cruelty. Such thoughts certainly did not come to mind while she was at the bullfight, for the spectacle of the event would have overwhelmed such thoughts. This discussion, then, is another example of Porter's shaping the facts in a fashion which will be of interest to the reader.

Page 155

"The Golden Age of the Broadway Musical"
A. Scott Berg

1. Explain why agent might well be the most important element in this selection.

Agent might not be the best term to apply to Goldwyn since the actors' agents must surely have been anathemas to him, but dramatistic terminology would appropriately designate Goldwyn as the agent. It would be a very strange biography if the agent were not the primary focus in a biography.

2. Characterize the central agent, Samuel Goldwyn, in this selection. What acts help you understand the man?

Goldwyn was an uneducated but savvy business man. His lack of formal education is reflected in his legendary use of malapropisms, such as "warmth and charmth" and "Southern Pacific" instead of "South Pacific." Goldwyn was in his seventies when he produced Guys and Dolls. No one in Hollywood could have lasted that long without a great deal of resourcefulness and power.

This selection deals with a crucial turning point in the history of the movies. Television was encroaching on the audience, which had before attended movies regularly, and the old studios were breaking up for a myriad of reasons besides the rise of television. Guys and Dolls was intended to be Goldwyn's great stand against the encroachment of the new realism which was introduced by actors trained in the Method, scriptwriters who were concerned with the average rather than the extraordinary person, and directors who were filming on location rather than in the controlled environment of the studio, which meant concentrating less on making a beautiful composition within the film frame and more on producing a realism never before seen on the screen. The elaborate gesture orchestrated by Goldwyn shows him to be a proud man who truly loved the movie business as he had come to know it. In addition, it revealed the amount of energy and self-will of the seventy-year-old man. (As the headnote on Goldwyn reveals, a person in his situation during the war might not have survived had he had less perseverance.) As one of the last of the great Hollywood pioneers, his pride pushed him on to make Guys and Dolls a spectacle.

3. What agencies does Goldwyn use to achieve his purposes?

The most important agency of Goldwyn or any other producer is money. As Berg notes, "Goldwyn spent $5.5 million overproducing the movie." Since a producer's function in Goldwyn's time was to provide the package for making a film, everything from raising the money to obtaining the talents, other agencies would include Joseph Mankiewicz, the director; the movie's stars (Marlon Brando, Frank Sinatra, and Jean Simmons); and the Broadway play upon which the movie was based.

4. Berg devotes a great deal of attention to purpose. Explain the purposes behind the following acts: (a) Goldwyn's decision to produce <u>Guys and Dolls</u>; (b) Goldwyn's decision to hire Marlon Brando and Frank Sinatra; (c) Mankiewicz's decision to hire Marlon Brando and Frank Sinatra; and (d) Goldwyn's decision to film within a studio even though the trend, even in musicals, was toward location shooting.

Goldwyn's decision to produce <u>Guys and Dolls</u> was the result of his attempt to show that he still had it in him to be a force in the movie industry and was, in addition, his manifesto against the trend in the current cinema to produce realistic films that presented slices of life.

"Goldwyn liked the ring of the stars' names," writes Berg of Goldwyn's decision to hire Brando and Sinatra for the two leading roles. The selection pays less attention to the reasons for selecting Sinatra, other than to note, beyond the ring of the names, that Sinatra was lobbying heavily to obtain a role in the film. The decision to hire Brando, however, is given greater emphasis. To begin with, Brando was one of the hottest actors around, having been nominated as best actor for each of the five roles he had taken on since his debut and receiving the award for <u>On the Waterfront</u>. Although it is not stated outright, the fact that Mankiewicz had directed Brando previously in the film version of <u>Julius Caesar</u> and that Mankiewicz had been impressed by Brando's talent and professionalism must also have had some bearing on Goldwyn's interest in the actor.

Mankiewicz wanted Brando because "he considered him the consummate actor," having worked with him previously in <u>Julius Caesar</u>. The incongruity of hiring an actor famous for his naturalism for a movie musical to be shot entirely on sets within a sound stage is diminished when one realizes that Brando had successfully acted in Shakespeare and had worked well with Mankiewicz on the project. The only reason advanced for Mankiewicz's acquiescence to hiring Sinatra is that when he met the actor at the Beverly Hills Hotel, he "found that 'Frank was just in love with it.'"

Goldwyn's decision to film on the sound stage was based on two major factors. First, as one of the last of the great movie pioneers, he "still believed movies should make magic," as Berg explains. He was very much opposed to the then current trend towards greater and greater realism. In addition, filming on the sound stage was Goldwyn's way of maintaining control of the production.

5. The scene (the time and place in history) in which Goldwyn resolved to make <u>Guys and Dolls</u> is very important. His son said of him, "Now he was living in a world he didn't like." What kind of world was that? "People don't want to pay good money," [Goldwyn] told Alfred Crown, "to see somebody else's kitchen." In what sense can it be said that scene creates the purpose for the act (producing <u>Guys and Dolls</u>)?

The scene, a rapidly changing Hollywood in the 1950s, was making a transition from the fantasy of the controlled sound stage to the naturalism of location shooting and the attendant acting styles and characters that were also in a more realistic vein.

Goldwyn, as noted previously, opposed this trend and produced <u>Guys and Dolls</u>, at least in part, as an act of opposition to the general trend of the day (purpose).

6. What kind of scene did Goldwyn create in <u>Guys and Dolls</u>? Do you find that scene ironic? Explain.

<u>Guys and Dolls</u>' main characters are New York grifters, bums, and petty crooks, regardless of their charm. However, instead of using the streets of New York for location shooting, and regardless of the trend toward location shooting exhibited even in such musicals as <u>On the Town</u> and <u>Oklahoma</u>, Goldwyn opted for the sound stage and the stylized sets constructed for the scenery. It is ironic that the style of the movie does not match its plot.

7. Explain this metaphor: "Hollywood was falling into the hands of men who had no passion for the 'garments' they manufactured, no feel for the material."

The metaphor refers to Goldwyn's original occupation as a glove salesman and manufacturer. Literally the metaphor refers to the corporate types who were taking over the production of movies even though these people, unlike Goldwyn, had not been involved with any aspects of production.

8. <u>Guys and Dolls</u> was not a critical success. Develop an explanation for this failure by considering the agents involved (producer, director, actors), the scene of filming (on a sound stage), the film script as an agency, and the purpose in filming the play.

Samuel Goldwyn was in his seventies when he decided to produce <u>Guys and Dolls</u>. Although he was a legendary Hollywood figure, Berg makes it evident that times had changed and that Goldwyn was out of touch with the current fashion. For example, the movie was filmed on stage sets at a time when the camera was breaking free of the constraints of the studio. Berg notes that the design was neither realistic nor stylized enough to be successful on its own but was, instead, a conglomeration of styles which failed artistically. The fault must lie with Goldwyn, at least in part, for he had input into many of the film's design elements and the power with which to enforce his decisions.

Mankiewicz's own contribution to the movie's failure resided in his lack of experience in directing a musical (<u>Guys and Dolls</u> was his first). In addition, Berg describes the director as "one of the most intellectual moviemakers ever to succeed in Hollywood." Intellectualism is certainly not a trait of great use in a genre in which music and dance are primary elements. Because of his nature, Mankiewicz wrote a script that was too long and did not make use of the songs to advance the plot but, instead, made them either redundant or superfluous. Finally, his camera work was often static during the large production numbers, making for a monotonous style. Goldwyn's son suggests that the immobile frame was a result of Mankiewicz's fascination with the spectacle of the production numbers within the frame rather than with the frame itself. (The fact that he was a novice musical director probably had a great deal to do with this.)

As for the actors, Berg thinks that the two major stars, Brando and Sinatra, were more suited to the role that the other had been given. In addition, Brando's singing voice was terrible.

The sound stage was appropriate for a musical if used correctly because it gave the director a great deal of freedom to move the camera and yet maintain control of any complex logistics. The sets, however, were a pastiche of realistic and stylized design. Berg quotes Stephen Sondheim: "As a result, they [the sets] have the disadvantage of both [the realistic and the stylized], and these disadvantages work against the very special nature of Runyonesque story-telling."

The film script was problematic; it was overly long and redundant because Mankiewicz had rewritten it so that it could play without the musical numbers even though the musical numbers were still to be included.

9. In "The Interior Life" and "White Days and Red Nights," the primary agent, as in any autobiography, is the author himself. In "The Golden Age of the Broadway Musical," a biography, the central agent is not the author. What are some of the advantages and disadvantages for authors of autobiographies? For authors of biographies?

For a discussion of the advantages of biography and autobiography, please see the discussion of question 11 concerning Dillard's "The Interior Life" immediately proceeding that selection.

10. Does the reader need any particularly background knowledge to understand the selection? Be specific.

The basic information contained within the selection does not require any special knowledge. However, a true appreciation of the drama contained within the selection does require some background information that many people, particularly those who are younger, might not possess.

It is hard to understand, for example, the influence which Marlon Brando's acting style had in the 1950s. No one else at that time save for James Dean had such charisma and presence on the screen. But whereas James Dean has become a legend due in large part to his death at an early age after making only three films, all of which were very good, Marlon Brando had to suffer the agony of growing old in the public eye and of living with the failure of film productions, with Guys and Dolls being only one of many. Today, many people know Marlon Brando only as an overweight, overpriced actor who is less an artist than an eccentric but forget that prior to his role in Guys and Dolls Brando had created two of the most memorable characters of that decade, that of Stanley Kowalski in A Streetcar Named Desire and of the motorcycle punk Johnny in The Wild One.

Berg explains to some degree the turmoil and change which the film industry was undergoing at the time, but he relies in large part on his reader's memory of the time to understand the scene in which the selection is set. The movies were beginning to free themselves from sound stages and were filmed on location. Along with this development was the great change in dramaturgy. Many important films of the 1950s began dealing with ordinary people in ordinary situations rather than setting them in extraordinary circumstances or portraying extraordinary personalities. These two developments are very important in understanding Berg when he writes, "It was a peculiar moment to produce Guys and Dolls."

11. In his biography of the American novelist Thomas Wolfe, David Herbert Donald explains his theory of biography as follows:

> **In telling Wolfe's story I have so far as possible avoided intruding my own comments on the events of his life. I believe that present-day readers no more desire moral judgments or psychoanalytical diagnoses from an author of a biography than they want heavy-handed moralizing and editorial pronouncements from a novelist. I am not persuaded that anything would be gained if I interrupted my account of Wolfe's attitudes toward Jews to announce that such bigotry is intolerable and uncivilized--as of course it is. Nor am I convinced that my portrait of Julia Wolfe would be more credible if I characterized her as an anal-retentive type.**
>
> **This does not mean, of course, that I have simply let the facts speak for themselves. The record of Wolfe's actions is so full that his biographer has constantly to make choices. Every quotation or incident included reflects my judgment of what is important and what is inconsequential in Wolfe's life. Throughout, I have interwoven interpretation with narrative. But I have tried not to stress an interpretive structure that would reduce Wolfe to a case study, whether psychological, literary, or sociological. My purpose has, instead, been to present him as a man, like all men full of contradictions and ambiguities.**

In your own words, state Donald's criteria for biography. Are they "rules of thumb" for writing successful biographies? Explain. In your opinion, does the selection from Berg's Goldwyn meet these criteria? Explain.

Donald is very much opposed to overt editorializing. The biographer's primary responsibility is to present the subject in the most complete detail possible and let the facts speak for themselves. This is not to say that the biographer simply puts down in print every event that occurs without any shaping of the material. Donald understands that the biographer must make value judgments when editing the chronicle of events in the subject's life and that certain events are more telling than others. What, finally, Donald calls for is the abolition of preconceived notions in structuring the biography.

Whether Donald's criteria are rules of thumb for writing successful biographies depends on how one defines success. Certainly, some of the current bestselling biographies are extremely tendentious and do not adhere to Donald's criteria. On the other hand, these bestsellers are not typically well received by the critics whereas those biographies which present a well-rounded portrait of the subject are judged successful. The instructor might discuss with the class whether Donald is simply being more devious than other biographers who are upfront in their admission that they have a particular ax to grind. Donald admits to shaping his material by judicious editing of the events and yet he apparently does not believe that he uses any particular paradigm or model with which to explain the subject's personality.

Berg adheres to Donald's dictum. There is no heavy-handed editorializing, and although Berg spends some time detailing the characters' motivations, the explanations are commonsensical rather than theoretical. Oftentimes, Berg will let others' opinions substitute for his own as a means of maintaining an objective tone while at the same time conveying his own thoughts on the matter.

Page 163

"A Tent at Maamba"
Elizabeth Salter

1. Why is it possible to view agent as the main element in this selection?

As with any biography, the primary element is agent. This does not mean to imply that all sections of the biography emphasize agent over the other dramatist elements for certain portions of the biography might very well emphasize one of the other elements. For example, "A Tent at Maamba" could have emphasized agency rather than agent and still maintained much of the same material: damper, tinned fruit, and magazines as agencies of exchange and expression of friendship; the <u>nowinning</u> magic stick as an agency of power. However, in all of these cases, Salter has decided to relegate the agencies to positions secondary to the agent.

2. The selection starts with a detailed account of Daisy Bates's camp. What does this scene tell you about the agent who inhabits it?

Daisy Bates obviously wanted as few of the trappings of civilized comfort as possible so that nothing would distract her from her studies. She must have been a no-nonsense person who was single-mindedly devoted to her research. For example, her entire wardrobe for a year was contained within one portmanteau, her cooking utensils consisted of a gridiron and pans, and her chair consisted of a packing crate placed against the trunk of a tree. She was practical in her arrangements. The portmanteau was placed under the table in her tent, and various pockets hanging from the sides of this same table held anything and everything that would fit.

3. What was Daisy Bates's purpose? What evidence do you have for your conclusion?

The selection explains that Bates was studying the Aborigines for the purpose of documenting their life stories. "Daisy took down all that they told her, used the material for her book and turned their personal histories into stories for the newspapers, 'Fanny Balbuk-Yooreel' and 'Policeman Jubytch' being two of the more successful." The reason that Bates thought it necessary to document these histories is also explained. "The breaking up of the native groups she saw as part of this inexorable process. Her certainty of their eventual extinction provided the incentive for the enormous effort she put into the next few years."

In addition, Bates also wished to help the Aborigines as much as possible, "believing that it was necessary to give all that she could of care and comfort in order to 'mitigate the guilt of one's race', as she put it." This is evident in the selection's explanation that "medicines were a constant expense" and in the story of Bates's arduous labor in cooking gruel for those stricken with the measles.

4. What character traits seem to have contributed to Daisy's success? Be specific.

Bates had the ability to appreciate the beauty of the bush country and organized her day in order to allow herself sufficient time in the morning to reflect on this beauty. Without her appreciation of nature, it is possible that her ability to continue to help the Aborigines in a level-headed and optimistic manner would be imperiled, given the depressing situation among the natives.

She was an extremely diplomatic person who respected the Aborigines. Salter writes, "Daisy behaved with politeness in their midst, never crossing the dividing hundred yards unless invited; because, she said, 'you must not go indiscriminately into a native camp if the friendship of the occupants is valued.'" Salter relates an anecdote which is an excellent example of the tact which Bates possessed. Ngilgee brought a gift of a damper and explained that it is customary for the recipient of the gift to reciprocate with one in kind. Bates, rather than immediately offering Ngilgee a gift, allowed an appropriate amount of time to pass during the visit before she asked Ngilgee if she would like a tin of fish. In waiting before offering the reciprocal gift, Bates spared Ngilgee any embarrassment in appearing to ask outright for a gift in exchange.

The description of Bates's camp and her daily routine makes clear that she was a disciplined person who did not allow herself to become distracted from her studies and writing. She was also very brave, and Salter describes several incidents in which this bravery was tested, once with Aborigines dressed for war and the other with three drunken whites on whom she had to draw a revolver.

The concluding paragraph, however, provides the greatest reason for her success and that is her cheerfulness, which Bates admits often helped her in that "miscrable camp" as she describes it when the natives were ill and there were few resources by which to help them. This cheerfulness is reflected in the humor that she puts into her writing such as her notebook description of marching the three drunks towards town in kimono and slippers and then passing the sergeant the next day unrecognized, dressed in clothes for church.

5. What part do agencies play in the narrative (for example, damper, the pistol)? In what sense is the rain ceremony an agency?

Damper is apparently a very important agency of exchange and is used as a token of friendship. It is practical for this purpose because it is easily made, is not terribly expensive, and is something that can be used by all. The pistol, like the nowinning stick, is an agency of power. The pistol was used by Bates to protect herself from, as it turned out, whites and the nowinning stick, while it could have been used for the same purpose with the Aborigines, was almost never used in such a way because she never felt the need for protection from the natives. Instead, the nowinning stick, along with her reputation as a sorceress, was used to cure the native ills through psychological means.

For the Aborigines of the rain totem, the rain ceremony was an agency of communication with their totem. It was a means by which they kept in spiritual contact with the totem and was thought to help increase the size of the totem group. For Salter, the rain ceremony and the subsequent cloudburst were a factor in establishing her great spiritual powers with the Aborigines.

There are other agencies which are important within this selection. Bates's reports and articles from the bush are agencies used to fund her stay at Maamba and also serve to document a culture and way of life which were quickly becoming extinct. The medicine purchased by Bates was an agency used to relieve the unjustifiable suffering of the Aborigines.

6. What sort of person (agent) is Ngilgee? How do her purposes clash or coincide with those of Daisy?

Ngilgee is an extremely independent and strong person. She lived successfully among the whites, having been brought up in white society, serving as a nurse to the future governor of Australia, and she spoke fluent English. Ngilgee also lived comfortably among her own people at Maamba even though she had not been raised among them. The Aboriginal customs are not explained in the selection, but Salter implies that it was an unusual action, and therefore another indication of Ngilgee's independence, in taking on "acting husbands." She was also fairly tactful as shown by her explanation of the custom of gift exchange. Instead of stating outright that Bates should exchange a gift for a gift, Ngilgee leads into her explanation by asking if Bates has learned all of the Aboriginal customs and gently explaining that Bates does not know all of the customs.

7. The last question regarding Berg's biography of Samuel Goldwyn quotes David Herbert Donald's theory of biography. Does this theory seem to characterize Salter's biography of Daisy Bates? Explain.

"A Tent at Maamba" appears to conform to Donald's theory of biography. The author does not have any preconceived notion of how to present Bates's life although it is obvious that the Salter admires her a great deal. Bates's motivations are explained in common sense terms without reference to any particular theory of personality. The reader might be slightly suspicious Salter might have idealized her subject as a result of her admiration. Whereas Donald was careful to present the reader with Wolfe's character flaws as well as the admirable qualities, the reader doesn't have any indication that Bates's personality had any drawbacks. She is a model of tactfulness in her dealings with the Aborigines and never seems to condescend when talking with them. Whatever problems arose as the result of her character flaws, and there is no better way to reveal one's character flaws than to encounter an alien culture, are kept from the reader.

8. In your own words, state the main point of the selection.

The selection's main point is that one must study an alien culture using tact and approach it with respect.

Page 171

"The Fire"
John Hersey

1. Explain why the agent-scene ratio--the relationship between the scene and the people in the narrative--is important in "The Fire."

Hersey's purpose is to portray the people of Hiroshima (agents) in the devastation (scene) after the bomb was dropped.

2. How would each of the following interpretations of scene influence your understand of "The Fire": (a) Hiroshima, (b) Japan, (c) Asia, (d) World War II, and (e) the dawn of the Atomic Age?

Here are just a few possibilities. (a) The focus is on one city and the devastation wrought by the atomic bomb. (b) If Japan is the scene, "The Fire" becomes a study of the Japanese character and way of life. (c) With Asia as the scene, the Japanese can be viewed as aggressors against the Chinese; the atomic bomb becomes retribution. (d) "The Fire" becomes a depiction of and commentary on the horrors of modern warfare. (e) "The Fire" is a warning about the perils of the new age.

3. If you were to choose agency (the bomb) as your pivotal term, how would your interpretation of the selection change?

For example, the focus would shift from the horrors undergone by the people to the power of the bomb and its consequences.

4. As a source of knowledge about the atomic bombing of Hiroshima, is Hersey's book reliable? Explain your judgment.

It is reliable. (a) It has stood the test of time. (b) It was first published in a highly respected magazine, The New Yorker. (c) Hersey is a highly regarded author. (d) Nothing in the account itself seems implausible.

5. In regard to manner, what are some of the ways in which Hersey makes his work easy to read and to understand?

His sentences are clear and uncomplicated.   His organization is clearcut, following first one person and then the next through the sequence of events.

6. Hersey's account of the chaos in Hiroshima is tightly structured. What structural principle does Hersey employ?   Do you find the contrast between the chaos of the subject and the "neatness" of the account ironic? Explain.

Regarding structure, see question 5. The problem of irony raises the question of matter and manner. How do you write an interesting story about a boring person? How do you convey chaos in a clearly structured narrative?

7. Hersey tells us that the magnitude of the catastrophe in Hiroshima inured many of the survivors to the horror. How does he try to avoid inuring his readers to the horrors?

He shows the reaction of various characters to those horrors.

Page 189

"The Long Egyptian Night"
Alan Moorehead

1. What are the primary scenes that Moorehead portrays in this selection? What does each of them tell you about Egyptian society during the Napoleonic era?

Moorehead begins and ends the chapter with a general description of Egypt in 1798, the year in which French forces under Napoleon invaded the land.   The introductory paragraphs portray the geopolitical regions of Egypt (the Nubian tribes of Upper Egypt, the Bedouin of the desert, the people of the delta, and the cities of Cairo and Alexandria) while the conclusion sums up the fatal, erroneous thinking which went into the decision to oppose the invading French forces.   Moorehead briefly describes Alexandria, but only in enough detail to explain that the once wondrous city had fallen on the worst of times.   Cairo, on the other hand, is given expansive treatment.   As a hub for the caravan routes which originated in this city, Cairo's brisk trade is detailed, and the Mamelukes and their warrior-governor position within the society are also given a good deal of consideration.   At the same time, Moorehead is careful to explain the feel for the culture.   The hot-house atmosphere of the society, and the fatalistic outlook of Cairo's citizens which helped to sustain such a view, are portrayed impressionistically but, one feels, also accurately.   Moorehead conveys the feel of the times, the organization of the society, and the actual look of the center of Egyptian society, Cairo.

2. What does "the long Egyptian night" refer to?

The long Egyptian night refers to the period of time during which Egypt was under Mameluke control. It is strange, by the way, that Moorehead does not explain just how long this night was since the Mamelukes seized Egypt in 1250 A.D. "Night" also refers to the torpor and stagnation to which Egyptian society succumbed. Egypt was one of the great birthplaces of civilization, and Alexandria became the intellectual and religious center of the Hellenistic world following the death of Alexander the Great. As mentioned by Moorehead, the French had invaded Egypt in the twelfth and thirteenth centuries, only to be routed. At the end of the eighteenth century, however, things were different, or rather, things were almost the same as they had been five hundred years earlier, with the exception of the introduction of the carbine rifle to the Mamelukes' weaponry. It is this lack of change within the Egyptian society that is referred to in the title of the chapter.

3. As Moorehead says, thousands of books have been written on the exotic East; this scene, as a result, has become a cliché. Does Moorehead's own account of Egypt add to the cliché, or is it original and informative? Explain. (What new aspects of Egyptian history and culture do you learn from the selection?)

Within most clichés lie elements of truth. Moorehead's portrait of Cairo and its bazaars certainly lends an exotic air to city and that great symbol of the sensual, mysterious East, the bellydancer, is given a great deal of attention. Such images, though, are put into some kind of perspective. The respectable women are noted to have worn black clothing from head to toe, and marriage, while it lasted, was taken as a serious contract between the husband and wife. Moorehead lists the seven deadly sins in Egypt (disobedience to parents, murder, desertion during an expedition against infidels, usury, falsely accusing a woman of adultery, idolatry, and the wasting of the property of orphans), and we agree with the author that they are very revealing, for they refute the idea that the Egyptians were simply sensualists who squandered their existences on pleasure.

Moorehead does directly take on some of the other clichés which he believes to be completely false. The image of the dull, apathetic sheik sitting cross-legged for hours on end is refuted by the author's statement that sheiks were the exponents of law and religion in the society and were widely respected. The author implies that they were widely read in the Koran and served to interpret the holy book for their people.

Certainly the Mamelukes and their lifestyle refutes the notion of the indolent Egyptian. Their training was in the art of warfare, and although Moorehead states that they were surrounded by luxury, they were abstemious. What such refutations add up to is a knowledge that with an apparently lackadaisical attitude, the Egyptians lived by a fairly strict and conservative code of conduct.

4. The author makes a number of value judgments concerning the Egyptian character during the late eighteenth century. What virtues does he find? What faults? Do you think it is fair or appropriate to judge as Moorehead does?

Among the virtues cataloged by Moorehead: holding marriage as sacrosanct, maintaining strong family ties, rarity of the vices of dissipation (drinking, drug taking), patience,   grace and beauty, modesty among the respectable women, and conservativism in attitude and conduct.

Among the Egyptians' faults as seen by Moorehead: "they lied, they stole, they were superstitiously ignorant, they were always lazy when they had the chance, and were probably cowards as well. . . ." Elsewhere, Moorehead also writes, "It was at the very core of their nature to resist all governments in a passive and dissembling way, to defeat the tax-gatherer, to cheat the magistrates and to avoid military service."

History is not simply an objective record of events but an interpretation of those events and the reason for their occurrence. In creating a history (as opposed to a chronicle or mere list of events), the writer must, like the biographer and New Journalist, make judgments. There is one basic fact about Egypt at the end of the eighteenth century: that it had not advanced in its science or arts for many, many years and there was every reason to believe that the society was stagnating. In this chapter, Moorehead has explained why the decline should have occurred after such a glorious history.

As noted above, Moorehead is also careful to explain the positive aspects of the Egyptian character. This attempt is not simply a false balancing of the scales of judgment, however. Many of the traits that account for the decline of the civilization are the very same that contribute to many of the positive aspects of Egyptian history (the conservative nature of the people, their quietude), and Moorehead is careful to point this fact out.

Moorehead appears to be more objective than Parkman. There could be many reasons for this, and the two readings themselves offer clues. A major objective of Moorehead's chapter is to analyze the reasons for the "long Egyptian night." He provides a thoughtful context within which the reader can begin to appreciate the reasons the stagnation of the Egyptian culture. In addition, the author comes to his subject from a distance of more than one and one-half centuries and has no personal stake in subject.

Parkman, on the other hand, provides a first-hand glimpse of the life on the Oregon Trail. He had every reason to fear the Pawnees since they could be expected to attack his own expedition at any time. He offers his negative view of the Pawnee without any attempt to understand the reasons for those peoples being as they are, probably because the book was written on the heels of the adventures it chronicles. Therefore, Parkman had no time for reflection.

5. Moorehead identifies two major influences on the Egyptians' fatalistic attitude. What were they, and how did they influence the character of the people?

According to Moorehead, the climate and topography of Egypt and the Moslem religion both helped shape the Egyptians' fatalistic attitude. Moorehead claims that the preservative nature of the dry and hot air, the lack of contrast such as mountains, gorges, or the like, and the cyclical rise and fall of the Nile all contributed to the peoples' belief that change was useless. The Moslem religion's absolute rules, which its adherents are to obey faithfully, also helped in preparing the people for an acceptance of what is.

6. Even if the reader does not have any knowledge of Egyptian history, the fate of the Mameluke's campaign against Napoleon is foretold at the end of the chapter, with Murad riding north to meet the French army on the Mediterranean coast. How does Moorehead foreshadow the outcome, and why does he do so?

The chapter begins, "Egypt was not easy to defend," and then goes on to explain this fact of geography. From the outset, then, the reader is aware that there would at least be great difficulties in stopping Napoleon's armies. Moorehead also writes in the last paragraphs, "It was in vain that Rossetti tried to make Murad realize who Bonaparte was, and to explain the power of modern arms. . . . Murad was not alone in suffering delusions. . . . And so one finds here all the makings of a major tragedy. . . ."

Like a good storyteller who wishes to foreshadow a major event in the plot, Moorehead wishes to prepare the reader for the French conquest. This invasion was the first time in hundreds of years that Egypt had come into close contact with western culture and marked the beginning of events which would eventually push the country into the modern world.

7. Viewing the Mamelukes from the standpoint of purpose, explain their values and their way of life.

Virtually the only purpose which the Mamelukes had in life was to rule the country of Egypt as a military oligarchy. Their training was certainly appropriate to such a purpose. As Moorehead notes, from their earliest years they were trained as horsemen and warriors. In order to keep their caste intact, they were persuaded not to marry or have a family. Instead, the Mamelukes purchased boys from southern Russia and trained them. The Mamelukes' currency was the power they wielded to maintain their style of life, which if not decadent was comfortable, and to secure material items and slaves. The Mamelukes were Muslims and adhered to the tenets of that religion (observing Ramadan, for example), yet they were not benign in their rule. Moorehead quotes another observer of Egypt who noted that the laborers did well simply to stay clear of the Mamelukes.

8.   Does Moorehead believe that Denon and Lane are sincere in their statements regarding Egyptian dancers? Explain.

Moorehead implies that Denon's shock is, at least in part, false, for he writes that Denon "affected to be shocked." Lane's statements cannot be reconciled because he talks of the immodesty of both the attire and the exhibitionism of the dancing girls and yet concludes that they are the "finest women in Egypt. . . ." If one were to choose between these opposite opinions, between outrage and admiration, Lane's opinion is probably the one to accept on face value for he would be going against the conventional morals of the society in which he lived.]

9.   In the foreword to A Distant Mirror, Barbara Tuchman's magnificent history of the fourteenth century, the author tells of the problems a historian has with sources. As a reader, what lessons about history do you learn from Tuchman's statement? In your opinion, can we ever know the "truth" about such a distant era? Explain your answer.

I come now to the hazards of the enterprise. First are uncertain and contradictory data with regard to dates, numbers, and hard facts. Dates may seem dull and pedantic to some, but they are fundamental because they establish sequence--what precedes and what follows--thereby leading toward an understanding of cause and effect. Unfortunately, medieval chronology is extremely hard to pin down. The year was considered to begin at Easter and since this could fall any time between March 22 and April 22, a fixed date of March 25 was generally preferred. The change over to New Style took place in the 16th century but was not everywhere accepted until the 18th, which leaves the year to which events of January, February, and March belong in the 14th century a running enigma--further complicated by use of the regnal year (dating from the reigning King's accession) in official English documents of the 14th century and use of the papal year in certain other cases. Moreover, chroniclers did not date an event by the day of the month but by the religious calendar--speaking, for example, of two days before the Nativity of the Virgin, or the Monday after Epiphany, or St. John the Baptist's Day, or the third Sunday in Lent. The result is to confuse not only the historian but the inhabitants of the 14th century themselves, who rarely if ever agree on the same date for any event.
    Numbers are no less basic because they indicate what proportion of the population is involved in a given situation. The chronic exaggeration of medieval numbers--of armies, for example--when accepted as factual, has led in the past to a misunderstanding of medieval war as analogous to modern war.... J. C. Russell puts the pre-plague population of France at 21 million, Ferdinand Lot at 15 or 16 million, and Edouard Perroy at a lowly 10 to 11 million. Size of population affects studies of everything else--taxes, life expectancy, commerce and agriculture, famine or plenty--and here are figures by modern authorities which differ by 100 percent. . . .

Discrepancies of supposed fact were often due to mistakes of oral transmission of later misreading of a manuscript source, as when the Dame de Coucy, subject of an international scandal, was mistaken by an otherwise careful 19th century historian for Coucy's second wife, at a cost, for a while, of devastating confusion to the present author. . . .

Isabeau of Bavaria, Queen of France, is described by one historian as a tall blonde and by another as a "dark, lively, little woman." The Turkish Sultan Bajazet, reputed by his contemporaries to be bold, enterprising, and avid for war, and surnamed Thunderbolt for the rapidity of his strikes, is described by a modern Hungarian historian as "effeminate, sensual, irresolute and vacillating."

Barbara Tuchman makes it fairly clear that there cannot be an absolute truth in the analysis of history. General truths, however, might be more attainable. If the historian will never know, for example, how many died in the black plague

10. Since many of the "facts" and interpretations of history are problematic, how can you, as a reader, make a judgment about the reliability of a historical text?

This question is intended to stimulate discussion about the reliability of sources. Students might now begin to check reviews and biographical information regarding the author.

11.   Does Moorehead provide all the information you need in order to understand "The Long Egyptian Night"?

Page 203

"The Platte and the Desert"
Francis Parkman

1. Explain why it could be argued that <u>scene</u> is the most important element of "The Platte and the Desert."

The great American prairie pervades the selection. Even the title indicates that scene is the focus of the piece.

2. Think of the various interpretations that you can give <u>scene</u> and how these differing viewpoints will influence your "reading" of the piece. For example, the scene can be (a) the area that Parkman describes in "The Platte and the Desert" (What effect does the location have on the acts of the agents? In what way is the "desert" symbolic? What is the region like now?); (b) the area traversed by the Oregon Trail (What was the route of the trail? Why was the trail established? Why were Parkman's group and the emigrant party on the trail?); (c) mid-nineteenth century America (In what way was the Oregon Trail related to the opening of the

West? What part did the trail play in the history of the period? In what way did the trail represent the spirit of the nation?)

The Oregon Trail ran from Independence, Missouri, to Fort Vancouver (now Vancouver, Washington), about 2,000 miles. During the 1840s and 1850s thousands of wagon trains and individuals followed the trail to the farmlands of the Willamette Valley. The trail went to Fort Kearney in Nebraska and west along the Platte and North Platte Rivers to Fort Laramie in what is now Wyoming. it crossed the Rockies and followed the Snake River to Fort Boise and along the Snake to the Columbia, where the pioneers usually took rafts to Fort Vancouver.

Explorers, fur trappers, traders, and missionaries opened the trail in the first third of the century. Father Pierre De Smet encouraged easterners to take the trail to the Northwest to establish farms. By 1846, more than 6,000 people had used the trail.

3. Survey the selection from the standpoint of how the actions relate to one another? In your opinion, are any sections irrelevant? Explain.

The organization is, of course, chronological.

4. Francis Parkman's historical account of the Oregon Trail is based on firsthand observation. Parkman was there. As a source of historical information, what are the advantages and disadvantages of eyewitness accounts?

Firsthand accounts have the advantage of immediacy and credibility. They have at least one disadvantage: the firsthand observer might lack the objectivity and disinterestedness of a detached observer.

5. If you know where the Platte is, you will suspect that the meaning of "desert" has changed since Parkman used the term more than one hundred years ago. Where can you find the mid-nineteenth century meaning of "desert"? (For a discussion of reference sources, see Appendix 1.)

The Oxford English Dictionary (OED), of course.

6. Parkman is obviously prejudiced against the Pawnees. What are his justifications for this dislike?

According to Parkman, the Pawnees were robbers--"a treacherous, cowardly banditti, who, by a thousand acts of pillage and murder, have deserved chastisement at the hands of the government."

7. Most American readers come to the Oregon Trail with preconceived notions of the westward migration: conceptions derived largely from motion pictures and television dramas. In what ways does "the Wild West" as portrayed in The Oregon Trail differ from the version in the popular media?

The contrast between the television and cinema versions of the Wild West and the Wild West of The Oregon Trail should stimulate discussion.

8. Find two or three examples of anecdotes in the selection, and explain what purpose they serve.

Page 213

"The Prussian Officer"
D. H. Lawrence

1. Explain why the agent-purpose relationship could be considered the most important element in this story.

The story centers on two main characters (agents), the captain and the orderly, and the reasons (purposes) for their acts. Readers ask, "Why did the captain treat the orderly in such a brutal way?" and "Why did the orderly finally kill the officer?" (In a sense, "The Prussian Officer" is a murder mystery, in which the reader, as detective, seeks motives rather than murder weapons or clues.) Most readers will use a "Freudian" interpretation: the captain as a repressed homosexual and the orderly as both the object of his desire and the scapegoat on whom he releases is frustration and anger.

2. One part of the scene, the mountains, is very important. What do the mountains symbolize for the young soldier?

> **He walked on and on in silence, staring at the mountains ahead, that rose sheer out of the land, and stood fold behind fold, half earth, half heaven, the heaven, the barrier with slits of soft snow, in the pale, bluish peaks. (par. 2)**

> **He was getting used even to his parched throat. That the snowy peaks were radiant among the sky, that the whity-green glacier-river twisted through its pale shoals, in the valley below, seemed almost supernatural. (par. 83)**

> **There, straight in front of him, blue and cool and tender, the mountains ranged across the pale edge of the morning sky. (par. 127)**

The mountains are almost an alternate world existing next to the one inhabited by the orderly. The colors of the mountains with their peaks of snow are described as pale, bluish, and grey while the valley is described in terms of the dark-green rye, pale green corn, and golden sunlight. In addition, the heat of the valley is contrasted with the coolness of the mountains. Lawrence writes that the mountains "rose sheer out of the land, and stood fold behind fold, half earth, half heaven, the heaven, the barrier with slits of soft snow. . . ." The mountains become an idee fixe to the orderly as the story progresses because they represent an escape from the hot, flat world through which he is tortuously trudging. They are also an endpoint and take on the qualities of death as the orderly deliriously flees from the troop of soldiers. (This association of snow and mountains with death also figures prominently in Lawrence's classic novel Women in Love.)

3.   From one point of view, the captain--an educated, cultured aristocrat--represents civilization, whereas Schöner--an uneducated peasant--represents nature. Does D. H. Lawrence seem to value civilization or nature more highly? Explain. You might think of this question in terms of an agent-scene relationship. What happens when the captain and Schöner are put into scenes that are not their natural habitat?

Schöner and the officer are a study in contrasts. That Schöner is an orderly indicates his rank with society. In addition, the scar on his thumb--the result of an accident with an ax--indicates that the youth was used to manual labor. Even though he was in the bondage of the Prussian military, he still exhibited "the free movement of the handsome limbs, which no military discipline could make stiff" and "there was something so free and self-contained about him. . . ." The captain, on the other hand, "was a man of passionate temper, who had always kept himself suppressed." His background was aristocratic (his mother had been a Polish countess) and he "was a gentleman, with long, fine hands and cultivated movements. . . ." Lawrence compares the natural man, the peasant Schöner, with the civilized man, the aristocratic officer. Schöner exhibits natural grace while serving the captain as an orderly; the captain, on the other hand, loses control of himself. Lawrence writes, "He [the captain] did not choose to be touched into life by his servant." The result of the captain's encounter with that which is outside of his usual experience is his failure to control his feelings and impulses, and he lashes out at the orderly in arbitrary and vicious ways. Lawrence seems to believe that civilization constrains and warps the natural qualities of man.

4. In what sense is Schöner merely an agency?

The captain uses the orderly as if he were a tool or a robot, not a human being.

5.   Might the scene in this story have believably been the United States of approximately 1900? Why or why not?

Much of the richness of the story would have been lost had Lawrence set the story in the United States. In order to contrast natural man with civilized man, the author relies heavily on the ancient class distinctions established in Europe through the centuries. In the United States class divisions result in great measure from economics, not bloodlines. Therefore, the contrast between the commander and orderly as a reflection of natural man versus civilized man would not be as comprehensible if the story were set in the United States. (Carson McCullers' novel Reflection in a Golden Eye is an interesting comparison to "The Prussian Officer." It, too, is set in the army, although this time it is the United States military, and it is concerned with attraction and force that a private unconsciously exerts over his commanding officer. Like "The Prussian Officer," the novel culminates in a murder. The differences, however, are telling. Lawrence's story looks at the problem of civilization as if it were an ill-fitting suit of manners and mores which bind and pull at natural man's body politic. McCullers' viewpoint is much more Freudian and looks at civilization from less a structural viewpoint as from a psychological one.)

6. Some scenes in the story are described realistically, in detail. For example:

At the next farmhouse, which stood low and broad near the high road, tubs of water had been put out. The soldiers clustered round to drink. They took off their helmets, and the steam mounted from their wet hair.

Some scenes, on the other hand, are misty and almost dreamlike. For example:

When, to his dumb wonder, he opened his eyes on the world again, he no longer tried to remember what it was. There was thick, golden light behind golden-green glitterings, and tall, grey-purple shafts, and darknesses farther off, surrounding him, growing deeper.

How do these scenes help us understand the agents and their acts?

The transformation of the story's scenic description from realism to impressionism and abstraction parallels Schöner's loss of mental stability after killing the officer. It allows the reader to understand more clearly that the act of murder was the result not only of passion but of a loss of mental equilibrium.

7. In what ways do the acts of the agents reveal their thoughts and feelings?

The Prussian officer's uncontrollable outbursts and the repeated badgerings directed against the orderly reveal the officer's fixation on Schöner. The relationship between Schöner and the captain changed suddenly after the orderly spilled a bottle of wine. The captain's outburst, along with blue fire of anger in is eyes, described only one paragraph after Lawrence writes of the officer's irritation at the "sureness of movement" with which the orderly poured wine, revealed to Schöner the officer's fixation with him. Schöner, as a result, avoided conversation with the officer or any attempts to meet him with his eyes so as not to fuel any of the antagonism which had suddenly flared.

8. What do you think is the main point of the story?

9. The overall scene for the story is Prussia before World War I. What sort of place was Prussia? What kind of symbolic value does the term "Prussian" have? (If

I were to call a government official a Prussian, what would I mean?) What reliable and easily accessible sources would you consult to find out about Prussia?

The adjective "Prussian" has been used as a symbol for a rigid, authoritarian character because Prussian society was militarized and bureaucratized. The authors consulted a desk dictionary, a The New Columbia Encyclopedia in one volume, and a one-volume history of the world in order to obtain the general information required to answer this question. The point of the question is to encourage students to use reference sources.

10.   The young soldier's name is Schöner, which in German means "more beautiful." What are the implications of that name for the story?

The story is concerned not only with the distinction between civilized and natural man but also the homosexual attraction of one man for another in a society which would consider such an attraction blasphemous. The use of this symbolic name is the only overt homosexual reference in the story. (Lawrence mentions only in passing the fact that the orderly was required to rub down the captain after riding on horseback although this could, of course, be a highly charged sexual situation.)

11.   Does Lawrence have an opinion of Prussia and Prussianism? If so, what is that opinion? How does Lawrence express it?

Lawrence's dislike for Prussia and Prussianism is made apparent in his use of the captain as a symbol for both and by making him a completely unsympathetic character.

12.   Explain why a spilled bottle of wine marks the turning point, or peripeteia, in the story.

As was mentioned earlier, this incident revealed the captain's obsessions to Schöner. As a result, Schöner became ever more withdrawn from the captain, forcing the captain to become even more aggressive in trying to break down the grace and ease he so resented in Schöner.

Page 232

"An Outpost of Progress"
Joseph Conrad

1.   What sort of people are Kayerts and Carlier? What do you learn about them from the scene in the first paragraph? What are their attitudes toward (a) their assignment, (b) each other, and (c) the natives and the land?

Kayerts is an effusive, gullible fool, an ex-administrator in the telegraph service, transplanted, without preparation, to the heart of darkness, three hundred miles from the nearest trading post. Carlier, an ex-noncommissioned officer, is a cynic, but no more prepared to run an isolated trading post than Kayerts. Each wants to reap as much as possible from the assignment, but Carlier is more skeptical than Kayerts. "We shall see, very soon," he says. They are wary of each other, subtly hostile. They scorn the natives and hate the land. They are archetypical colonials: white men in the tropics. As Conrad says, "They were two perfectly insignificant and incapable individuals, whose existence is only rendered possible through the high organization of civilized crowds" (par. 3).

For another view of colonialism, students should be encouraged to read "Heart of Darkness."

2. What is the turning point in the story (peripeteia)? How do the attitudes and actions of Kayerts and Carlier change after the peripeteia?

The turning point comes when Makola trades the station men for ivory. After this, Kayerts and Carlier lose all semblance of morality.

> As they were going back to the house Kayerts observed with a sigh: "It had to be done." And Carlier said: "It's deplorable, but, the men being Company's men, the ivory is Company's ivory. We must look after it." "I will report to the Director, of course," said Kayerts. "Of course; let him decide," approved Carlier.

3.   During the nineteenth century, Europeans "invaded" Africa in force, colonializing, exploiting, and "modernizing." (The slave trade is just one aspect of the impact of "civilization" on the "Dark Continent.") How is Makola symbolic of nineteenth-century Africa? How does the agent represent the vast scene?

Makola is the corrupted African. European commercialism created the Makolas and changed Africa forever. Many Africans were eager participants in the slave trade, which continued even after abolition in Great Britain (1807) and America. According to the Grolier encyclopedia,

> In the mid-19th century . . . Arabo-Swahili caravan leaders from Zanzibar were scouring the lands within the distant Congo basin for slaves to supply the developing markets of Arabia and the Indian Ocean islands, where sugar was being grown, as well as the clove plantations of Zanzibar itself. Earlier the hinterlands of Malawi and Zambia had been crisscrossed innumerable times for slaves and ivory, and virtually no part of Africa was unacquainted with the horrors of enslavement.

4. Is Makola the perfect "company man"? Explain.

Makola puts commercial interests above all others. His own interests and those the company are inseparable. He is as indifferent to the fortunes of the company men whom he sells into slavery as the director is to the fortunes of Kayerts and Carlier.

5. Give specific examples of background knowledge that one must have in order to understand this story.

For example: a general understanding of colonialism; some knowledge of slavery. The term "colonialism" could be a prompt for a discussion of the significance of the tale--its "moral."

6. What is the main idea of the story? How does the title relate to the main idea?

The ironic title sums the story up: an outpost (at the very frontier) bringing progress (in the form of inept Europeans and rapacious commercialism) to the heart of darkness.

7. What is Conrad's attitude toward European civilization?   Cite specific evidence for your opinion.

The Europeans in the story are less than admirable: the foolish and greedy Kayerts and Carlier; the heartless, rapacious director.   Even the symbol of technological progress, the steamboat, is "an enormous sardine box with a flat-roofed shed erected on it." (Conrad, of course, had a master's license for sailing vessels, but he never did qualify for a master's license in steamships.)

8.   The story conveys Joseph Conrad's opinions about nineteenth-century colonialism in Africa, among other subjects. Give examples of passages in which he directly states his opinions. How do the characters and their actions further develop the author's opinions about his theme?

Conrad says, for instance:

The courage, the composure, the confidence; the emotions and principles; every great and every insignificant thought belongs not the individual but to the crowd: to the crowd that believes blindly in the irresistible force of its institutions and of its morals, in the power of its police and of its opinion. But the contact with pure unmitigated savagery, with primitive nature and primitive man, brings sudden and profound trouble to the heart. (par. 3).

9. In what ways does the author withhold information to build suspense?

For example, we do not learn what transpired between Makola and the threatening strangers until Kayerts and Carlier find the company men gone and the ivory trove enriched.

10.   Conrad frequently uses irony to convey his meaning.   Point out some instances and explain them.

For example, par. 14: "For days the two pioneers of trade and progress would look on their empty courtyard in the vibrating brilliance of vertical sunshine." It is deeply ironic to call the two "heroes" pioneers of trade and progress. They are not pioneers, they are unsuccessful as traders, and in no sense do they represent progress; in fact, they represent decadence.

Page 252

"The Yellow Wallpaper"
Charlotte Perkins Gilman

1. Do a thumbnail sketch of the husband. Cite the parts of the story that revealed his traits to you. Are they opinions expressed by the narrator/wife, are they the actions or reactions of the husband, or are they some other aspect of the narrative? What acts does the husband perform? What is his relationship to the scenes? Is some agency important? What are the purposes of the husband's acts?

The narrator of the story, the wife, says of her husband's character: "John is practical in the extreme. He has no patience with faith, an intense horror of superstition, and he scoffs openly at any talk of things not to be felt and seen and put down in figures." Because the narrator says that John chides her about losing proper self-control and is always giving his wife special instructions, the reader gains an understanding of the husband as one who wants to keep all matters which affect him within his own rigid control. Because he doesn't trust anything but the tangible, he has no understanding of his wife's mental instability. As she herself writes, "John does not know how much I really suffer. He knows there is no reason to suffer, and that satisfies him." He is unable to empathize with others, which is the reason that he refuses to repaper the room or to move to another room. He is terribly condescending; in attempting to be affectionate, he calls the wife a little girl and his blessed little goose.

The husband's major act was to take his wife to the country in order to provide her with a rest since she had started exhibiting "a slight hysterical tendency." However, the husband's true importance in the story is less for what he does than for what he does not do. Whether or not he had brought his wife to the colonial mansion for a rest, the wife nonetheless would surely have suffered a breakdown. The husband's adamant refusal to accept mental illness as a treatable disease is the important act of the story. By insisting that his wife confront her fears, especially those having to do with the bedroom wallpaper, the husband ensured her quicker decline into madness. In addition, even though the wife wished to travel and visit relatives, the husband refused even though the insular nature of the wife's existence exacerbated her mental breakdown.

The wallpaper, since it is the focus of the wife's attention, could be considered an agency.

2. Now do a thumbnail sketch of the wife.

The wife is a passive person who is aware of her husband's condescending attitude but tends to accept it as a token of his love for her. In addition, she is probably a fairly well educated person since she makes reference to the fact that she writes as a pastime and that she has some knowledge of the principle of design. Such activities would have been regarded as something which benefits and improves the character of a person who was born into a well-to-do family. Therefore, the narrator has probably been financially comfortable her entire life. The wife has very few, if any, responsibilities since the husband, with his controlling personality, would surely be the one to make the major decisions and conduct the business 8affairs of the household. The narrator lets the reader know that she even is not responsible for the care of her own baby since she has a person who does that for her.

3. In doing your characterizations of the husband and the wife, did you find that some relationships among the critical questions were more useful than others? Explain.

The relationships between the wife (agent) and the scene (the room with yellow wallpaper) and between the wife and the husband (agents) are the most important.

4. The primary scene of the story, the room with the ugly yellow wallpaper, is unusual. What other strange elements are there about the room? Do you believe that these features actually exist, or are they figments of the wife's imagination? Explain your reasoning. Explain how these details of scene enhance the story.

The narrator calls attention to the barred windows. There are "rings and things" in the walls, the wallpaper is peeled off in spots, the plaster is has fallen off in places, the floor is scratched and gouged, and the bed is nailed to the floor.

There is no reason for the reader to suspect that these features of the room exist only in the narrator's imagination. The reader, in fact, must trust the accuracy of most of the narration in order to understand the story. We see the husband only through the eyes of the narrator, and none of her statements about her husband's actions are contradicted later in the story. The only imaginary element is the figure held prisoner within the wallpaper's design.

These unusual features create a bit of mystery for readers and allow them to empathize a little bit more with the narrator. Not all of the features can be explained by the narrator's supposition that the room was a gymnasium because that doesn't explain why the bed had been nailed to the floor.

5. Was any of your world knowledge about the era during which the story takes place useful (or essential) when you were evaluating the relationship between the husband and wife? Explain.

Some knowledge of the relationship between men and women and of the upper middle classes of one hundred years ago is necessary to understand the characters: that women would have been educated in the arts and that men were the preeminent power both in the workforce and in domestic situations. In general, a knowledge of feminist history is useful, if not essential, to the reader of "The Yellow Wallpaper."

6. Does the story itself provide you with essential background information? What is this information?

The story provides information about the disorder called "nervous depression" and its treatment in the nineteenth century.

7. What clues in the story, besides references to historical personalities, tell you that it was not written recently?

The medicines: phosphates or phosphites and tonics. The spelling of <u>draught</u> for <u>draft</u>.

8. The story is told by a character who is mentally ill. At what point in the story do you realize that the wife is seriously ill and not just suffering from a slight nervous disorder? What clues and foreshadowing are presented before this point of revelation? How does the unreliability of the narrator in the story affect your interpretation of it.

By paragraph 35, readers know that the narrator is seriously disturbed. Just before paragraph 35, we learn that the windows of the room had been barred to keep children from falling out; now, however, the bars keep the narrator in. The unreliable narration is the very stuff of the story, for we see the world through the eyes of a seriously disturbed woman.

3. Thinking Critically about Exposition

Background and Sources

The analytical questions in this chapter fall into two categories: a group based on the Pentad (which is central to Chapter 2) and a group derived from the widely influential essay "Logic and Conversation," by philosopher Paul Grice.

Critical Questions about Exposition

Page 268. How Can Knowledge about the Author(s) Help Me Read Critically?

The author is the <u>agent</u> (or the authors are the agents) who performed the action of writing the text. In the case of narratives, the author is the agent <u>of</u> the text and the characters are the agents <u>in</u> the text. Thus, Conrad as author is the agent <u>of</u> "An Outpost of Progress," but the characters are the agents <u>in</u> the text. We can study the text as an <u>act</u> of the author or the <u>acts</u> that the characters (agents) perform in the text.

Page 268. Exercise: Author

The exercise encourages students to think about the reasons for authors' beliefs. The daily newspaper or a newsmagazine can be a resource for students who need a bit of help.

1. **Name one national figure whose opinion on a current issue is obviously influenced by religious beliefs. Explain the issue and the influence.**

2. **Name a national figure whose opinion on a current issue is obviously influenced by a political philosophy. Explain the issue and the influence.**

3. **Name a national figure whose viewpoint on a current issue is, in your opinion, merely a prejudice. Explain why you think the figure is prejudiced.**

Page 269. How Can Knowledge about the Time and Place in Which the Text Was Written or Published Help Me Read Critically?"

The <u>scene</u> in which the text is composed influences the author, and the scene in which it is read influences the readers. For example, in a politically conservative community, a letter to the editor advocating a radical cause is likely to be less forthright than such a letter written in a liberal community--or perhaps the reverse would be the situation, the conservative scene influencing the radical author to pull all stops. The point is that the influence of scene is important when one evaluates a text.

Page 269. Exercise: Time and Place

1. Explain how time and place have influenced your own writing (or what you say in public). Be specific rather than general.

Almost every student will recall, when prompted, that an English teacher made demands, either reasonable or unreasonable. (To require correct spelling--except for occasional lapses--is quite different from banning sentences that end with prepositions or insisting that students not use first person.) Language that is appropriate in the dormitory room is often inappropriate in church. The point is this: to demonstrate to students that situation influences language use and that they have a variety of "registers."

2. In a current issue of a national magazine such as _Time_ or _Newsweek_, find an example of the influence of time and place on the publication of some text and explain that influence. (If you prefer, you might explain the influence of time and place upon a film or television program.)

One obvious example: the television series on Columbus, celebrating the 500th anniversary of his voyage.

Page 270. How Can Knowledge about the Medium Help Me Read Critically?

The medium is the _agency_, and the term includes publisher, genre, and format. The statements from Bethany House and Sierra Club Books demonstrate the influence of the agency on the author (agent) and his or her act of composing.

Page 271. Exercise: Medium

Discuss one of the following magazines as a medium. What sorts of articles does it publish? What sorts would it _not_ publish? How might its readers be classified (lowbrow, middlebrow, highbrow)? Does it seem to have a political bias? Explain.

Alaska Outdoors
B'Nai B'Rith International Jewish Monthly
Child Life
Discoveries
Esquire
Family Circle
Good Housekeeping
Harper's Magazine
Insight
Jack and Jill
Mademoiselle
Ms.
National Review

<u>Outdoor Life</u>
<u>Paris Review</u>
<u>People</u>
<u>Road and Track</u>

For example, <u>Harper's</u> (November 1991): It publishes a series of brief articles or extracts under the general heading "Readings." These include offbeat pieces (such as "L. A. Crises," a list of oddball calls received by Los Angeles fire dispatchers on the 911 number--"Slept wrong on neck"), serious essays ("The Objects of Childhood," by John Updike), and short oddities such as an announcement from the Harvard Divinity School's recycling coordinator:

> Someone changed the recycling sign in Rock entryway from "colored paper" to "paper of color." If this was meant as a joke, I don't think it's funny. If it was done because of a legitimate concern about language usage, please let me know by leaving a note in my mailbox.

The magazine typically contains at least one article on a serious and timely subject such as "Mixed Blood," by Richard Rodriguez, in the November 1991 issue. There is also a whimsical article, classed as criticism, by E. L. Doctorow: "Standards," comments on "how great songs name us." There is also an article on the civil war in Sri Lanka.

The editor, Lewis Lapham, always writes a column, and he is a liberal in politics.

Clearly, the magazine is aimed at a fairly intellectual audience; a person who subscribes to <u>People</u> and regularly buys the <u>National Enquirer</u> would be unlikely to read <u>Harper's</u>. The magazine is aimed at a given social class: middle-class liberals.

Page 271. How Can Knowledge about Purpose Help Me Read Critically?

When students question purpose, they begin to unravel the tangle of motives that usually fuel human actions.

Page 271. Exercise: Purpose

The mysteries of purpose are often more difficult to unravel than they are in most advertisements. For example, Ernest Hemingway wrote "The Torrents of Spring," a parody of the work of his friend Sherwood Anderson. If you read carefully and think about what is <u>not</u> said as well as what is said, Hemingway's explanation of why he wrote this book illustrates the complexity of motives that underlie some texts. After you have carefully read the selection, discuss your perceptions of Hemingway's motives. (Explain how knowledge of Hemingway's biography would help you determine his purpose in the selection.)

> I wrote it because I was righteous which is the worst thing you can be. And I thought he was going to pot the way he was writing and that I could kid him out of it by showing him how awful it was. I wrote 'The Torrents of Spring' to poke fun at him. It was cruel to do and it didn't do any good and he just wrote worse and worse. What the hell business of mine was it if he wanted to write badly.

None. He had written good and then lost it. But then I was more righteous and more loyal to writing than to my friend (qtd. in Plimpton 36).

The following questions will prompt discussion of this complex statement.

1. What is a parody? Do you think that parodies are usually just good-natured humor or kidding?

2. What sort of person was Hemingway? Do you think that he would have written "The Torrents of Spring" as a charitable act, to save his friend from deteriorating as a writer?

3. Do the following two sentences indicate that Hemingway actually regretted the parody, or was he simply making an apology because that would be the expected action? "It was cruel to do and it didn't do any good and he just wrote worse and worse. What the hell business was it of mine if he wanted to write badly."

Page 272. The Writer-Reader Contract

The following background discussion is adapted from The Culture and Politics of Literacy, by W. Ross Winterowd:

> When I speak or write, I use words in conventional structures. However, I also have an intention: to promise, to state, to ask, to apologize, to threaten, to explain. . . . Thus,
>
> (1) I promise I'll wash the dishes tonight.
>
> and
>
> (2) I promise I'll disinherit you if you don't mow the lawn.
>
> are--or at least could be--quite different kinds of speech acts: 1 we would normally take as a promise, and 2 is undoubtedly a threat. And we can determine these values because we have a sense of the way the world works.
>
> In the jargon of speech act theory, the illocutionary force of 1 is that of a promise; the illocutionary force of 2 is that of a threat.
>
> So part of the meaning of every speech act (whether oral or written) is its illocutionary force, the user's intention.
>
> However, this formulation leaves out an essential component: the hearer or reader. Since you cannot read my mind, you must interpret my illocution. Take the following exchange as an example:
>
> (3) Wife to husband (at a party): It's getting late.
> Husband to wife: It's only eleven.
>
> The wife, we can assume, was not merely making a statement, giving information, but was intending "It's time to go." And the husband was not correcting misinformation, but was really saying, "Let's stay a bit longer." Yet at face value, according to the dictionary, the husband and wife were merely exchanging information. In fact, the husband interpreted his wife's illocution and

responded with his own perlocution: perlocutionary act is the response to the illocutionary act.

We can see, then, that the tapestry of language comes about through the warp of illocution and the woof of perlocution, an intricate weaving of intention and response.

Since conflicts among nations and races often come about through misunderstanding of illocution and perlocution, the subject is worth pursuing through two classic examples:

> (4) Gracie: On my way in, a man stopped me at the stage door and said, "Hiya, cutie, how about a bite tonight after the show?"
> George: And you said?
> Gracie: I said, "I'm busy after the show, but I'm not doing anything now," so I bit him.
> George: Gracie, let me ask you something. Did the nurse ever drop you on your head when you were a baby?
> Gracie: Oh no, we couldn't afford a nurse, my mother had to do it. (Pattison 14)

In this comic drama, Gracie's first problem is her misunderstanding of "bite." She takes an intended metaphor literally. But when George asks her if she had been dropped on her head when she was a baby, his illocutionary intention was an insult, something like, "You're nuts!" Gracie takes his utterance as a request for information and gives him a "straight" answer.

> (5) A young man on a train to Lublin, Poland asked a prosperous merchant, "Can you tell me the time?"
> The merchant looked at him and replied: "Go to hell!"
> "What? Why, what's the matter with you! I ask you a civil question in a properly civil way, and you give me such an outrageous answer! What's the idea?"
> The merchant looked at him, sighed wearily, and said, "Very well. Sit down and I'll tell you. You ask me a question. I have to give an answer, no? You start a conversation with me--about the weather, politics, business. One thing leads to another. It turns out you're a Jew--I'm a Jew, I live in Lublin, you're a stranger. Out of hospitality, I ask you to my home for dinner. You meet my daughter. She's a beautiful girl--you're a handsome young man. So you go out together a few times--and you fall in love. Finally you come to ask for my daughter's hand in marriage. So why go to all that trouble? Let me tell you right now, young man, I won't let my daughter marry anyone who doesn't even own a watch. (Farb 109-110)

This classic Jewish anecdote gives an analysis of a speech exchange that didn't work because the perlocutionary response to the illocutionary intention was not understandable. The point of the humor is the merchant's explanation of his response.

But we can pile complication upon complication.

Suppose a private says to a general, "Stand at ease, soldier." Granted, the private would probably be reprimanded or court-martialed, but our question is this: did the private give a real order? If the private somehow thought he had the authority to give an order to a general, then his speech act was a genuine order (as misconceived as it might have been). If the general believed that the private _intended_ a real order--not just wise-cracking--then the general would conclude that the private was not insubordinate, but somehow misinformed or unbalanced, and would perhaps recommend psychiatric therapy.

However, we can turn to a real-life situation involving modes of _mitigation_ and _politeness_. When a teacher says to a middle class child,

> (6) "Junior, this is very sloppy work. Now you take that composition and write it over again."

The child is likely to reply politely with some kind of mitigating term, such as

> (7) "Aw, do I have to?"

or

> (8) "I'll do it tomorrow."

The illocutionary force of either **8** or **9** might well be complete denial, the intention being "I won't do it." In any case, we would not expect a middle class student to give an out-and-out "No!" to the teacher. On the other hand, some children not in the middle-class speech community might well respond simply (and candidly) "No!" The usages they have inherited from their language group do not include _certain_ modes of mitigation and politeness, though every language has its own ways of expressing these niceties. The result of such discrepancies between language communities is often confrontation, brought on by failures in understanding.

And this is how language progresses: my intention, your interpretation of that intention. For any of it to work, we must share the language system and world knowledge. You must be able to guess what my response will be, and I must be able to guess what your intention is. When cultures clash, this cooperative endeavor breaks down, and conflict ensues, for we project and understand intentions on the basis of our cultural heritage.

Language transactions progress within an unwritten, but clearly perceivable set of "laws," which we might call "the cooperative principle." When we speak or write, in effect we give the hearer or reader a four-part guarantee, which Grice explains in this way:

> Quantity: If you are assisting me to mend a car, I expect your contribution to be neither more nor less than is required. If, for example, at a particular stage I need four screws, I expect you to hand me four, rather than two or six. [Our translations of the principle for speech and writing: I will give you all of the information you need to understand what I'm getting at, and no more than is necessary.] (28)

Quality: I expect your contributions to be genuine and not spurious. If I need sugar as an ingredient in the cake you are assisting me to make, I do not expect you to hand me salt; if I need a spoon, I do not expect a trick spoon made of rubber. [Our translations of the principle for speech and writing: I will be reliable and truthful.]

Relation: I expect a partner's contribution to be appropriate to the immediate needs at each stage of the transaction. If I am mixing ingredients for a cake, I do not expect to be handed a good book, or even an oven cloth (though this might be an appropriate contribution at a later stage). [Our translations of the principle for speech and writing: Everything in my discourse will relate to my point.]

Manner: I expect a partner to make it clear what contribution he is making and to execute his performance with reasonable dispatch. [Our translations of the principle for speech and writing: I will be as clear as possible.] (28)

Now a language user can violate these principles for one of two reasons: purposely, to create a special effect, or inadvertently, through inattention or lack of skill in language use. For example, in the following marvelous course description, Woody Allen primarily violates the principle of relation--and does so zanily:

(9) Fundamental Astronomy: A detailed study of the universe and its care and cleaning. The sun, which is made of gas, can explode at any moment, sending our entire planetary system hurtling to destruction; students are advised what the average citizen can do in such a case. They are also taught to identify various constellations, such as the Big Dipper, Cygnus the Swan, Sagittarius the Archer, and the twelve stars that form Lumides the Pants Salesman. (58-59)

Virtually nothing in the passage relates to what we might conceive as a course in astronomy, but when Woody tells us that the sun is made of gas, a fact that all of his readers know, he violates the principle of quantity, giving us more information than we need.

Or think about manner. "The Gettysburg Address," with its eloquent language, is considered one of the world's great masterpieces of public address: "Fourscore and seven years ago, our fathers brought forth upon this continent a new nation, conceived in liberty and dedicated to the proposition that all men are created equal." Certainly nothing could be more appropriate to the occasion. However, on another occasion, the reaction to a child's spilling orange juice on the parlor rug, elevated language is comic:

(10) On Sabbath last, the first son of my first son, inadvertently and without malicious intent, did overturn the vessel containing his orange juice, thereby staining the carpet in the parlor of our dwelling.

Sometimes, of course, language that should be perfectly clear in <u>manner</u> is opaque, for reasons that we cannot determine. The following--quoted in the August 25, 1986, <u>New Yorker</u>--is from the Iowa City <u>Press-Citizen</u>:

> (11) A woman wearing a bold gold bracelet, a well-crafted lapel pin and tasteful earrings shows attention to detail and quality. The rings that catch one's eye as she points to her chart or pensively balances her gold pen on her chin make her ring as good as gold.

The last sentence of this examples <u>does</u> make sense if you think about it in the right way.

It might be said that the problem with grammatical and spelling errors in writing is one of <u>manner</u>; in most writing situations they are simply inappropriate. But more about this later.

The principle of <u>quality</u> is easily illustrated. We tend to place more credence in information from the New York <u>Times</u> than from the <u>National Enquirer</u>. Most people place great confidence in the statements of professionals about their fields: lawyers, engineers, physicians, architects. When we consider the quality of a statement or piece of writing, we are really asking about its credibility.

James Boyd White, a professor of law at the University of Chicago, discusses the difficulty of legal language for laypersons. The law is difficult to understand, he says, not because we don't know the definition of the words, but because of what he calls the "invisible discourse" of the law. "Behind the words, that is, are expectations about the ways in which they will be used, expectations that do not find explicit expression anywhere but are part of the legal culture that the surface language assumes." It might be said, in other words, that nonlawyers do not know how the cooperative principle works in legal language.

Page 272. Exercise: The Writer-Reader Contract

Before you read the examples, explanations, and analyses that follow in this chapter, explain your initial reaction to these "terms" of the writer-reader contract. Might not some writers intentionally give more information than is necessary? Don't some writers lie? Do writers always stick to the point? Do you know of texts that you think are intentionally written to violate one or more of these rules? In light of these questions, does the writer-reader contract seem valid to you?

See the discussion under **The Writer-Reader Contract** on page 80, above.

Page 272. Exercise: Quantity

Discuss the quantity of information in the following brief texts. For what sort of readers are they apparently intended? For example, an article in a general encyclopedia is intended for nonspecialists. In your opinion, do the texts provide enough information for those readers? Do they contain more information than is

necessary?   For example, an ichthyologist would not need the nonitalicized information in the following sentence:

> <u>Last year, I caught a fifteen-pound steelhead</u>, a trout that, like a salmon, spends its life in the ocean, but returns to its native stream to spawn.

However, an ichthyologist would probably need the nonitalicized information in the following sentence:

> <u>Last year, I caught a fifteen-pound brown trout in Rock Creek</u>, a tributary of the Clark Fork of the Columbia, which flows into the Clark Fork about thirty miles west of Missoula, Montana.

1. Mercury, the nearest planet to the sun, is the second smallest of the nine planets known to be orbiting the sun. Its diameter is 3,100 miles and its mean distance from the sun is 36,000,000 miles. (<u>The World Almanac and Book of Facts,</u> <u>1991</u>)

The text is intended for general readers.   One bit of conclusive evidence: astronomers and other experts would know that Mercury is the nearest planet to the sun and is the second smallest of the nine planets.

2. The Flesch scale does not give grade level equivalents. You end up instead with a number between 0 and 100. The higher your text rates on the Flesch scale, the easier it should be. A Flesch score of 40 is called "difficult," while 75 is fairly easy. The FOG index and the Dale-Chall formula do give grade level equivalents. (Janice Redish, <u>Readability</u>)

The text seems to be intended for specialists since general, educated readers could not be expected to know about the Flesch scale, the FOG index, and the Dale-Chall formula.   General readers would need some explanation of these technical terms.

3. To us, layman and scholar alike, writing is <u>written language</u>. Ask a man in the street and he will not even hesitate about giving his answer. The same definition is expressed poetically by Voltaire: "L'écriture est la peinture de la voix; plus elle est ressemblante, meilleure elle est," and by Brébeuf: "Cet art ingénieux de peindre la parole et de parler aux yeux."   The French authors are in good company here because they can back their opinion with the authority of the reliable Aristotle, who centuries ago, in the introductory chapter of <u>De Interpretatione</u> of his <u>Logic</u>, said: "Spoken words are symbols of mental experience and written words are the symbols of spoken words. (I. J. Gelb, <u>A Study of Writing</u>)

The text is intended for a highly specialized audience: those who are interested in the history of writing systems--primarily scholars such as linguists and paleographers. The untranslated French quotations are a clue to the expectations that Gelb has of his readers. Translations: <u>Writing is painting with the voice; the</u>

more the resemblance, the better. That ingenious art, to paint the word and speak with the eyes.

4. More than a hundred million years ago there were some kinds of ants scurrying about on the earth much as they do today. A hundred million years! In this great length of time many other kinds of animals came into being, flourished for a while, then died away leaving only fossil remains as evidence that they ever existed. It is not surprising, therefore, that we sometimes wonder about the success of these little insects.

In general, people are apt to think that ants thrive because they are constantly busy. Certainly their reputation for industry is widespread, being noted even in Biblical times when King Solomon gave the advice, "Go to the ant, O sluggard, consider her ways and be wise." Because the quotation often is ended here, it may be thought that the mere hustle and bustle of ants were the only "ways" Solomon had in mind. But the words that follow concern a harvest, and indicate that the King was thinking of an ability to provide for the future during fair-weather months. However, it is not likely that he really had an understanding of all the remarkable ways of ants. Did he know that some kinds do not harvest but eat only meat, while others keep plant lice as "cows," obtaining nourishment through them? Did he realize that certain ants enslaved others? Did he know of the fine cooperation between the members of an ant colony and of their talents in constructing homes and caring for them? (Dorothy Shuttlesworth and Su Zan Noguchi Swain, The Story of Ants)

This is a fairly complicated text, not in the information that it conveys, but in its implications about the intended readers. The Story of Ants is, of course, a children's book, and in tone it is aimed at either young readers or listeners, particularly the series of questions following Solomon's quotation. However, a young reader or a child listening as the book was read to him or her would need a great deal of world knowledge for comprehension: the concept of millions of years and of evolution; the dying-out of species; King Solomon and Biblical times; the word sluggard. The authors assume what amounts to adult cultural literacy in a book that simplifies entomology for children. If an adult and a child somehow share interpretation--the adult providing world knowledge that the child could not be expected to have--The Story of Ants could be a successful piece of writing.

Page 274. Exercise: Quality

This is the first sentence in the preface to the New International Version of the Bible, copyrighted in 1978: "The New International Version is a completely new translation of the Holy Bible made by over a hundred scholars working directly from the best available Hebrew, Aramaic and Greek texts" (vii).

1. Why did the editors feel that such a statement was necessary?

From the standpoint of quality, it was necessary to assure readers that this translation of the Book is absolutely reliable.

2. Explain why the quality of the New International Version depends on other texts.

It is important to base translations on the best available and most authentic versions of a text. Thus, Biblical scholars use the texts that they believe most nearly represent the original intent. If, for instance, the New International Version were simply a translation of the King James version, it would be a translation of a translation and thus would be less credible than a translation that relies on original sources.

3. Explain how judging the quality of the New International Version or any other version of the Bible is similar to judging the quality of a secular covenant such as the United States Constitution. Another way of looking at the question is this: In what way or ways are theologians who study the Bible like the members of the United States Supreme Court?

The question takes us back to the first chapter of this book and the discussion of reading--such matters as world knowledge and the inferences we draw from texts. The question might well prompt discussion about determinacy of meaning. Does the Bible or the Constitution have one final meaning, or does meaning evolve? Biblical interpreters and Supreme Court justices are constrained by traditions and institutions: the church, and the structure of the United States government.

The question should stimulate a great deal of discussion and debate.

Page 276. Exercise: Manner

Without worrying about technical language, explain how the following examples violate the principle of manner. If possible, rewrite the examples so that they are easier to understand.

1. "The system of 'hearing (understanding) oneself speak' through the phonic substance--which presents itself as the nonexterior, nonmundane, therefore nonempirical or noncontingent signifier--has necessarily dominated the history of the world during an entire epoch, and has even produced the idea of the world, the idea of world-origin, that arises from the difference between the worldly and nonworldly, the outside and the inside, ideality and nonideality, universal and nonuniversal, transcendental and empirical, etc." (Jacques Derrida, _Of Grammatology_, translated by Gayatri Chakravorty Spivak)

Anyone who has attempted to read Derrida--either in French or in an English translation--can attest that he is a furiously difficult writer. However, if one is familiar with the project that he has undertaken--the deconstruction of Western metaphysics--the passage becomes decipherable. In brief, Derrida argues against the belief in Western philosophy that writing is secondary, a representation of speech, and that speech is primary, the expression of truths that are present to consciousness.

In our translation:

Spoken language--which seems to come directly from our minds, unmediated by print, conveying our thoughts directly--has dominated the history of the world during an entire epoch and has even given us our concept of the world and the origin of the world. Speech is: nonworldly (spiritual), existing only for the moment, as contrasted with the permanence of writing; it arises from the interior of oneself, whereas writing is only the physical, external representation of speech; it is ideal, having no visible manifestation; it is a universal attribute of humanity (for not all people or all societies have writing); it is associated with the transcendental as opposed to the empirical.

2. "Dr. Lisa Eichler, my psychology professor, criticized Susanne Langer's concept of symbolism. She said that she did not adequately differentiate verbal knowledge from nonverbal." (Advanced Composition student)

The problem, of course, is pronoun reference. Here is a "translation" of the text: Dr. Lisa Eichler, my psychology professor, criticized Susanne Langer's concept of symbolism, saying that Langer did not adequately differentiate verbal knowledge from nonverbal.

3. "Of the exercises which the rules of the University required, some were published by him in his maturer years. They had been undoubtedly applauded; for they were such as few can perform: yet there is reason to suspect that he was regarded in his college with no great fondness. That he obtained no fellowship is certain; but the unkindness with which he was treated was not merely negative. I am ashamed to relate what I fear is true, that Milton was the last student in either university that suffered the public indignity of corporal correction. (Samuel Johnson, Milton)

Revising sentence structure makes the passage easier to read--not necessarily better! That is to say, clarity and accessibility are valuable only in relation to the author's semantic intention. Changing the vocabulary also simplifies the passage. In revising these sentences to make them easier to read, we are also muting the distinctive "voice" of Samuel Johnson. Nonetheless, here is a rewrite:

In his maturer years, he published some of the exercises which the rules of the University required. Even though they had undoubtedly been praised (for they were such as few can perform), yet there is reason to suspect that in his college he was not well liked. It is certain that he obtained no fellowship, but the unkindness with which he was treated was not merely negative. Though I fear it is true, I am ashamed to relate that Milton was the last student in either university who suffered the public indignity of corporal punishment.

Page 276. Exercise: Relation

Below is a "doctored" version of the first paragraph of an enigmatically titled book that you would probably enjoy, The Dancing Wu Li Masters, by Gary Zukav. Point out the irrelevancies in the paragraph, the material that has no relation or

only a tenuous relation to the point of the text.   Don't consult the original paragraph, which follows the "doctored" version, until after you have made your decision.

Irrelevant material is italicized:

> My first exposure to quantum physics occurred a few years ago when a friend invited me to an afternoon conference at the Lawrence Laboratory in Berkeley, California. At that time, I had no connections with the scientific community, so I went to see what physicists were like. To my great surprise, I discovered that Chinese restaurants in Berkeley are just as good as those across the Bay in San Francisco, and I discovered also that (1), I understood everything the physicists said, and (2), their discussion sounded very much like a theological discussion. When I was in college, I was very religious and talked theology to my roommates for hours. I scarcely could believe what I had discovered. Physics was not the sterile, boring discipline that I had assumed it to be. It was as interesting as history, my favorite subject. (Since I was in high school, I have been a Civil War buff.) It was a rich, profound venture which had become inseparable from philosophy. Incredibly, no one but physicists seemed to be aware of this remarkable development. As my interest in and knowledge of physics grew, I resolved to share this discovery with others. This book is a gift of my discovery. It is one of a series.

Works Cited

Burke, Kenneth.   A Grammar of Motives.   Berkeley and Los Angeles: U of California P, 1969.

Farb, Peter. Word Play. New York: Bantam Books, 1975.

Grice, Paul. "Logic and Conversation." Studies in the Ways of Words. Cambridge, Mass.: Harvard UP, 1989. 1-143.

Pattison, Robert. On Literacy. New York: Oxford UP, 1975.

White, James Boyd. "The Invisible Discourse of the Law: Reflections on Legal Literacy and General Education." Literacy for Life. Ed. Richard W. Bailey and Robin Melanie Fosheim. New York: MLA, 1983. 137-50.

Winterowd, W. Ross. The Culture and Politics of Literacy. New York: Oxford UP, 1989.

Page 285

"Popular and Scholarly Views of 'Good English'"
Edward Finegan

1. Regarding the principle of quantity: At any points in this essay does Finegan give you less information than you need to understand him? Does he ever give you more than necessary? (Be specific in your answers.)

Finegan does not explain in each of his examples why the use of the word in question is incorrect. In regard to John Ciardi's dictum that <u>as</u> should be substituted for <u>like</u> in the Winston slogan, Finegan states the rule which is broken by Kipling's "Recessional." However, he does not explain the problem of usage for the following: the phrases <u>drive slow</u>, <u>I'll try and go</u>, <u>different than</u>, <u>who did you see</u>, and <u>It's me</u>; the problem with split infinitives; the use of <u>hopefully</u> in the sense of <u>I hope that</u>. Technically, grammar consists of three elements: syntax, semantics, and phonetics. Most people would not be aware that phonetics is part of grammar.   However, Finegan provides an example of bad grammar in which the rules of phonetics are broken (the pronunciation of the words <u>realtor</u> and <u>nuclear</u>). The students might very well be confused by Finegan's example because he did not note prior to his example that phonetics is part of a language's grammar. This essay is the introductory chapter to Finegan's book <u>Attitudes Toward English Usage</u>. Towards the close of the chapter, the author begins laying out some of the issues that will be addressed in future chapters. As a result, the reader might have a general sense of what the author is referring to but would not have a complete understanding without further clarification: "Besides straightforward differences of opinion, we find that misunderstanding, hostility, and bigotry have contributed at times in this century--as before--to the confusion surrounding the composition of dictionaries and grammars and the teaching of English usage. Philosophical differences over the nature of language, the purposes of education, the function of science (especially its role in language studies), the value of democracy, and ultimately the character of human society have obscured discussions ostensibly about English usage." The second to the last sentence also contains more information with scant detail: "Besides the standard of authority, he [Otto Jespersen] noted appeal to geographical, literary, aristocratic, democratic, logical, and esthetic standards."

2. Regarding the principle of quality: What reasons do you have for trusting (or distrusting) Finegan's knowledge of his subject or his honesty?

The author is writing about a subject which is within his area of expertise, and his level of expertise should be considerable given the fact that he is a professor of linguistics at a major university. The essay is written so as to present both sides of the argument (descriptive/prescriptive) in a fair and impartial manner. There is nothing to suggest that the author has slanted the presentation to benefit the side of the argument with which he agrees, if indeed he has even chosen a side in the debate.

3. Regarding the principle of manner: If you think the essay is sometimes unclear, indicate where and explain the difficulty.

The manner in which Finegan writes is clear and straightforward. He provides the reader with an ample background to the descriptive/prescriptive debate and is careful to supply common, everyday examples which help the reader understand the nature of the debate.

4. Regarding the principle of relation: Are any parts of the essay irrelevant to the topic? Explain.

There are no major (or even minor) irrelevancies.

5. The controversy over Webster's Third New International Dictionary had to do with its purpose. Contrast the publisher's purpose with what Mario Pei and other "traditionalists" believe the purpose should have been.

The traditionalists believed that the Third should have recorded only the best usage, whatever that might have been. In effect, the traditionalists held that the dictionary should regulate or at least have a normative influence on language. The publisher and editors, on the other hand, believed that the dictionary should be an accurate description of the language used by English-speaking peoples. Thus, strict traditionalists would deplore the inclusion of dove as the past tense of dive (I dive from the bank right now, I dove from the bank yesterday). The editors would argue that dove is a form used by native speakers of English and thus should be included in a comprehensive dictionary.

6. State the main point of "Popular and Scholarly Views of 'Good English.'"

One of the most fundamental differences between students of language is the way in which they regard their role or mission: the members of one group believe that it is the purpose of language study to regulate usage; the members of the other group believe that it is the purpose of language study to describe usage.

7. Should dictionaries try to describe language as it is used, or should they attempt to set standards?

There is, of course, no definitive answer to this question. It should be pointed out that even Webster's Third made distinctions in the types of usage, noting, for example, that the pronunciation of the word nuclear as "nu-cu-lar" was chiefly substandard. That is to say, even with the descriptive tack taken by the editors, distinctions in usage were made, and the student searching for the most generally accepted educated usage would have no difficulty finding it in Webster's Third.

8. Explain "doctrine of correctness" and "doctrine of usage."

The instructor might bring into the discussion the terms prescriptive and descriptive in defining the two doctrines. Very important to the discussion of the doctrine of usage are these two sentences: "They [Webster's Third's compilers] claim that the setting of value on linguistic forms is a social, not a lexicographic, matter" and "Descriptive linguists do not recommend that a grammar of nonstandard English be taught in schools and colleges, where a command of standard English is assumed as the accepted goal." That is to say, descriptivists and prescriptivists both agree on the educational goal of achieving fluency in standard English within the classroom. Two reasons for such a relativistic viewpoint are the "dramatic increases in the numbers of students from lower socioeconomic levels and from foreign cultures. . . ."   Very important to the doctrine of correctness: "They [Webster's Third's compilers] must carefully elect the words and meanings they list, rigorously weeding out every questionable usage."   To differentiate the two, Finegan says that   "the view of descriptive linguists may be summarized thus: the correctness of 'grammar' or 'English usage' is relative."   On the other hand, by implication the correctness of grammar or English usage for prescriptive linguists is absolute.   If the discussion is involved and the class is interested in the topic, the instructor might ask that they relate usage and correctness to the variables which Finegan itemizes towards the end of the chapter: "Philosophical differences over the nature of language, the purposes of education, the function of science (especially its role in language studies), the value of democracy, and ultimately the character of human society have obscured discussions ostensibly about English usage."

9. Explain "school grammar."

Finegan notes the existence of three grammars: (1) a systematic and complete description of a language, (2) the psychological system that not only contains the decoding rules for understanding language but also the heuristics for continuously generating unique communication (transformational-generative grammar), and (3) school grammar. A major difference between school grammar and the other two types is that unlike the others, school grammar "must be taught in the schools because it is not much observed in ordinary spoken communication and therefore cannot be acquired the way a child absorbs the vast bulk of his internalized linguistic system--without conscious effort or formal instruction."   School grammar can be regarded as almost the linguistic equivalent of social manners.

10. Explain your reaction to "bad grammar" such as "Me and him played on the same team," "Louella don't have no time for extracurricular activities," and "George ain't been here since May."

This question is, in many ways, the most powerful argument for the school of prescriptive usage. Many people, when they hear such usage, find it difficult to get beyond the language form to understand exactly what the person is trying to express, no matter how valid the idea or sentiment. Because of this, nonstandard usage is almost as much a barrier to true communication as a sentence whose literal meaning cannot be determined.

11. Why do many people value "correct" grammar so highly?

There is a certain elitism in valuing correct grammar since it is an indication of a good deal of education at the public level and of good breeding at the private level.

12. What are your own opinions about "correct" grammar? Do you believe that there is an absolute standard of correctness to which one should aspire? Explain the ways in which you agree or disagree with Finegan's viewpoint.

13. **How would a linguist determine whether a disputed word or phrase should be used or avoided? Relate your answer to the critical questions that readers of texts should ask themselves. For example, a critical reader considers the scene in which a text was written and in which it is read; a linguist also considers scene. Think about other questions regarding critical reading, and apply them to the problem of word usage.**

For example, slang is both appropriate and effective in given scenes (e.g., bull sessions among professors in the coffee room) but inappropriate in others (a formal lecture before a professional society). Purpose also determines the appropriateness of usage; if my purpose is to insult a writer, I might call him or her a "hack." Agency influences usage: the vocabulary in a popular tabloid will be quite different from the vocabulary in the Times Literary Supplement.

Page 299

"U, Non-U, and You"
John Simon

1. **Regarding the principle of quantity: At any points in this essay does Simon fail to give you enough information? Does he ever give you more than necessary? (Be specific in your answers.)**

Simon is very good about giving the reader sufficient information with which to understand his writing. He provides an adequate description of such terminology as U, non-U, amphibrach, and dactyl. Simon also provides a brief but comprehensible description of the premises for the books U and Non-U Revisited and Noblesse Oblige.
Perhaps Simon provides too much information when he discusses the origins of the word snob. The etymology is unclear and the several hypotheses concerning the source of the word are not relevant to the discussion.

2. **Regarding the principle of quality: What reasons do you have for trusting (or distrusting) Simon's knowledge of his subject or his honesty?**

There is no reason to dispute the facts presented in Simon's essay. He is careful, in fact, to cite both the sources of his facts and the opinions of other people. From the headnotes, one can also gather that Simon is a learned man who would probably be careful to check his facts if he were ever in doubt.
The principle of quality applies to opinions as well as facts, however, as shown by Jonathan Swift's violation of the contract in "A Modest Proposal." Because Simon uses hyperbole and strongly inveighs against mispronunciation, the reader becomes unsure as to how truly serious Simon is being in his condemnation. (See the next question.) It is in this respect one might conclude that Simon violates the contract.

3. Regarding the principle of manner: If you think the essay is sometimes unclear, indicate where, and explain the difficulty.

The hyperbole of some of Simon's statements is confusing. For instance, he half-jokingly decries the low status of the snob who cannot even enjoy the "semifavorable publicity accorded bank robbers, necrophiliacs, and starters of forest fires." The authors are avid readers of the Metro section of our large daily newspaper where most of the paper's lurid crime coverage appears, but we are at a loss to remember any publicity, "semifavorable" or not, about forest fire starters or necrophiliacs. (Now bank robbers are another matter!) The comparison is so off the wall that it is difficult to determine, at least initially, whether Simon is in favor of the snob or just the opposite.

Later in the essay Simon becomes so vicious in his attack as to be shocking. He writes, "What makes <u>influence</u> so ghastly is not necessarily its sound (though I think it is ugly) but its demonstration of the existence of people so uneducated, so deaf to what others are saying, so unable to learn the obvious that they are bound to be a major source of verbal pollution, linguistic corruption, cultural erosion." This extremist rhetoric would tend to alienate readers except for those who are already won over to Simon's viewpoint.

4. Regarding the principle of relation: Are any parts of the essay irrelevant to the topic? Explain.

Simon begins the fifth paragraph of his essay, "What concerns me here, however, is whether there is such a thing as linguistic snobbery: the use of language to achieve or assert social superiority." The previous paragraph, however, is devoted to a discussion of the etymology of the word <u>snob</u> without ever arriving at the word's definitive origins and without shedding any particular light on the application of a word within the realm of linguistics. The paragraph before that discusses the use of <u>snob</u> as a tool for demagoguery.

Neither of these paragraphs is particularly relevant to the issue at hand. This article reads very much like a column written for a regular deadline with the author grabbing a particular idea or book, <u>U and Non-U Revisited</u> in this particular case, as a springboard for a few thoughts of his own on the same subject.

In another section, Simon discusses how the pronunciation of the word <u>squalor</u> has changed from rhyming with tailor to rhyming with holler. Simon then lets loose this vitriolic comment, "Nowadays, I suppose, you don't need to know even the meaning of <u>squalor</u> to teach English anywhere; the assumption may be that you'll learn the meaning from experiencing it on the job." Nowhere else in the essay has Simon made any reference to the misuse of words.

5. Explain your reaction to Simon's advice: "If you are the sort of person who thinks that to sound well brought up, educated, fastidious, and perhaps even old-fashioned is not shameful but distinguished, go ahead and be a linguistic snob."

Simon's article is concerned with the pronunciation of words, with "sounding" well brought up, educated, and so forth. His article does not concern itself with usage or grammar. The discussion with the class will probably focus strictly on Simon's argument regarding pronunciation.

6. Explain why Simon considers Edmund White's use of the word gay a "dreadful abuse."

Simon believes that White purposefully confuses the issue of a reaction against the sexuality of transvestites with that of elitism and racism. In addition, there is something very basic about the very word gay which Simon dislikes although he does not explain his reasons in the essay.

7. In the argument between Richard Buckle and Philip Howard, whose side are you on? Explain.

The argument itself is a debate over whether language is organic and changes over time with changes in society itself. Howard argues that language "is a living thing" which changes and that it is foolish to wish it to remain the same. Buckle argues the other side: "I know the laws of beauty change, like everything else, but I should fight against that to the end." The question, of course, could also be rewritten to ask whether you agree or disagree with Simon.

8. Explain instances of snobbery in a group with whom you are associated (e.g., a sports team, social organization, your family).

9. State the main point of "U, Non-U, and You."

The main point is that some varieties of language are universally correct and that it is a mark of distinction to uphold the standard of correctness.

Page 304

"Politics and the English Language"
George Orwell

1. Regarding the principle of quantity: At any points in this essay, does Orwell fail to give you enough information? Does he ever give you more than is necessary? (Be specific in your answers.)

When he analyzes the faults in the passages on pages 305-306 of this book, Orwell, in our opinion, does not provide enough information. His diagnosis of the faults as "staleness of imagery" and "lack of precision" needs clarification and examples; furthermore, the difficulties in the passages result from a variety of problems that Orwell doesn't mention--for instance, the piling up of negatives in the passage by Laski.

2. Regarding the principle of quality: What reasons do you have for trusting (or distrusting) Orwell's knowledge of his subject or his honesty? (Remember that Orwell is one of the most respected writers in English.)

Paradoxically, great writers are not necessarily great or even competent students of language. For example, Janice Redish, whose essay appears in the first chapter of this book, could undoubtedly do a more thoroughgoing analysis of the unreadability of the passages than the one that Orwell provides. There is, then, reason for questioning Orwell's competence, but there is no basis for questioning his honesty.

3. Regarding the principle of manner: If you think the essay is sometimes unclear, indicate where and explain the difficulty.

It will be interesting to discover students' opinions about the clarity of this classic essay.

4. Regarding the principle of relation: Are any parts of the essay irrelevant to the topic? Explain.

Will students find that parts are irrelevant?

5. In the second paragraph of the essay, Orwell explains his view of the decline of English. What specifically does he do to help the reader understand his point?

He uses an analogy: "A man may take to drink because he feels himself to be a failure, and then fail all the more completely because he drinks. It is rather the same thing that is happening to the English language. It becomes ugly and inaccurate because our thoughts are foolish, but the slovenliness of our language makes it easier for us to have foolish thoughts."

6. Use the terms of the writer-reader contract to explain the point of the paragraph on page 306, beginning, "Each of these passages has faults of its own."

Quality: As we said in regard to Question 2, we have reason to doubt Orwell's competence as an expert on language. (He is not a linguist or lexicographer.) But there is no reason to doubt his honesty or sincerity. Quantity: Readers need more explanation and examples. Stale imagery? Lack of precision? The paragraph contains nothing irrelevant (Relation), and it is perfectly clear (Manner).

7. Use the terms of the writer-reader contract to explain why you agree or disagree with each of the six rules that Orwell sets forth on page 314.

(i) If a writer uses stale metaphors and similes, readers begin to doubt the quality of his or her mind. Lack of originality bespeaks stereotypical thinking.

(ii) This rule is too vague to be useful. It is merely saying, always use the right word. Thus, Orwell himself violates the principle of quantity. He needs to be more specific. (Many factors influence a writer's diction or word choice: the intended audience, the writer's purpose, the agency of publication, among others.)

(iii) This rule also is too vague. It is quantitatively inadequate.

(iv) This rule is downright wrong! At times, the passive is preferable to the active. In the final paragraph, Orwell writes (in passive voice), "Political language--and with variations this is true of all political parties, from Conservatives to Anarchists--is designed to make lies sound truthful and murder respectable, and to give an appearance of solidity to pure wind." Following his own dictum, Orwell should have framed the sentence thus: "All political parties, from Conservatives to Anarchists, design political language to make lies sound truthful and murder respectable, and to give an appearance of solidity to pure wind." The quality of the rule is obviously questionable.

(v) Once again, this rule is at best misleading. Experts writing for experts should use the technical terminology of their respective fields.

(vi) Who could disagree with this one?

8. What is Orwell's purpose in "Politics and the English Language"? Is he trying to persuade, explain, amuse, horrify, convince?

Interestingly enough, the reader can legitimately assign any one of several purposes to the essay. For example, Orwell is no doubt explaining his contention that the English language is decaying, but from another point of view, he is arguing, trying to convince the reader. The essay is tinged with anger; Orwell is expressing himself, getting the matter off his chest.

9. Reread the quotation from Ecclesiastes and Orwell's corruption thereof. Which version is more difficult to understand? To answer this question, ask yourself, Are there words whose definitions I don't know? Are there greater gaps to be filled in one version or the other?

The corrupt version contains no particularly unusual vocabulary, though commensurate and innate might not be in most students' lexicons. The problem, of course, is the abstractness of the rewrite. The original is concrete, specific, and visual and thus easier for the reader to grasp. It is a well-established principle that ideas and information are more accessible and memorable when embodied in images and narratives than when presented abstractly. (See, for example, Linda S. Flower, John R. Hayes, and Heidi Swarts, Revising Function Documents: The Scenario Principle, Document Design Project Technical Report No. 10 (Pittsburgh: Carnegie-Mellon U, 1980).)

10. Does the fact that the essay was written four decades ago in a foreign country (the United Kingdom) make the piece less relevant today? Explain. Are the examples that Orwell cites less relevant today?

The subject of the essay--readability--is as timely now as it was when it was written. In fact, the essay by Janice Redish in the first chapter of this book might be viewed as a modern version of "Politics and the English Language." The examples might well have been taken from publications that appeared in 1991.

11. State the main point of the selection.

Through purifying one's language, one can help straighten out the politics of the nation.

12. Explain why Finegan would disagree with Orwell's first sentence. What is your own opinion?

Finegan would probably argue that language does not decay or become corrupt--even though the people who use the language might be decadent and corrupt. That is, a linguist would not set out to improve the moral character of a nation by attempting to purify the language. On the other hand, feminists have successfully changed usage and thus have greatly influenced attitudes about gender throughout the world. Until quite recently, such usage as the following was universal: "Will everyone who wants to attend the concert raise <u>his</u> hand"; "<u>Mankind</u> longs for peace." Because of the feminist movement, normal usage now demands, "Will everyone who wants to attend the concert raise <u>his</u> or <u>her</u> hand"; "<u>Humankind</u> longs for peace."

13.   In what ways do Orwell and Simon agree in their attitudes toward language?

They both feel that language is decaying and that conscious effort can stop this process. They also hold to absolute standards of correctness and usage.

14. Give examples of overused dying metaphors.

Golden parachutes (retirement plans for executives). Country-club prisons. Fat farms. "The freeway is a parking lot" (i.e., very crowded).

15. Give examples of language usages that annoy you. For example, many find the repeated use of "ya know" in conversation to be objectionable.

16. Is Orwell's argument merely one of aesthetics? Explain.

Orwell's point is that some usages are politically subversive; he is not concerned exclusively with aesthetics.

17. Explain how politics enters into Orwell's discussion.

See paragraphs 13 and 14. The language of politics supports the party line, whatever that might be. Fresh, vivid language would be revolutionary in that it would reveal true meanings. In paragraph 16, Orwell says, "The inflated style is itself a kind of euphemism. A mass of Latin words falls upon the facts like soft snow, blurring the outlines and covering up all the details."

18. Orwell says that political speeches often "mechanically repeat familiar phrases." Might politicians have valid reasons for repeating familiar phrases over and over again? Explain.

Repetition is not necessarily bad. After all, the most meaningful rituals are repetitive: the Pledge of Allegiance, the Lord's Prayer. To be meaningful, however, discourse must contain "news"; that is, it must contain some new information. Paradox on paradox: each time a slogan is repeated, it is to a certain extent new, in that the scene has changed.

Page 317

"The Country of the Mind"
Barry Lopez

1. Regarding the principle of quantity: At any points in this essay, does Lopez fail to give you enough information? Does he ever give you more than is necessary? (Be specific in your answers.)

Many people will be unfamiliar with the various species of life that are briefly mentioned in the text but are not described in enough detail for readers to understand exactly (e.g., common eider/duck; phalarope/a bird resembling a sandpiper; peregrine/falcon; bowhead/whale). On the other hand, Lopez provides much more detail about the arctic fox than is necessary to make his point about the animal's Umwelt. Out of interest in the species, Lopez provides a short history of the arctic fox's encounters with man, first as an animal largely ignored by the native Eskimo people, then as a severe problem for Vitus Bering's expedition, and finally as a hunted animal during modern times.

2. Regarding the principle of quality: What reasons do you have for trusting (or distrusting) Lopez's knowledge of his subject or his honesty? Does the discussion that precedes this selection relate to this question?

It is apparent that Lopez had done a good deal of background research before heading into the Arctic. For example, note his reference to the microhabitats of hydric (wet), mesic (balanced supply of moisture), and xeric (dry) tundra and his historical references to the explorers Ernest Leffingwell, (Vilhjalmur) Stefansson, and Vitus Bering. In addition, as the headnote indicates, Lopez has written a good deal about natural history in general and so would probably have a good working knowledge of arctic wildlife. The research for his previous book on wolves, in particular, would have provided him with some relevant background material for writing about the Arctic. Lopez is not reluctant to note the limitations of his perceptions. ("I am aware that I miss much of what I pass, for lack of acuity in my senses, lack of discrimination, and my general unfamiliarity." "A more thoughtful inquirer, someone dependent upon these bits of information in a way that I am not, would find out why.") Writers aware of their limitations earn the reader's trust. Finally, Lopez has apparently done some research in the field because he refers to the observations of a tundra botanist, Eskimos with whom he has traveled, a Canadian scientist, and a whale biologist.

3.   Regarding the principle of manner: If you think the essay is sometimes unclear, indicate where, and explain the difficulty.

It seems to us that this essay is a model of clarity. However, there are some concepts that Lopez does not spend a great deal of time elucidating. For example, in his anecdote about the arctic botanist who dissected a tussock, Lopez writes, "She said she remembered looking up at one point, at the tundra that rolled away in a hundred thousand tussocks toward the horizon, and that she could not return her gaze because of that sight, not for long minutes," but he provides no further elaboration on the point which he is making, which is that the vastness of the tundra can oftentimes be overwhelming. In another example, one of Lopez's major points of the entire piece is the difficulties in understanding a creature's <u>Umwelt</u>, and yet he defines and clarifies this uncommon term only in a footnote. On the other hand, Lopez's explanation of the pitfalls that biologists must face in trying to get a comprehensive view of a species is extremely clear: "They know that while experiments can be designed to reveal aspects of the animal, the animal itself will always remain larger than the sum of any set of experiments. They know they can be very precise about what they do, but that does not guarantee they will be accurate. They know the behavior of an individual animal may differ strikingly from the generally recognized behavior of its species; and that the same species may behave quite differently from place to place, from year to year." In this example, the first two sentences are general statements that require the reader to make a significant effort to understand the ways in which the study of animals can miss important aspects of their existence. Although these two statements could reasonably stand alone in the paragraph without further explanation, the third sentence makes crystal clear the reasons for making the first two statements. This section goes on to support the author's premise by quoting three different scientists and providing evidence for an additional means by which the animal can be studied (use of anecdotal information such as that given by the Eskimos of the region).

4.   Regarding the principle of relation: Are any parts of the essay irrelevant to the topic?   Explain.   For example, what is the relevance of the long passage regarding the arctic fox?

As previously noted, some details about the arctic fox are not completely pertinent to the point Lopez eventually wants to make, which is to discuss the concept of <u>Umwelt</u>. Nevertheless, the information is interesting and is within the general topic of discussion, that of arctic fauna. However, the piece as a whole is very clearly and interestingly related. The writer discusses his own ability to perceive and understand his environment (his walk across the tundra), compares it with the

Eskimo's own ability (more meticulous), speculates about the arctic fox's <u>Umwelt</u>, discusses the scientist's difficulty in studying fauna in the wild (the animal is always greater than the sum of the experiments; corporate sponsorship's own conditions of quick, quantitative analysis), and then details the variables that influence one's understanding of a region (what one knows; what one imagines; how one is disposed). In sum, the parts add up to a discussion about the limits of knowledge in the natural environment.

5. What sorts of readers do you think Lopez had in mind? (Their levels of education? Their socioeconomic status? Their interests?) Explain your answer.

Lopez assumes a fairly educated, curious, and critical readership. As noted previously, he fails to describe many creatures mentioned in passing, presumably assuming that the reader will already be familiar with them or will take enough time to use a dictionary or encyclopedia. He expects the reader to understand the concept of <u>Umwelt</u> and to grasp certain issues and questions that are corollary to the concept. These two points are another way of saying that the author assumes an educated readership. The content also assumes such a readership. While some of the essay concerns itself with natural history in a general way and thus should interest a wide audience, the philosophical questions concerning knowledge and perception are issues that fewer people would be interested in. And regardless of the level of education and intellectual interests, certain readers would be more inclined to be interested in the piece because of its philosophical outlook than others. For example, an actuarial statistician working at an insurance company is certainly well aware that no one individual conforms to the norm or average that guides company's policies, but such a person would probably argue that the numbers do describe the species (humans) in general and that a general description, in the end, is of greater value than a case history. After all, the actuary might argue, the individual case history can be used to discuss only the individual, and once that particular being is no longer in existence, one has no basis to discuss other individuals of the species without having made the same kinds of generalizations that actuarial science makes. Obviously, the naturalists whom Lopez has talked with would disagree, at least in part, with this viewpoint.

6. Which details in the selection did you find particularly vivid? In what ways do these details contribute to the meaning and effect of the piece?

Lopez supplies many details and examples to make his points come alive. The overwhelming nature of the tundra is shown in the story of the botanist, working from almost a microscopic perspective in analyzing a tussock for hours on end, who looks up and sees "a hundred thousand tussocks toward the horizon." Other memorable details: subtle differences in the land at each step, described by scientific terms (<u>mesic</u>, <u>xeric</u>, and <u>hydric tundra</u>); cultural disparity as shown by the Eskimo's question about the binoculars seeing into the future; the keener or at least different way in which the wolf holds space in its mind, discovered first hand by a friend who tried to locate the wolf's cache; the Eskimo's own enhanced perceptive abilities on the tundra as revealed by the ability to glass the landscape for an hour at a time.

7. What is the main point of "The Country of the Mind"?

Lopez states his main point in a two-sentence paragraph towards the end of the selection. "The perceptions of any people wash over the land like a flood, leaving ideas hung up in the brush, like pieces of damp paper to be collected and deciphered. No one can tell the whole story."

8. What is the most prominent theme of the selection?

The concept of <u>Umwelt</u> is the most prominent theme of the selection. The <u>Umwelt</u> allows the wolf to find its hidden cache and, for the individual human, it is partially dictated by what one knows of a region, what one imagines of a region, and how one is disposed.

9. In your own words, explain Lopez's critique of modern science. (It starts on page 323 with the paragraph beginning "A belief in the authority of statistics. . . . ")

One of the major methodologies of scientists is to analyze the subject in a controlled environment such as would be used in experiments. In addition, a major assumption of any experiment is that it should be able to be repeated with the same results. Both aspects of the scientific process ignore the individual; in trying to establish the rule, they tend to ignore exceptions. In addition, the scientist looks at the parts and not the sum of the parts. In doing so, the scientist often overlooks the subtle ways in which the parts fit together and influence each other.

10. In paragraph 40, Lopez begins a discussion of language. What would Edward Finegan and George Orwell say about his ideas?

Orwell would, presumably, agree with Lopez: language determines culture, and changing language can change culture. Finegan would probably argue that language and culture interact; a change in culture demands a change in language. For example, Latin is a perfectly adequate language for science, provided the vocabulary expands to include words for modern concepts and devices.

11. Lopez writes, "All else being equal, a Hopi child would have little difficulty comprehending the theory of relativity in his own language, while an American child could more easily master history." In response to Lopez, Edward Finegan asked this question: "What was Einstein's native language?" Explain what Finegan meant by his response.

English is a Germanic language, in the same family as modern German, and the propounder of the theory of relativity spoke German, not Hopi. Apparently, his native language did not impede or determine Einstein's thought process.

Supplementary Questions

A. Compare Lopez's method of observation and learning with that of Matthiessen's. How are they alike? Different?

In oxymoronic terms, both authors made conscious attempts to let their unconscious minds take over. Lopez lets his mind release "its fiduciary grip on time" in order to transcend the distances of the tundra. Lopez wants this to occur so that he can appreciate the land as it is without having to concern himself with worry. It also appears that his mind is less consciously surveying the land than wandering over it. In many ways, his descriptions of surveying the land make it appear that the land itself directs his eyes. ("And there is something, too, about the way the landscape funnels human movement. . . ." "And when you fall into the habit [of scouring the land with your eyes or field glasses], find some way like this to shed your impatience, you feel less conspicuous in the land.") Matthiessen sits "in meditation, doing [his] best to empty out [his] mind" in order take in the presence of the Universe (nature). Matthiessen's techniques, however, are more passive. He is truly not attempting to seek something out but is interested in letting in anything that comes to him. On the other hand, Lopez, even though the rational, conscious mind might not be as predominant in his thought, is active, physically striding across the land or systematically glassing the landscape for signs of life.

B. Why do you think the title of the chapter from which this piece was excerpted is "The Country of the Mind"?

As is also apparent in the writing of Matthiessen, explorations in strange and distant lands are means by which the author can understand himself better. The vastness of both the tundra and the Himalayas seems constantly to call upon the authors to justify themselves in terms of the landscape. It is this constant questioning that spurs the authors to contemplate their existence in ways that would not be possible in the quotidian world of the city. Within this selection, Lopez comes close to answering this question when he writes, "Whorf, Boas, and others in this tradition urged people after the turn of the century to see human culture as a mechanism for ordering reality. These realities were separate, though they might be simultaneously projected onto the same landscape. And there was no ultimate reality--any culture that would judge the perceptions of another, particularly one outside its own traditions, should proceed cautiously." These authors consciously step outside of their culture in order to gain further insights into reality.

Page 330

"November 6"
Peter Matthiessen

1. Regarding the principle of quantity: At any points does Matthiessen give you less information than you need? Does he ever give you more than necessary? (Be specific in your answers.)

How much world knowledge should students be expected to bring to this selection? For example, they should certainly know what sherpas are, but what is a gompa? Context should reveal that it is some kind of dwelling. Argali, as an ordinary desk dictionary tells us, are Asiatic wild sheep with large horns. In other words, either context or a dictionary supplies all of the background information that one needs. Should Matthiessen have supplied this information? Explaining his terms would have ruined the effect of the text. Should the editors of this book have supplied footnote glosses? Probably.

The Snow Leopard is, of course, a travel book, and like all good travel writers, Matthiessen gives us a vivid sense of scene. The journey begins, at the end of September, in the lowlands of Nepal, where "Green village compounds, set about with giant banyans and old stone pools and walls, are cropped to lawn by water buffalo and cattle; the fresh water and soft shade give them the harmony of parks" (14-15). Children play in the warm sun, "and women roll clothes on rocks at the village fountain and pound grain in stone mortars, and from all sides come reassuring dung smells and chicken clatter and wafts of fire smoke from the low hearths" (15). Here is fecund easiness, life growing like the "yellow-flowered pumpkin vines" and the maize and the rice "spread to dry on broad straw mats." However, the way lies upward and northward toward the snowy peaks of the Himalayas.

The scene becomes progressively more austere, mystical. After a long climb, "A pine forest drifts by in breaths of mist, and on the mountain face just opposite, seen through shifting clouds, ribbons of water turn from white to brown as they gather up soil in the fall to the roaring rivers. On a corner of the trail is a weird shrine where horns of many slaughtered goats are piled high in a kind of altar, with red ribbons tied to branches of the trees" (37).

The climax of the journey and of the scenic progression is in the vicinity of Crystal Mountain, where, on an adjoining peak, Matthiessen has found a place for meditation, "a broken rock outcrop like an altar set into the hillside, protected from all but the south wind by shards of granite and dense thorn" (217). "Now the mountains all around me take on life; the Crystal Mountain moves. Soon there comes the murmur of the torrent, from far away below under the ice: it seems impossible that I can hear the sound. Even in the windlessness, the sound of rivers comes and goes and falls and rises, like the wind itself" (217). This is the scene of the epiphany, but we will return to discuss that moment hereafter. The point is that scene in The Snow Leopard is never gratuitous and never merely for information but is always the right setting for the acts that make up the narrative.

2. Regarding the principle of quality: What reasons do you have for trusting (or distrusting) Matthiessen's knowledge of his subject or his honesty? (What tests could you apply to determine whether or not Matthiessen is reliable? The discussion of evaluating the source, on pages 579-583, relates to this question.)

The headnote that introduces the selection should be evidence in Matthiessen's behalf--if students trust the coauthors of this book! What reason do they have for trusting Winterowd and Winterowd? They can find biographical information about W. Ross and reviews of his other books, but Geoffrey is unknown. Might it be that The Critical Reader, Thinker, and Writer is unreliable? The point, of course, is that students should critically question all texts.

3. Regarding the principle of manner: If you think the selection is sometimes unclear, indicate where and explain the difficulty.

It is impossible to predict what students might find unclear. However, lack of clarity arises from one or a combination of these sources, among others: (a) ambiguity in the text, (b) faulty syntax, (c) unfamiliar vocabulary, (d) inadequate background information on the part of the reader.

4. Regarding the principle of relation: Are any parts of the selection irrelevant to the topic? Explain.

In the question, the word explain is the operator. If a student finds irrelevancies, he or she should be able to explain.

5. Considering the complexity of his intention, do you think that Matthiessen expressed himself as clearly as possible? Explain.

Writing clear instructions for operating a new VCR is difficult, but obviously possible. It is more difficult to explain a belief or opinion, but still quite possible. It is very difficult to convey, in language, the texture of an experience, which is exactly why poetry is necessary, for it is often an attempt to say the unsayable, and to paraphrase the poem is to strip it of its poetry. How could Matthiessen have been clearer? By forsaking truth for clarity, by changing poetry into exposition. But in losing the poetry, the journal entry would have lost everything.

The unbelievably difficult trek--through snow-clogged mountain passes, often with nothing to eat except a "white diet" of rice and millet--is a quest symbolized by two animals: the bharal, or Himalayan blue sheep, which George Schaller has set out to study, and the near mythic snow leopard, which Matthiessen hopes to see.

Schaller is "'single-minded, not easy to know' and 'a stern pragmatist,' unable to muster up much grace in the face of unscientific attitudes; he takes a hard-eyed look at almost everything" (4). His purpose is to confirm his belief that bharal is the common ancestor of both sheep and goats but that the animal itself is more of a goat than a sheep (3). Schaller undergoes the severe test of the journey to establish zoological fact.

And Matthiessen's reason for the trek? In Katmandu he and Schaller had visited with a young biologist, who automatically comprehended Schaller's motive. But Matthiessen's? "How could I say that I wished to penetrate the secrets of the mountains in search of something still unknown that, like the yeti, might well be missed for the very fact of searching?" (131). How, indeed, could Matthiessen advance a logical reason for the rigors and hazards of the expedition? Could he claim that the possibility of glimpsing a snow leopard was explanation enough?

As the bharal are symbols of rationality, so the snow leopard becomes the symbol of suprarationality, and in the psychic territory between rationality and suprarationality is the legend of yeti. The evidence in favor of its existence is strong enough to convince even the skeptical Schaller--and yet, if yeti exists, why have all expeditions pursuing these creatures failed (128-31)?

6. No one doubts that Peter Matthiessen did trek into the Himalayas with the zoologist George Schaller. Suppose, however, that Matthiessen had taken the journey only in imagination, not in reality. How would that fact affect your judgment of the quality of information in the text?

As long as Matthiessen represents himself as having been there, the facts of his journey are stable. Either he did reach Shey on his trek with George Schaller or he is lying. If the journey was imaginary, the facts are no longer stable but serve to develop the theme and plot. The author can invent whatever he or she chooses. Shey then no longer counts as a geographical location, any more than Oz; its value is fictional.

7. Does one of the following sentences express the main point of the selection? All of them? None of them? Other sentences from the selection? Explain.

Though I am blind to it, the Truth is near, in the reality of what I sit on--rocks.

These hard rocks instruct my bones in what my brain could never grasp in the Heart Sutra, that "form is emptiness and emptiness is form"--the Void, the emptiness of blue-black space, contained in everything.

The mountains have no "meaning," they <u>are</u> meaning; the mountains <u>are</u>.

The theme of the book is the search for enlightenment, the diverse elements of the narrative relating always to that theme, building it, giving it the depth and complexity of a lived drama.

All of the sentences relate to Matthiessen's semantic intention. The problem is that paraphrasing simplifies to the point of mawkishness: "I learned to accept the universe as it is and to be a part of the totality." "Pure form has no content; it simply is." "When I really experience the universe, I become one with it."

8. Now that you have read a brief selection from <u>The Snow Leopard</u>, explain why you would or would not like to read the whole book.

9. What is the principle of structure or organization in a journal such as The Snow Leopard, from which "November 6" is extracted? How does this structure compare with that of Barry Lopez's "Country of the Mind"?

The basic structure is, of course, chronological. Matthiessen's journal is a day-by-day record of his trek. The Snow Leopard is a magnificent achievement, having all the power of a great novel with a first-person narrator as well as the inherent appeal of informativeness. One reads the book as "fact," not fiction, but becomes totally immersed aesthetically. Three simultaneous movements provide structure for The Snow Leopard: through time, space, and free association of ideas. We are continually reminded of the temporality since the book is in the form a journal, starting with the entry of September 28, 1973, and ending with the entry of December 1, the same year (though a brief anachronistic interpolation takes the account to December 10).

The story records a field trip to an area in Nepal, near the border of Tibet, that Matthiessen took with the zoologist George Schaller to study bharal or Himalayan blue sheep.

Even though the books are different in structure, the ingredients of The Snow Leopard are like those of Arctic Dreams, narrative pausing for the "radical particularity" of images, and information about flora and fauna leading to philosophical musings. The great difference between them is the way in which the particulars "add up" in The Snow Leopard. Arctic Dreams has something of the disunity of Irving Stone's Passions of the Mind, whereas The Snow Leopard has the total unity necessary for a work of art to achieve maximum power.

10. If you wanted general, reliable information about Zen Buddhism, to what source or sources would you turn?

For example, The Encyclopedia of Religion and Ethics, the Britannica and the Americana.

Page 334

"The Angry Winter"
Loren Eiseley

1. Regarding the principle of quantity: At any points in this essay does Eiseley give you less information than you need to understand him? Does he ever give you more than necessary? (Be specific in your answers.)

Eiseley's essay runs on two different levels. First, as a scientist, he discusses very concrete, fundamental issues of geology, physical anthropology, evolution, and natural history. Simultaneously, he discusses the meaning of these scientific facts on a metaphysical level, in broad generalities that sometimes don't provide the reader with enough of a context to fully understand the author's meaning. For example, the anecdote that opens the essay refers to the shadows of both Wolf's and Eiseley's past. This concept is nebulously explained because Eiseley himself is unclear about it.

A fundamental problem with this essay for the layperson is that most people have very little concept of geological time. Eiseley opens Part 2 of his essay by mentioning the influx of spectacular events in the form of life on a formerly barren planet: "The evolution of a lifeless planet eventually culminates in green leaves. The altered and oxygenated air hanging above the continents presently invites the rise of animal apparitions compounded of formerly inert clay." These two sentences refer to the following developments and their approximate times of occurrence:

> "evolution of a lifeless planet" -- Between 4.55 billion and 3.8 billion years ago the crusts and oceans of the world were formed.

> "culminates in green leaves" -- Between 3.8 billion and 700 million years ago the earliest forms of life appeared. Between 435 million and 395 million years ago the first land plants developed.

> "The altered and oxygenated air hanging above the continents presently invites the rise of animal apparitions compounded of formerly inert clay." -- Between 395 million and 345 million years ago the first land animals appeared.

Then, in the following paragraph, Eiseley states, "We are the final product of the Pleistocene period's millennial winters. . . ." This is the period between 1.8 million and 10,000 years ago when the species Homo sapiens arose (approximately 100,000 years ago). This survey of time is presented without any perspective on the orders of magnitude between events.

Nor are absolute values of time explained. In Part 2, Eiseley mentions the various eras without giving the time scale. In explaining the cycle which is synchronous with one complete revolution of our galaxy, Eiseley mentions the pre-Cambrian era (3.8 billion to 700 million years ago), the Pleistocene period (1.8 million to 10,000 years ago), and the Permian period (280 million to 230 million years ago).

The writing gets even more confusing when Eiseley mentions a geological era in the same sentence as a geological period (a subdivision of an era): "The Pleistocene episode [a period existing from 1.8 million to 10,000 years ago], so long unguessed and as insignificant as a pinprick on the earth's great time scale, signifies also, as did the ice of the late Paleozoic [an era of 470 million years which contained the Permian period and the previous great glacial age], the rise of a new organic world."

2. Regarding the principle of _quality_: What reasons do you have for trusting (or distrusting) Eiseley's knowledge of his subject or his honesty?

The headnote should provide answers to this question.

3. Regarding the principle of _manner_: If you think the essay is sometimes unclear, indicate where and explain the difficulty. Was it difficult for you to relate the images so that they would add up to a coherent whole?

We have already noted above that Eiseley has not explained the geological time line. As a result, the manner in which the following sentence is written makes it ambiguous to the layperson: "For the Permian glaciation, however, we can derive a rough estimate of some twenty-five to thirty million years, during which the southern continents periodically lay in the grip of glacial ice." Is thirty million the number of years ago that the period began or ended? Is it the length of that period's duration? Is it the length of time for glaciation to develop? Only by knowing that the Permian period existed more than 200 million years ago and that it was 50 million years in duration can one eliminate the first two possibilities. Even so, it remains unclear what Eiseley meant by glaciation. We are unsure at that point in the essay whether thirty million years is the amount of time for glaciation to begin or to reach its apex, or whether the number is the length of duration. Later in the essay, Eiseley clarifies matters: "I have said that the earlier Permian glaciation appears to have fluctuated over perhaps thirty million years."

Then, too, Eiseley never makes clear that the recurrent cycle (It "comes once in two hundred and fifty million years--about the time, it has been estimated, that it takes our sun to make one full circle of the galactic wheel") is a cycle of one ice age. Instead, he writes, "That circle and its recurrent ice have been repeated back into dim pre-Cambrian eras. . . ." Without carefully rereading the selection and possibly consulting a geographical time line, the reader is unsure about how many ice ages occur within one circle/cycle.

Eiseley obviously wanted to avoid explaining some of the scientific terms because it would hurt the flow of his prose and the reader would get tripped up with the details while overlooking his main points. However, as we have seen above, it is necessary to understand some of the terms in greater detail that Eiseley provides.

4. Regarding the principle of <u>relation</u>: Are any parts of the essay irrelevant to the topic? Explain.

See question 7.

5. How does Eiseley's method (manner) affect the credibility of his argument (quality)?

See question 7.

6. In "The Country of the Mind," "November 6," and "The Angry Winter," a winter landscape is the setting, or scene. How does this scene contribute to the meaning and effectiveness of Eiseley's essay?

See question 7.

7. Eiseley creates brilliant metaphors, such as this one:

Every man contains within himself a ghost continent--a place circled as warily as Antarctica was circled two hundred years ago by Captain James Cook. ("The Ghost Continent," in <u>The Unexpected Universe</u>.)

This metaphor means that all of us are afraid to explore some parts of our psyches. Point out the metaphors in "The Angry Winter" that you think are most striking. Paraphrase them, and explain what you gain or lose with the paraphrase. Is the paraphrase easier to understand than the original metaphor? Is the paraphrase as powerful (vivid, memorable) as the original?

The entire essay is based on the idea that mankind as a species arose during an ice age, so Eiseley makes use of the metaphor of winter to discuss issues concerning our development. A winter storm rages in Part 1 while Eiseley and Wolf, his dog, contemplate what images and shadows the fossil bone conjures up in their (genetic?)h memory. Thus, the entire essay opens up with images of winter. From Part 2: "Illiterate man has lost the memory of that huge snowfall from whose depths he has emerged blinking" (par 15). Eiseley quotes Thoreau, agreeing with that philosopher on a more literal level than Thoreau could have imagined at the time of writing this sentence: "The human brain is the kernel which the winter itself matures" (par. 16). Says Eiseley: "We are the genuine offspring of the sleeping ice, and we have inherited its power to magnify the merely usual into the colossal" (par 21). A metaphor links the ice age and man's intellectual development, the emergence of language: "And as that mantle [of ice] encased and covered the final strata of earth, so, in the brain of man, a similar superimposed layer of crystalline though substance superseded the dark, forgetful pathways of the animal brain" (par 30). "[M]an has been matured by winter; he has survived its coming, and has eaten of its marrow. But its cold is in his bones. The child will partake always of the parent, and that parent is the sleeping dragon whose kingdom we hold merely upon sufferance, and whose vagaries we have yet to endure" (par 32). Within this sentence is a second metaphor which Eiseley maintains throughout his essay, that of glaciation as a dragon (see below).

Further examples of metaphors: "He sensed uncannily the opening of a damp door in a remote forest, and he protested that nature was too big for him, that it was, in reality, a playground of giants" (par. 17). A short while later in the essay, Eiseley explains: "Modern man, for all his developed powers and his imagined insulation in his cities, still lives at the mercy of those giant forces that created him and can equally decree his departure" (par 19). "The sorcerer's gift of fire in a dark cave has brought us more than a simple kingdom" (par. 21). "[T]he claws of a vast dragon, the glacial ice, groped fumbling toward him and blew upon his thc breath of an enormous winter" (par. 18). Eiseley compares the concentric ripples in a pond during a rain to time's progression (par. 33). His metaphor becomes elaborate, with man's beginnings described as a drop of water and his subsequent evolution and development as "a great hasty wave that swept [the mammoths] under." There are small ripples which are likened to "the fauna of isolated islands" and the drops which disturb the surface of the water come in surges, just as geological periods have times of quiescence as well as great change. Finally, the pond and the images that it conjured up within the author's imagination is likened to a crystal ball in which one sees the past, not the future. Eiseley, by way of showing that magnitude is a relative matter, immediately after his discussion of the pond goes on to compare a spider's web to a universe, a swarm of midges to a galaxy, and a canyon to a backward look into time.

The following comments are from W. Ross Winterowd, <u>The Rhetoric of the</u> <u>"Other" Literature</u> (Carbondale, Southern Illinois UP, 1990), 107-109:

Leafing through the works of Loren Eiseley, one finds, on page after page, brilliant metaphors, such as this one from the first page of <u>The Unexpected</u> <u>Universe</u>: "Every man contains within himself a ghost continent--a place circled as warily as Antarctica was circled two hundred years ago by Captain James Cook," or this one from the first page of <u>The Immense Journey</u>: "Some lands are flat and grass-covered, and smile so evenly up at the sun that they seem forever youthful, untouched by man or time. Some are torn, ravaged and convulsed like the features of profane old age." And throughout the essays, one finds anecdotes from which the teller draws lessons. One of the most dramatic, though too long to quote in its entirety, is the beginning of "The Angry Winter": "I had been huddled beside the fire one winter night with the wind prowling outside and shaking the windows. . . ."

There follows an essay, concerning evolution and ecology, among other topics, which ends with another anecdote. When he was a young man, Eiseley set out for a long walk on a "sullen November day," finally, at twilight, reaching the town cemetery. There among the dead, he finds life: a jackrabbit.

> We both had a fatal power to multiply, the thought flashed on me, and the planet was not large. Why was it so, and what was the message that somehow seemed spoken from a long way off beyond an ice field, out of all possible human hearing?
>
> The snow lifted and swirled about us once more. He was going to need that broken bit of shelter [provided by a slab]. The temperature was falling. For his frightened, trembling body in all the million years between us, there had been no sorcerer's aid. He had survived alone in the blue nights and the howling dark. He was thin and crumpled and small.
>
> Step by step I drew back among the dead and their fallen stones. Somewhere, if I could follow the fence lines, there would be a fire for me. For a moment I could see his ears nervously recording my movements, but I was a wraith now, fading in the storm.
>
> "There are so few tracks in all this snow," someone had once protested. It was true. I stood in the falling flakes and pondered it. Even my own tracks were filling. But out of such desolation had arisen man, the desolate. In essence, he is a belated phantom of the angry winter. He carried, and perhaps will always carry, its cruelty and its springtime in his heart. (119)

It would appear that Eiseley the essayist is a practicing Romantic, following the leads of his anecdotes and metaphors, not aiming them--as does Stephen Jay Gould, for instance--toward a clear-cut semantic intention.

As a long-time admirer of Eiseley's work, one who has with great pleasure been reading and rereading the essays for twenty years, I can say without intending criticism that the essays are structurally a-logical. . . . They gain their structure through the "perspective by incongruity" that results when Eiseley follows the implications of his "representative anecdotes."

8. Eiseley uses anecdotes (brief stories) to make his points. For example, Eiseley draws this "lesson" from the anecdote about the author and his dog: "I think there is something in us that we had both better try to forget." Point out other anecdotes in the essay.   Is this anecdotal method of explaining ideas and establishing points effective or ineffective? Explain your answer.

See question 7 above.

9. What is the main point of "The Angry Winter"? Could Eiseley have conveyed this gist more effectively? If you think he could have, explain how.

The last paragraph in the essay states the main point, which, in paraphrase, is that we are the result of an evolutionary heritage that we cannot overcome and should not ignore: "In essence, [humankind] is a belated phantom of the angry winter. [We] carried, and perhaps will always carry, its cruelty and its springtime in [our] heart[s}."

Page 350

"The Bleeders"
Earle Hackett

1. Where could you find out about Hackett, the author (aside from the scant information that precedes the selection)?

For a discussion of using the libraries and its resources, see Chapter 5. Direct students to Contemporary Authors.

2. In your opinion, what might have been Hackett's purposes in writing the book from which "The Bleeders" is taken? On what do you base your opinion?

The author's profession as a hematologist provides evidence with which to answer this question. Hackett is obviously fascinated with his chosen field of study and probably wished to convey this interest and excitement to others by writing a general treatment about blood. By writing such a book, Hackett has the ability to answer to the best of his ability that proverbial question, "What do you do [for a living]?" It is likely also that Hackett wanted to make money from the book.

3. As a "thought experiment," place "The Bleeders" in the following variety of scenes. Does it "fit"? Why or why not?

a. Hackett reads the paper to a group of hematologists at a convention of the American Medical Association.

b. Hackett has been invited to speak about his field at a meeting of the Jefferson High School PTA. He reads "The Bleeders" and uses an overhead projector to show the chart.

c. Hackett is visiting a faculty member at Utopia University. This faculty member invites Hackett to speak to a freshman class in biology. Hackett reads "The Bleeders."

d. Hackett has been invited to speak at an anti-abortion rally. Three hundred noisy participants fall silent when he takes the microphone. He reads "The Bleeders."

The students should immediately recognize that this question deals with the writer-reader contract. At issue is whether manner and relation have been upheld or broken in the contract. The principle of manner is broken in the first example. Although the subject matter is one that is appropriate for a presentation to the AMA, the discussion is on such a basic level for people trained in the field that it would be of absolutely no interest except perhaps in his discussion of the hemophilia in Queen Victoria's family. An argument could be made that the principle of relation is also broken because the subject matter expected to be presented at an AMA convention would be so much more complex than the information in Hackett's overview.

On the other hand, the information presented by Hackett would be too complex in the second scene. Parents, most of whom have very little training in biology, could not be expected to follow the discussion, even if Hackett used his chart. In any case, the specificity of the material is not appropriate. The layperson would be more interested in a general overview of the profession and the issues at hand. If the parents were interested in a complex discussion of a medical problem, the topic would not be hemophilia per se but instead something more topical, such as how the AIDS epidemic has affected the hemophiliac population. It is primarily the principle of manner which is broken in this instance.

In the fourth scene, the principle of relation is broken. The people at the rally would not be interested in any discussion of hemophilia, no matter on what level of complexity it was conducted. It is only in the third example, that of a freshman biology class, that the writer-reader contract is upheld. The students would have enough background to understand Hackett's explanation of sex-linked recessive genes and are presumably interested enough in the subject to follow the discussion closely. Finally, the students wouldn't have so much knowledge of the subject that Hackett's presentation would be trivial.

4. Point out and explain some ways in which Hackett attempts to make his technical subject understandable to nonexperts.

The diagram explaining the inheritance of hemophilia is the most successful device for making the presentation comprehensible to the layperson. It is a model of graphic clarity. However, the layperson could not understand the diagram without the background information on sex determination and other genetic principles:

An egg contains one X chromosome.

A sperm cell contains either one X or one Y chromosome.

A female of the species is determined when the egg is fertilized by an X sperm cell.

A male of the species is determined when the egg is fertilized by a Y sperm cell.

The hemophilia mutation occurs in a region of an X chromosome which does not have a counterpart in the Y chromosome.

The hemophiliac defect can be countered with the pairing of a normal X chromosome.

The hemophiliac defect cannot be countered when paired with a Y chromosome.

Hackett has provided enough information that the reader can follow the deductive steps in the explanation of the transmission of hemophilia.

Even with this careful preparation and the clear diagram, an the reader needs further explanation of an important aspect of the transmission of hemophilia. In the past, females did not typically develop hemophilia. The essay explains that in the past the male hemophiliac often did not live long enough to father children and pass his mutant X to a daughter.

5. Evaluate "The Bleeders" from the standpoint of quantity. At any point, do you need more information? Less information?

Hackett's discussion of Christmas disease and devil's pinches are disturbingly brief. The author states that there are two forms of hemophilia, one of which is named Christmas disease after the doctor who discovered one of the forms. However, the only explanation of the differences in the two forms is that they have different blood-clotting factors in the plasma. By giving this section a subheading, the author sets up expectations in the reader that the discussion will be more involved than the one paragraph which actually deals with Christmas disease. The subheading "Devil's Pinches" creates expectations of exotic problems and yet the term simply refers to bruises on a woman's body which cannot be immediately explained. This section is one paragraph, yet it discusses three types of bleeding diseases, in addition to bruising. The discussion of these bleeding problems is far too sketchy to merit its own section of the chapter. These summary discussions would be more appropriate as an introduction to this chapter. The author could explain that there are many bleeding diseases, list them as he has done, and then devote the remainder of the chapter to hemophilia, the most infamous of these disorders.

The question of whether too much information has been provided is more subjective. Certainly, readers might feel that the elaborate explanation of how the hemophilia gene is passed through the generations is too much for a general discussion. Likewise, even if the reader has willingly followed Hackett's explanation in order to understand the general principle of recessive, sex-linked genes, his subsequent discussion of the British and Russian royalty's transmission of hemophilia is technical and requires most readers to go back and review the principles of transmission in order completely to understand the manner in which Victoria's descendants have inherited and transmitted the disorder. The reader might believe that this is too technical for such general purposes. The reader might also believe that the discussion is tangential and should not have been included in the chapter in the first place.

6. Hackett violates the principle of relation. Point out where. Do you believe that the violation is justified? Explain.

The second to the last section of "The Bleeders" is not directly related to the subject matter of genetically inherited bleeding diseases or problems. In fact, the subsection "Cousin Marriages" is a tangent to the discussion of bleeders, taking off as it does from the immediately preceding discussion about the line of hemophilia in Queen Victoria's family and descendants, in order to discuss the transmission of various recessive genes among relatives. The final paragraph/subsection titled "Devil's Pinches" doesn't discuss recessive genes at all but does deal with the issue of hemorrhaging.

In general, these two tangents are appropriate within this section even though they are not strictly relevant. This is because Hackett's intent is to provide an interesting overview for the layperson, and such sidelights enlarge the subject at hand and make it more interesting. They also make important scientific distinctions for readers who would not typically make them themselves. For example, Hackett explains that other hemorrhaging problems and diseases are not necessarily the result of genetic defects. (Women naturally bruise more easily than men, and liver disease can reduce the amount of the clotting agent prothrombin.) Hackett explains in "Cousin Marriages" that hemophilia's recurrence within a family's generations is not a result of inbreeding, whereas other non-sex linked genetic defects are more likely to occur with inbreeding.

7. What criteria can you apply to evaluate "The Bleeders"? What do experts in medicine think about the book? What do laypeople think? Where could you find such information?

The reader could first look at the dustjacket, which might contain critical quotes from reviews. This could very well be the reason that the reader, browsing through the bookstore or library, selected the volume in the first place. The author's credentials tend to ensure that the factual information presented in the book is accurate. Since the book is not speculative, the reader can be assured that the principle of quality has been observed. However, hematologists may or may not like the way the information has been presented. That is, they might argue that the principle of manner has been violated. Reference materials in the library collect reviews of books, and the student could look through these in order to see if any doctors of medicine have done reviews. The Reader's Guide would also list reviews of the book.

8. What world knowledge must a reader have in order to understand the technical explanation of the inheritance of hemophilia?

The general principle of genetics is assumed: that the chromosomes contained in the cell's nucleus carry the information required to construct and duplicate the organism. The reader is also presumed to have some understanding that mutations of the genetic information sometimes occur and significantly affect the inheritor of the mutation. Knowledge of certain basics of sexual reproduction is also required. This information was provided in a previous section of Hackett's book, and Hackett alludes to this fact when he writes, "Genetically, as we have seen, the maleness of men is determined by their inheriting two different sex chromosomes. . . ." The ovum and sperm cells contain one-half the number of chromosomes found in the species' non-sex cells, and the union of the two gives the offspring that develops from the fertilization one-half of the father's genetic information and one-half of the mother's. Without this information, Hackett's subsequent discussion might be confusing to the reader.

9. Point out ways in which Hackett attempts to make this technical subject interesting to nonexperts.

Hackett purposefully digresses in his discussion in order to cover related topics of interest. (He violates the principle of relation to some degree in order to maintain interest.) As a result, he discusses Devil's pinches and non-sex linked genetic diseases in addition to the main topic of hemophilia. His discussion of hemophilia within the British and Russian royal families lends the disease an exotic aura and, in the case of the Russian lineage, offers a possible aid in determining whether the man and woman claiming to be children of the Grand Duchess Anastasia are telling the truth (a daughter would be carrying a hemophiliac gene and a son would be a hemophiliac).

Hackett also discusses some of the broader issues surrounding the subject. For example, he analyzes ethical issues concerning a hemophiliac's decision to have children, given that the outcome can be predicted based on the sex of the child. In the section about cousin marriages, Hackett provides an interesting summary of small, closed societies and recessive genetic defects. Surprisingly, these defects are not magnified by the inbred ways of the society because, Hackett surmises, the sufferers of the genetic disease do not have as good a chance of surviving and hence of passing the defect to future generations.

10. State the main point of "The Bleeders."

The main point: Many bleeding diseases are genetic in origin rather than the result of infection.

Page 358

"The Nature of Theories"
Stephen Hawking

1. **As a "thought experiment," place the selection in the following variety of scenes. Does it "fit"? Why, or why not?**

    a. At a convention of the American Astrophysical Society, Hawking is brought to the platform in a wheelchair. Because of Lou Gehrig's disease he is unable to speak in such a way that the crowd will understand him, so he has one of his associates read the essay to a group of astrophysicists.

    b. Hawking has been invited to speak about his field at a meeting of the Jefferson High School PTA. His associate reads the selection.

    c. Hawking is visiting a faculty member at Utopia University, who invites him to speak to a freshman class in physics. Hawking's associate reads the essay.

    d. Hawking has been invited to speak at an anti-abortion rally. Three hundred noisy participants fall silent when the associate starts to read Hawking's paper on the nature of theories.

Interestingly, much of the writing could easily be the subject of an address to a group of astrophysicists. Hawking's discussion of some of the paradoxes of a unified theory would certainly interest his colleagues because they are unresolved issues (e.g., working on partial theories as a wrong approach if everything depends on everything else; the determination of the outcome of our search for the unified theory by the theory itself; reasons why such a determination must necessarily be the correct one). However, the astrophysicists would be offended if Hawking presumed it necessary to define the elements of a good theory for them or discuss in anything but a passing reference the difference between Einstein's and Newton's theories or the mutual exclusivity of the relativity and quantum mechanics theories. In short, the facts mentioned in the piece are inappropriate, but the wider philosophical questions which are discussed are very appropriate.

The piece is probably too dense to be given in a speech to an audience of high school parents. Although it might be something that many people in the audience would understand if they read it, there are too many subtleties to be captured in oral statements. In such a case, many PTA members would be an appropriate audience, but the medium would not.

The freshman physics class is probably the most appropriate audience and scene. The class would have enough education to follow the issues presented, particularly those that are philosophical, and yet would probably have little experience with Einstein's theories or with quantum mechanics. As a result, Hawking would not appear to be talking down to them. As a matter of fact, much of the material might be stretching the class because of its density, but this would be more appropriate in a college classroom than at an after-school function for families of high schoolers.

The subject matter is obviously not appropriate at the anti-abortion rally. However, there are also several other incongruities. The medium is inappropriate. At rallies, the purpose is not to raise doubts, as Hawking intentionally does in his essay, but just the opposite. Rallies are designed to banish all doubts on an issue and to bolster support through appeals to authority and use of the bandwagon effect. Finally, the intellectual and educational backgrounds at such a rally would be so diverse that his remarks would not be understood by a good part of the audience.

2.   **Regarding author: How does your knowledge of Hawking's physical condition affect your reaction to his essay?**

3.   **On the basis of the following statement, what can you conclude about Hawking's purposes in writing A Brief History of Time? Relate those purposes to the author and to the time and place which he has chosen for the book.**

> I decided to try and write a popular book about space and time after I gave the Loeb lectures at Harvard in 1982. There were already a considerable number of books about the early universe and black holes, ranging from the very good, such as Steven Weinberg's book, The First Three Minutes, to the very bad, which I will not identify. However, I felt that none of them really addressed the questions that had led me to do research in cosmology and quantum theory: Where did the universe come from? How and why did it begin? Will it come to an end, and if so, how? These are questions that are of interest to us all. But modern science has become so technical that only a very small number of specialists are able to master the mathematics used to describe them. Yet the basic ideas about the origin and fate of the universe can be stated without mathematics in a form that people without a scientific education can understand. That is what I have attempted to do in this book. The reader must judge whether I have succeeded.
>
> Someone told me that each equation I included in the book would halve the sales. I therefore resolved not to have any equations at all. In the end, however, I _did_ put in one equation, Einstein's famous equation, $E = mc^2$. I hope that this will not scare off half of my potential readers. (vi-vii)

In another forum, Hawking has remarked that he is lucky, considering the severity of his incapacitating disease, that his intellectual pursuits do not involve a tremendous amount of writing (relative to other scientists), such as with equations and formulas, but only a tremendous amount of thinking. His concerns border on the same questions which are posed in philosophy and religion.

4. **Why should anyone want to find a unified theory?**

The final paragraph of the essay provides Hawking's answer to this question: "the search for the ultimate theory of the universe seems difficult to justify on practical grounds. . . . Humanity's deepest desire for knowledge is justification enough for our continuing quest." In addition, Hawking notes that seemingly impractical scientific searches in the past have resulted in nuclear energy and the microelectronics revolution, implying that practical benefits could also result from the search for a unified theory.

5. Evaluate the selection from the standpoint of quality.

The preeminence of Hawking in his field virtually assures one of the quality of information in the essay. Even if one disagrees with Hawking's philosophical outlook, especially in regard to predestination, the point is well argued and must be given serious consideration.

6. Evaluate the selection from the standpoint of manner. What are some of the ways in which Hawking tries to make his subject understandable?

This is an excellent example of how to write about science for lay readers. Instead of discussing issues in the abstract--for example what constitutes a good theory--Hawking provides concrete examples that clarify his points. In this instance, he compares Aristotle's theory of the constituency of matter with Newton's gravitational theory.

7. Does Hawking give you enough information about both the general theory of relativity and the theory of quantum mechanics? In other words, do you believe that he violates the principle of quantity? Does he violate the principle elsewhere?

8. State the main point of the selection.

It is a clarification of the ultimate goal of science and the important issues that pertain to such a pursuit.

9. What world knowledge does one need in order to understand the selection? (What theological debates relate to the selection?)

In the opening discussion of theories, some world knowledge of some scientific theories (particularly those which have subsequently been discredited) and the scientific method is probably necessary in order to truly understand Hawking's point that (a) no theory is synonymous with reality but, instead, is only a model of reality, at best only approximating truth but never fully obtaining it and (b) theories are provisional. A general knowledge of the theory of natural selection is also probably necessary if the reader is to understand Hawking's assumption that our search for the unified theory would be guided by right thinking:

> [T]here will be variations in the genetic material and upbringing that different individuals have. These differences will mean that some individuals are better able . . . to draw the right conclusions. . . . These individuals will be more likely to survive and reproduce. . . . we might expect that the reasoning abilities that natural selection has given us would be valid also in our search for a complete unified theory. . . .

To paraphrase the above argument, natural selection has thus far led humankind to develop towards the right conclusions. There is no reason to believe that the search for the unified theory would be conducted in a different environment than that of any other search for answers. Therefore, natural selection would also operate within the search for the unified theory and lead us towards right, rather than wrong, conclusions.

10. According to Hawking, what two qualities must a good theory have?

"It must accurately describe a large class of observations on the basis of a model that contains only a few arbitrary elements, and it must make definite predictions about the results of future observations."

11. What is the easiest way to disprove a theory?

"[Y]ou can disprove a theory by finding even a single observation that disagrees with the predictions of the theory."

12. Explain what Hawking means by a unified theory of the universe. Would such a theory necessarily invalidate other partial theories, such as the theory of evolution, to which Hawking alludes in the latter part of the essay? To the theory of supply-side economics? To the theory of relativity or quantum mechanics?

Hawking explains the unified theory thus: "a single theory that describes the whole universe." Such a theory would unify the general theory of relativity and quantum mechanics.

13. Explain how Hawking rescues himself from this paradox: "[I]f there really is a complete unified theory, it would also presumably determine our actions. And so the theory itself would determine the outcome of our search for it!"

As explained above, everything leads one to believe that the evolution of knowledge is directed towards correct conclusions, and since there is no reason to believe that such would be an exception to the rule when searching for the unified theory, there is no reason to believe that the outcome, if predetermined, would not itself also be correct.

Do you see a certain contradiction in the search for a unified theory and Hawking's statement that "any physical theory is always provisional" (par. 2)? How do you think that Hawking might answer this question? (Before answering this question, reread his comparison of Newton's theory of gravity with Einstein's theory of relativity.

Page 364

"Ice Pond"
John McPhee

1. What is McPhee's purpose? To provide information about the technology of ice ponds? To do a character sketch of Theodore B. Taylor? Are both of these statements inadequate? If so, give a better one.

McPhee is obviously interested in the technology of the ice pond, going to great lengths to explain many of the technical aspects. He explains the basic idea early in the piece but then goes on to discuss the method of making ice ponds and, more technically, the economies of scale, measured in terms of the net energy savings, that would be obtained in cooling cheese factories, natural gas, concrete as it hardens, and even seawater for purposes of mining the elements dissolved in it.

McPhee is also interested in Taylor, admiring the grandiosity of his thinking, from his idea for a spaceship sixteen stories high designed to transport humans to the perimeter of the solar system to ice ponds containing several million tons of ice. Writes McPhee, "A man who could devise atomic bombs and then plan to use them to drive himself to Pluto might be expected to expand his thinking if he were to create a little hill of ice." McPhee undoubtedly admires a man whose career began with designing instruments of destruction and who is now using his expertise to benefit mankind and the environment. He also admires the understated way in which Taylor conducts himself in spite of the tremendous scope of all his projects, ice ponds included. Taylor self-deprecatingly describes the ice pond concept as simple-minded, and McPhee good-naturedly describes Taylor as "replete with technology but innocent of technique." (McPhee's very funny turn of phrase in mentioning "unskilled laborers such as Taylor and Freeman Dyson" is along these same lines.) McPhee might very well have had a higher purpose than to describe a clever application of technology by an interesting man. The optimism and largeness of spirit in the work contrasts with much of the literature concerned with energy alternatives, which is pessimistic in its outlook and narrow in its vision.

2. What is McPhee's purpose in using vivid descriptive language? Point out instances of such language.

"Taylor's hair is salt-and-peppery now but still stands in a thick youthful wave above his dark eyebrows and luminous brown eyes. He is tall, and he remains slim." The spaceship Orion's shape is said to "resemble the nose of a bullet, the head of a rocket, the ogival hat of a bishop." Taylor's ice pond is a "five-hundred-ton Sno-Kone," and the mound of ice and its wrapping is said to be "as if the tip of the Finsteraarhorn had been wrapped by Christo."

This description of the Prudential's new buildings is marvelous:

They are low, discretionary structures, provident in use of resources, durable, sensible, actuarial--with windows shaded just enough for summer but not too much for winter, with heat developing in a passive solar manner and brought in as well by heat pumps using water from the ground--and incorporating so many other features thrifty with energy that God will probably owe something to the insurance company after the account is totted up.

Vivid descriptive language is simply good writing, regardless of the subject matter or purpose. In many case, it is the only way that one's idea can be communicated, and it is certainly the only way in which one can hold most readers' attention. The low-key style in this selection is extremely attractive. McPhee seems to be saying that energy independence will involve many success stories such as the one he is telling; it will not come in one revolutionary discovery.

3. **In regard to author, "The Bleeders" is impersonal; Hackett is almost completely in the background. "Sounding" is very personal; the author, Mark Twain, is central to the piece. Is McPhee, like Hackett, almost invisible in "Ice Pond," or is he, like Mark Twain, a central element in the essay? Or does McPhee's "authorial presence" fall somewhere between these two poles? Point out references that McPhee makes to himself, either overtly or by implication. What is the effect of "authorial presence"?**

There are very few allusions to the author's presence, but the writing makes the reader feel as if he or she is right there in the field standing side by side with Taylor as he works on the ice pond. McPhee achieves this immediacy by writing in the present tense ("Taylor, up on the foam, completes his inspection of the ice within . . ."), by using the vivid language which was the subject of the previous question, and by including direct quotes from Taylor and Freeman Dyson which are obviously responses to McPhee's questions. The final paragraph is an answer Taylor gives to a question presumably posed by the author: "'What do you do with the ice?'" This, and the opening sentence ("At Princeton University, off and on since winter, I have observed the physicist Theodore B. Taylor standing like a mountaineer on the summit of what appears to be a five-hundred-ton Sno-Kone") is the only instance in the piece in which the author makes his presence overt. McPhee appears to the reader as an interested layperson who is intelligent enough to ask probing, perceptive questions of the experts.

4. **In your opinion, is the quality of the information adequate? Why do you think that McPhee is or is not a reliable source of information on this subject?**

McPhee liberally quotes directly from Taylor, an eminent scientist who has worked at the prestigious Los Alamos Scientific Laboratory and served on the President's Commission on the Accident at Three Mile Island. In addition, it is clear that McPhee has paraphrased a good deal of Taylor's own discussion and explanation. Importantly, McPhee himself does not render any verdict or pass judgment on the ice pond project or the other projects for which Taylor envisions using the snow machine's capabilities. This would clearly have been outside of his authority. The proof is in the pudding; as Freeman Dyson points out, "The first rule of technology is that no one can tell in advance whether a piece of technology is any good." Within the essay itself, McPhee does mention that a prototype pond "worked too well to be forgotten," providing evidence that the ice pond is practical.

5. In regard to manner, most readers feel that McPhee's prose is exceptionally clear and easy to read. What are some of the reasons for this clarity? (Sentence structure? Vocabulary? Figures of speech? Examples?)

McPhee uses everyday language. The structure of the piece is also helpful in making things clear. The opening introduces the reader to Taylor, the concept of the ice pond, and the reason for building it. The immediate reason is that Taylor "wants to take the 'E' out of OPEC." In addition, McPhee briefly charts the course of Taylor's career, from building bombs and constructing dreamships in the sky to the practical and important issue of increasing security within the nuclear industry and reducing our energy dependence, implying that in some ways the scientist is atoning for the errors of science itself if not his particular endeavors. The next section details the technical aspects of the ice pond, from the description of the prototype and its successor to the savings possible with the use of the ice pond. The third section then expands on the application of the ice pond concept of providing air conditioning to offices to that of using it to cool milk, cheese, natural gas in the pipeline, cement dams, and mining the ocean's waters. There is a certain symmetry in the construction of each of these sections because each starts out discussing Taylor himself before going to the main thesis of the section: Section One starts with McPhee's mentioning that he has observed Taylor at Princeton from winter until summer of 1981; Section Two starts with McPhee's joke on Taylor's ineptness with his hands; Section Three begins with the notion that someone like Taylor can be expected to expand his thinking beyond the scope of the immediate project.

6. With regard to scene, how have the issues of the day shaped Theodore Taylor's career?

Students should think of scene in terms of the Atomic Age, the energy crisis, the ultimate exhaustion of fossil fuels, and so on.

7. What is some of the world knowledge readers must have in order to understand "Ice Pond"?

Students undoubtedly understand <u>Sno-Kone</u>. Do they have world knowledge about the following?

<u>Los Alamos Scientific Laboratory</u>: Government-established nuclear research center in New Mexico where the first atomic bombs were made.
<u>Institute for Advanced Study</u>: Center for graduate study and research in the fields of mathematics and natural and social sciences located in Princeton, New Jersey.

Three Mile Island accident: Accident which occurred on March 28, 1979, in Harrisburg, Pennsylvania, involving the partial melting of a nuclear reactor's uranium core.

fission: The splitting of an atom's nucleus. It is the basic process in today's nuclear reactors.

fossil fuel: Fuel such as oil, natural gas, and coal which is the product of prehistoric organisms.

OPEC: Acronym for Organization of the Petroleum Exporting Countries, established in 1960 to coordinate oil policies among many of the third-world oil-producing states.

polyethylene: a plastic polymer.

Dacron: A synthetic cloth fiber.

Finsteraarhorn: A tall mountain in the Swiss Alps.

Christo (Javacheff): Artist known for projects which involve completely wrapping or covering large areas of ground or historical buildings with cloth.

8. In your opinion, how does Taylor's earlier plan to build a sixteen-story spaceship affect his credibility?

Such a grandiose plan tends to detract from Taylor's claims for the practical applications of his cooling technology on a large scale. The students might note that this piece was written a decade or more ago, and yet there hasn't been a hint of the technology's being used by the mainstream as a valid method of cooling.

9. In the opening paragraph, McPhee writes, "His [Taylor's] has been, at any rate, a semicircular career." The final paragraph also concerns itself with matters coming back around. In the latter instance, what matters will come back around? Why do you think the piece ends as it does?

The use of ice as a commodity, once a "cash crop" for Boston, could easily become economically important once more, according to Taylor. The practices of the past are mentioned in order to buttress Taylor's argument about the benefits of ice as a product and, stylistically, such an ending gives the piece a balance that it wouldn't have otherwise.

10. What images show the semicircular nature of Taylor's career?

11. What do you suppose are the author's qualifications for writing "Ice Pond"? Explain.

Page 372

"The First Cure"
Black Elk

1. Explain why one can argue that the selection resulted from the effect of time and place on the author.

The oral history would never have been transcribed if Black Elk and his people had not been placed on an Indian reservation, a result of the domestication of the western frontier by whites.

2. In this selection, language is presumably spoken. How does this spoken language differ from the written language in, for instance, the selection by Hawking?

The Black Elk selection is more discursive than that by Hawking. For example, the explanations of why Black Elk's people perform and construct things in circles and why they go from left to right are digressions--interesting though they are--from the main narrative thrust of the essay. And the fact that this piece is narrative changes the structure from one that is hierarchical (main point, supporting statements, evidence, etc.) to one that is chronologically ordered.

3. Discuss the effect of Black Elk's language on our perception of him (the author) and of the time and place that he talks about.

The language is simple and very direct. In discussing the fact that it takes longer for adolescents to mature in the square houses on the reservation than in the round teepees, Black Elk concludes, "Well, it is as it is. We are prisoners of war while we are waiting here." The times when Black Elk elaborates on points are those when he wishes to explain how the tribe's culture is in harmony with what he perceives to be the natural state of things (circular). As a result, Black Elk is a man who appears to be resigned to the defeat of the tribe at the hands of the white man. He also impresses the reader with the earnestness with which he communicates his story, obviously taking great care to tell the story properly and clearly.

4. Many literature courses now include works by native Americans (such as Black Elk) and black Americans (such as Zora Neale Hurston, whose piece "How It Feels to Be Colored Me" appears later in this chapter), whereas twenty years ago these authors were virtually unknown. In what way have changes in the American scene brought about changes in the literature curriculum?

Multicultural diversity is one of the great issues currently being debated on college campuses. The melting pot concept of giving up one's uniqueness as an ethnic group in order to fit in with the general population is now seen by many as relinquishing control to those in power.

5. In what ways does the discussion of the circle as a sacred element of Lakota culture violate the principle of relation?

See question 2.

6. Do you trust the quality of information in the selection? Explain.

There is no reason for distrust. The fact that Black Elk Speaks, first published in 1932, has established itself as an important historical document indicates that critics have had ample chance to attack the work's credibility.

7. The literal medium used in Black Elk Speaks is, presumably, written transcriptions of interviews. On a less literal level, the medium is an oral history. How do you think each medium influences the other?

It is important to realize that a third member was involved in the writing of this book, namely, Black Elk's son, who interpreted and translated his father's stories. In editing the piece, Neihardt probably also added or interpolated words and phrases in order to make the piece more fluent.

8. In your opinion, what is the most important theme in "The First Cure"?

There are several major themes in this selection: the achievement of one's destiny in life; the importance of living in harmony with and learning from nature.

9. Some texts are valuable for the information they contain. For example, the manual that comes with a new computer contains absolutely essential information. Other texts are valuable because of the imaginative experience they provide readers. And some texts, of course, are both informative and imaginative. From your point of view, why is "The First Cure" valuable?

John Neihardt's purpose was probably to obtain as much information as possible about Black Elk's tribe. As the headnote mentions, Black Elk was of the last generation of his tribe to be born before their defeat, and it was important to get his first-hand accounts before his generation completely died out. That Neihardt was a poet allowed him to recognize the great literary merit of Black Elk's accounts. It was presumably Neihardt who edited the history. At the least, this means that Neihardt punctuated the book and created paragraphs. It also probably means that he filled in with his own writing where the transcription was not in complete sentences. Such editorial shaping is primarily aesthetic, and certainly this selection reads exceptionally well.

10. The Black Elk and Hawking pieces illustrate the differences between a belief and a theory. Use the two selections to explain this difference.

According to Hawking, a good theory satisfies three requirements: it describes a large body of observed phenomena, it has very few arbitrary elements (i.e., it makes very few assumptions), and it must make definite predictions. A belief, like a theory, generally describes a large body of observed phenomena, which is why people retain the belief in the first place. A belief, however, does have arbitrary elements. Belief in a religion, for example, generally requires that the adherent simply possess faith. In addition, beliefs do not necessarily have predictive value. For example, belief in God does not allow one to predict the outcome of events.

Page 378

"The Vassar Girl"
Mary McCarthy

1. The principle of quantity: At any points in this essay does McCarthy give you less information than you need to understand her? Does she ever give you more than necessary? (Be specific in your answers.)

The answers will depend upon students' individual backgrounds of world knowledge.

2. The principle of quality: What reasons do you have for trusting (or distrusting) McCarthy's knowledge of her subject or her honesty?

This selection is subtly tinged with a nostalgia which the author herself might not have admitted to. Bluntly stated, one of the major points that McCarthy makes in her essay is that "things were better back then." This emotional side to her essay does make one suspicious of her analysis of Vassar in the fifties. Oddly enough, this nostalgia seems less prejudicial to the author's discussion of her own years at the college. There also seems to be something close to envy when McCarthy talks of the current Vassar student who is all too perfect, all too poised. Compare her description of the fifties Vassar student "who lives in an ideal present" and whose "plans are made" with the description of herself as she is about to enter Vassar. She describes herself as "an ardent literary little girl" who smoked on the fire-escape and contemplated suicide. McCarthy seems to begrudge the new generation their greater security and sense of self.

On the other hand, there appears to be no reason that the reader would suspect McCarthy's knowledge. The author seems to have kept current with the events at Vassar. Instead of relying simply on the newsletter from the college to inform herself, McCarthy states that she has sat in on classes in order to obtain a sense of the college in the fifties. In addition, as a professed intellectual, she certainly kept abreast of the current scene in education and in the world view that would allow her to assess the state of education at Vassar.

3. The principle of manner: If you think the essay is sometimes unclear, indicate where and explain the difficulty.

4. The principle of relation: Are any parts of the essay irrelevant to the topic? Explain.

5. What sorts of readers do you think McCarthy has in mind? (Their levels of education? Their socioeconomic status? Their interests?) Explain your answer.

6. Which details in the selection did you find particularly vivid? In what ways do these details contribute to the meaning and effect of the piece?

7. McCarthy notes that Vassar was founded in 1861, the same year as Lincoln's inauguration and the emancipation of the Russian serfs. What purpose does the author have in providing this seemingly extraneous information? (Has she violated the principle of relationship?)

McCarthy states in the same paragraph that the school was conceived as a declaration of rights and proclamation of equality, concerns which were also central to Lincoln.

8. Explain how differences in the scene at the time of writing this piece and the scene described within the piece have influenced this autobiographical essay.

9. Is the purpose of this essay autobiographical? Or is McCarthy explaining something? Is she arguing? Explain your answer.

10. Do you understand the following? What world knowledge do you need? If you did not understand why, for instance, the date October 1929 is significant, where could you find out about this date?

"After October, 1929, some of us had smaller allowances. . . ."
Date of the great stock market crash.

"[T]he off-campus shops still prospered, selling grape lemonade, bacon-and-tomato sandwiches, and later 3.2 beer."
Prohibition, enacted in 1919, was repealed by the 21st amendment in 1933.

"With the impetus of the New Deal and memories of the breadlines behind us, even we aesthetes began reading about Sacco and Vanzetti and Mooney. We wrote papers for Contemporary Prose Fiction on Dos Passos."

New Deal: Franklin Roosevelt's domestic program designed to rescue the nation from the Great Depression through public works and other methods and to enact reform through such social legislation as the Social Security Act (1935).

Sacco and Vanzetti: Nicola Sacco and Bartolomeo Vanzetti were two immigrants sentenced to death in 1921 for the killing of a paymaster and his guard during a robbery. Many believed their trial to be unfair and their sentencing, despite conflicting evidence, to be the result of their political belief in anarchism. They were executed in 1927.

Mooney: Thomas J. Mooney (1883-1942), American labor leader convicted as a participant in a bombing that killed several people in San Francisco. He was sentenced to death, but because of perjured testimony in his trial, the sentence was commuted to life imprisonment. In 1939, Governor Culbert L. Olson of California pardoned him unconditionally.

Dos Passos: (John Roderigo Dos Passos, 1896-1970). American novelist whose major work is U.S.A., a trilogy of novels portraying American life in a collage by incorporating standard narration, stream of consciousness, and quotations from the newspapers and magazines of the day. These works expressed a leftist viewpoint.

11. Does McCarthy's Vassar College experience represent your own idea of the role colleges should play in the lives of students? Do you think that the changes at Vassar are for the better? Why or why not? Which Vassar, that of the late 1920s and early 1930s or that of the early 1950s, do you feel most closely corresponds to the mission of the college, as stated by its founder?

McCarthy typifies her own Vassar experience as one requiring independence of mind and self-reliance in order to succeed:

"A wistful respect for the unorthodox is ingrained in the Vassar mentality."

"[A]t Vassar, by and large, the student is almost forbidden to take her direction from the teacher."

"An arresting performance in politics, fashion, or art is often take by the Vassar mind to be synonymous with true accomplishment."

"[T]here is a challenge in the Vassar atmosphere that makes her graduates feel that they owe it as a positive duty to the college and to the human community to be outstanding, aggressive, and secure."

"[I]n my day, the roadster, the trolley car, and the taxi bore us off the campus and away from the supervisory eye."

"During the early thirties, a single psychiatrist, a psychologist, and a visiting consultant from Riggs Institute took care of the emotional problems of 1,250 students."

The college students of her day were all too eager to escape the bounds of the college campus whenever they could, in order to drink in speakeasies or eat at picturesque inns along the road. In the 1950s, the students don't want to escape from the pull of the campus or the watch of the campus official. Instead, they prefer to remain at the Alumnae House or drink in the lounge-living room under the eye of the alumnae secretary or one of her assistants.

"Their plans are made. . . . There is none of the conflict and indecision that harried us in the thirties. . . ."

"[T]hey have decided to help the world, but not to change or destroy it."

"[T]he college is businesslike."

"[T]hey have an air of placid aloofness from what is currently going on in the world of arts and letters."

"Reversing the situation in most colleges, the faculty is ahead of the student body in its awareness of the times."

"And this itself is less lively than formerly; a Peck & Peck, a drugstore, an eating place or two, and the Vassar Bank are the principal remains of a once-spirited commercial area, where teashops, inns, and dress shops once flourished on Vassar extravagance."

"[T]oday's undergraduates flock up the hill to Alumnae House. . . . [T]hey join their young men in the big lounge-living room for a cocktail or two, under the watchful eye of the alumnae secretary or her assistants."

"This increasing dependency on the college and its auxiliary agencies to furnish not only education but pleasure, emotional guidance, and social direction is reflected in nearly every sphere of the current Vassar life."

"The college is a miniature welfare state. . . . Now Vassar's 1,350 girls have been endowed with a two-million-dollar grant by Paul Mellon . . . for a guidance and counseling program under the direction of Dr. Carl Binger, the psychiatrist who testified in the second Alger Hiss trial."

"The extracurricular side of Vassar life has already expanded to the point where solitude and self-questioning seem regulated out of existence."

The changes are summarized by McCarthy in the following paragraph:

This intensification of the extracurricular life, in which every hour is planned for and assigned to some scheduled group activity, in which no one is left out or discriminated against (there are no secret societies or sororities), is the most striking feature of the current scene at Vassar. To the returning alumna whose college years were both more snobbish and sectarian, on the one hand, and more Bohemian, rebellious, and lyrical, on the other, the administrative cast, so to speak, of the present Vassar mold is both disquieting and praiseworthy. A uniform, pliant, docile undergraduate seems to be resulting from the stress on the group and the community that prevails at Vassar today. The outcast and the rebel are almost equally known. There has been a leveling-off in the Vassar geography of what was once a series of ranges, peaks, and valleys, so that Vassar, formerly known for the extremities of her climate, is now a moderate plateau. The vivid and extraordinary student, familiar to the old teachers and the alumnae, is, at least temporarily, absent from the scene.

In addition, 216 Yale men were brought in for the Vassar freshman dance. Such action would have been unthinkable in McCarthy's day, when one was expected to act on one's own initiative. The Vassar of the 1950s is seen to be more conservative and matter of fact.

12. Most of McCarthy's readers haven't attended Vassar nor do they have much knowledge of the institution, yet the essay deals in large part with a discussion of the changes in the campus over the course of two decades. Briefly list these changes and explain how the author has given the reader enough information to understand these changes.

13. McCarthy makes repeated allusions both to classical mythology and to classic literary personae. Why? What are the purpose and the effect of these allusions?

The allusions:

"Like Athena, goddess of wisdom, Vassar College sprang in full battle dress from
     the head of a man."

"[A]ll this seems to foretell four years of a Renaissance lavishness, in an academy
     that was a Forest of Arden and a Fifth Avenue department store
     combined."

"This older Vassar career woman is nearly as familiar to American folklore as
     the intrepid young Portia or Rosalind she may at one time have passed for."

"Other private colleges have turned to the literary avant-garde and found
     Abelards to substitute for the Heloises--young male critics, philosophers,
     poets, novelists, short-story writers, trained, for the most part, in the New
     Criticism. . . ."

The reason for these references is stated by McCarthy herself: "The essence of Vassar is mythic. Today, despite much competition, it still figures in the public mind as the archetypal woman's college."

14. McCarthy obviously enjoyed her years at Vassar a great deal and has great admiration for the institution, but she also is clear-eyed about its drawbacks. What were they at the time she attended and what are the drawbacks the author sees in the early 1950s? Do you yourself see these as drawbacks?

15. In typifying the Vassar student, McCarthy writes, ". . . the Vassar girl is thought of as carrying a banner. The inscription on it varies with the era or with the ideas of the beholder and in the final sense does not matter--the flushed cheek and tensed arm are what count" (par. 5). Explain what McCarthy is getting at here.

16. McCarthy notes that Vassar in the 1950s is a hubbub of planned activity. List the activities mentioned. What point is McCarthy emphasizing by itemizing to such a great extent?

Page 395

"How It Feels to Be Colored Me"
Zora Neale Hurston

1. It can be argued that time and place are the most important elements of this essay. What are the important scenes that Hurston portrays? Do these scenes symbolize aspects of America? Explain.

Hurston presents two scenes: her native town Eatonville, Florida, and Harlem, although she also briefly mentions Barnard College and Jacksonville, Florida. The contrast between Eatonville and Harlem is great. Hurston's home town is small, rural, and fairly backwards. (She mentions that even the white Floridians rode through town on horses. Only northern tourists drove through the town's sandy road in automobiles.) The people of Eatonville were apparently very reserved because they would peer at the Northerners from behind curtains and frowned on Zora's outgoing tendencies. Harlem, on the other hand, was a major section of the largest city in the United States. In addition, the ambience of the jazz club and the image of Zora sauntering down Seventh Avenue with her hat set at an angle portray a jauntiness.

These two contrasting scenes mirror the lives of many blacks who migrated from the agrarian, rural South to the industrial and urban North in the hopes of finding a better life. When she writes that her days in Eatonville were a part of her life that existed prior to the Hegira, Hurston makes it clear that her move to the North was for this same purpose. In this case, Hurston's reference is not an allusion to persecution but to the pursuit of a better life. From an even wider perspective, the shift from a rural to an urban scene mirrors the change in America as a whole from an agrarian society into an industrial power.

2. How does change of scene affect Hurston?

Although Hurston does not emphasize the Jacksonville scene, the move to that city affected her greatly. It was upon arriving in Jacksonville that she "became colored," that is, that she suddenly realized the disparity between blacks and whites in American society. Her attendance at nearly all-white Barnard College accentuated the realization.

Hurston writes, "I do not always feel colored. Even now I often achieve the unconscious Zora of Eatonville before the Hegira." She provides an example of this loss of self-consciousness when she writes about walking down Seventh Avenue, Harlem City. "The cosmic Zora emerges." The scene in the jazz club is meant as an example of Hurston's sense of race in the contrast with the white friend accompanying her. However, in her description of the music and her reaction to it, the "cosmic" Zora emerges in the ecstasy of the event. The change of scene to Harlem, therefore, allows Zora to lose her self-consciousness, her coloredness, if but only for a few moments at a time.

3. Explain the "brown bag" metaphor with which the essay concludes. (Who is the Great Stuffer of Bags?) In regard to manner, what does Hurston gain through using a metaphor to express this idea?

The Great Stuffer of Bags is obviously an allusion to God and the different colored bags are the various races of people. By using this metaphor, Hurston is able to distance the reader from confronting the emotional issue of race directly and yet still make her point that all peoples are essentially alike regardless of the color of their skin.

4. What was Hurston's purpose in writing the essay? What evidence do you have for your conclusion?

The title "How It Feels to Be Colored Me" reveals part of Hurston's purpose for writing the essay. The author provides examples of times when she has been self-conscious of her race and how she has felt in those situations. At Barnard, she was overwhelmed by the number of white students, but because of her self-assurance she was able to maintain her identity. ("Among the thousand white persons, I am a dark rock surged upon, and overswept, but through it all, I remain myself.") In a jazz club, the author is transported by the music to Africa where her primitive emotions take over. These emotions of "colored me" are compared to "great blobs of purple and red" while her white friend remains emotionless and "pale with his whiteness."

Hurston also wishes to reveal that there are many times when she is totally unaware of her color. She states that she did not become aware of her color until the age of thirteen, when she was sent from her hometown of Eatonville to Jacksonville in order to attend school. Until that time, she greeted all passers-by, white and black alike, as simply objects of interest and as an audience for her spontaneous performances. The only distinguishing features of the whites were that they did not live in Eatonville and that they rewarded Zora's dancing and singing with dimes. The author notes that she has the same lack of self-consciousness as she walks down Seventh Avenue in her new hometown of Harlem.

The gist of Hurston's essay, that "[she is] not tragically colored," also provides the larger, overriding purpose. In tone, the essay resembles a coach's pep talk:

> Slavery is sixty years in the past. The operation was successful and the patient is doing well, thank you. The terrible struggle that made me an American out of a potential slave said "On the line!" The Reconstruction said "Get set!"; and the generation before said "Go!" I am off to a flying start and I must not halt in the stretch to look behind and weep.

Hurston is probably addressing both white and black audiences. The author, by implication, asks that African Americans avoid seeing themselves as victims. Instead, she suggests adopting a constructive attitude. ("No one on earth ever had a greater chance for glory. The world to be won and nothing to be lost.") Hurston purposefully avoids any specific mention of racism which might make the tone of the essay ugly. The only mention is in the penultimate paragraph when she states that racism surprises her rather than makes her angry. It is interesting to compare this viewpoint with contemporary opinions of some influential African American intellectuals who also call for blacks to become self-sufficient and avoid the stigma of victimization. Such opinions can be contrasted with the viewpoint which stresses the victimization of African Americans and society's remedies.

To whites, Hurston appears to be offering a hand of friendship and an invitation for all races to unite in harmony. The essay is diplomatic in that it does not accuse but, rather, forgives. The author, in essence, asks that bygones be bygones.

5. Hurston calls herself "colored." What term do "colored" people now apply to themselves? Why do you think the terminology changed?

"Black" and "African American" are the two most common terms currently used. One reason for the change in terminology is the need for succeeding generations to grapple with the issue of race and to adopt their own methods for resolving the problem. The new terminology immediately helps clarify the change in perspective and makes clear that previously held conceptions have been discarded.

The terms themselves incorporate these changes in perspective. Whereas "colored" implied that one people were "painted" and therefore stigmatized, "black" is simply one of many possible colors of the human skin. "African American" stresses the place of origin, which is especially important for a people who were uprooted and taken to another continent against their will.

6. What forces in contemporary America prompted the editors of the <u>Norton Anthology of American Literature</u> to rediscover Zora Neale Hurston and to include her work in their collection?

As greater numbers of minorities enter college, their call for multicultural diversity has been the greatest force in expanding the university curriculum beyond the study of the "Western tradition," with its emphasis on European culture. This trend is not, however, endorsed solely by minorities but also by those who are disappointed in the results of the Western tradition. These people would argue that it was the Western tradition which has created the ecological crises and which has endorsed the conquering and subordination of native peoples. Advocates of multiculturalism hope that the study of different cultures and viewpoints will bring about a greater understanding and respect for other people, in turn reducing the level of hatred and distrust that exists in our society.

7. Paraphrase the following passage, making it easier for the casual reader to understand:

It is quite exciting to hold the center of the national stage, with the spectators not knowing whether to laugh or weep.

The position of my white neighbor is much more difficult. No brown specter pulls up a chair beside me when I sit down to eat. No dark ghost thrusts its leg against mine in bed. The game of keeping what one has is never so exciting as the game of getting.

From the standpoint of manner, would you say that Hurston has expressed herself as clearly as possible? What does your paraphrase gain? What does it lose?

To paraphrase:

It is quite exciting to be directly involved in an issue which is the focus of the nation's attention even if the public does not know whether it should be glad or regret that the issue of race has arisen.

The issue of race relations is more difficult for whites. Blacks, unlike whites, <u>are not haunted by the thought of another race gaining on them</u> or <u>do not have the burden of guilt that whites must bear</u> [Hurston's point is ambiguous]. In addition, it is a better feeling to be striving for advancement than to be guarding against the loss of what one already has.

Hurston has not expressed herself as clearly as possible. She does not make clear the reason that the spectators should laugh (out of derision? out of joy for the advances made by blacks? out of joy for the manner in which the advances are being made?) or cry (out of guilt or sympathy with the blacks' cause? because of the gains the blacks are making?).

Hurston is also unclear about why whites should be haunted by blacks. Immediately after raising the issue of the brown specter/dark ghost, Hurston states that there is less excitement in keeping what one has than in striving for gains. This juxtaposition might imply that gains for blacks are losses for whites, and it is this possibility that frightens whites. On the other hand, Hurston might be making separate points. For example, blacks might haunt white people for any number of reasons (e.g., guilt arising from the past inequities; the pressure whites feel when blacks exert their rights). Furthermore, whites have already reached reasonable levels of achievement and do not have the optimism created by advancement but instead, for any number of reasons unrelated to the gains obtained by blacks, fear the loss of that which they have already achieved.

The paraphrase has no advantages over Hurston's text because it is every bit as ambiguous and does not contain lively images, such as that of holding the national stage or of dark ghosts haunting white people, nor does it have the pithy impact of the sentence, "The game of keeping what one has is never so exciting as the game of getting."

8. Do you believe that Hurston has satisfied the writer-reader contract for quantity when she describes how she feels to be colored? What would you delete or add to the text?

Hurston does not satisfy the reader's expectation that the author will explain what it feels like to be colored. The only real discussion of how the author feels is the description of her reaction to the music of a jazz band. Two other situations which brought home the fact that the author was black are given only cursory attention. The description of her stay at Barnard is simply the image of a dark rock over which a river flows. The author delicately avoids any direct mention of racism and her reaction to it, even though racism was the reason that she first felt colored at the age of thirteen. She simply writes, "I was now a little colored girl. I found it out in certain ways."

Readers would probably be interested in learning about the "certain ways" in which the young Zora learned that she was colored and her reactions to those events. Also, Hurston has a surprisingly optimistic and positive outlook on life, and it would increase the impact of the essay if she were to outline her reasons for optimism and the battles that she surely must have waged against despair, fear, and anger before coming to terms with her situation.

9. Does Hurston's vignette in the jazz club violate the principle of relation? Explain.

Hurston is very clear that the scene is meant to show how she is different from whites. Her enthusiasm for the music is contrasted with the cool reaction that her white friend has to the same jazz club performance. Seen in this light, the passage upholds the principle of relation. What is not clear, however, is how much of Hurston's emotional reaction to the music is mirrored by her external actions. Although she does not believe that her friend shares her enthusiasm for the music, she offers few objective clues. As a matter of fact, it is the friend who states that the music at the club has been good. It could be argued that the scene does violate the principle of relation in some ways if one believes that the author's reaction to good music is typical of most people's, not only blacks', and that she inappropriately compares her own subjective feelings with what she can observe of her white friend. On the whole, however, the principle of relation is upheld in this section of the essay.

10. What world knowledge must the reader have in order to understand the essay?

The reader must have some general knowledge of the history of race relations in the United States.

11. Characterize Hurston's attitude toward her race. How does that attitude compare with the attitudes of blacks today?

The answers to this question might form a substantial volume, but Hurston is probably more sanguine about her race's prospects than are many black leaders today. After all, in the essay (as question 4 indicates) Hurston says, "Slavery is sixty years in the past. The operation was successful and the patient is doing well, thank you. . . . "

Hurston died (in 1960) in a welfare home, poverty stricken and forgotten. In view of this irony, would the Hurston of the 1950s have the same attitudes as the young Hurston?

Page 400

"On the Pilgrim's Path to Lourdes"
Eleanor Munro

1. **The author states that if you "steep yourself instead in the geography, architecture and massed population of the sacred precinct, you may gain an inkling of the meaning of this ancient and universal human practice [of making pilgrimages]." In short, if you steep yourself in the time and place, you might gain some inkling. Explain the unique characteristics of the geography of Lourdes and the pilgrims who journey there.**

Lourdes is set in a valley surrounded by cliffs whose waterfalls create "ethereal rainbows and ghostly low-hanging clouds." Many of those who travel to Lourdes are afflicted with disease or disfigurement and are in hopes of a miracle cure. The gloomy surroundings mirror the misery of the pilgrims.

2. **The author concludes her essay with a comparison of the pilgrims' faith to the orbiting of the earth around the sun. Find another place where the author makes a similar comparison. Do you think that this repetition is effective? What is the author's purpose in the repetition? Explain.**

The essay's third paragraph discusses the pilgrim's visitation as making a circular path around the object of adoration in the same direction as the clockwise course of the sun and compares the lights of the nighttime pilgrims as a galaxy of stars revolving in the darkness. This use of celestial metaphors at the beginning and end of the essay gives it an order which people naturally find pleasing and alludes to the "harmonic order we on earth find both beautiful and eternal." In addition, the use of metaphor in the final paragraph serves to sum up and conclude the essay in a tidy manner.

3. **What is Munro's purpose in the essay?**

The author wishes to understand the act of making pilgrimages and the reason that Lourdes holds such an attraction.

4. **In what sense could we say that "On the Pilgrim's Path to Lourdes" is about the relationship between the time and the place and what occurs at that time and place?**

This question, of course, asks students to consider the relationship (ratio) between act (what happens) and scene (time and place) and refers to Chapter 2 (specifically, pages 114-18). Historically, Lourdes has become a holy site, endowed, for believers, with the mystery and power of all such shrines. Is Lourdes an agency, a therapeutic spot like a physical therapy clinic, or is it imbued with supreme Agency?

5. **Munro writes in the first paragraph, "Among sacred pilgrimage sites of the world . . . the French shrine of Lourdes in its gloomy mountain setting may be one of**

the most instructive." Do you believe that Munro satisfies the principle of relation throughout the essay in supporting this statement? Why, or why not?

In order truly to support the contention that Lourdes may be one of the most instructive pilgrimage sites, the author would have to do two things. First, she would have to explain just how Lourdes is instructive, and second, she would need to compare Lourdes with other well-known shrines. Because the author addresses only the first issue, she does not in the strictest sense uphold the principle of relation.

The second section of the essay, which provides a succinct and interesting history of the shrine, does not relate directly to the lessons Munro believes can be learned from the shrine at Lourdes. Nonetheless, because the reader would be naturally curious as to why Lourdes is regarded as a holy shrine, the background information is appropriate even if it does not absolutely adhere to the principle of relation.

Otherwise, the other sections of the essay adequately maintain the principle. The first section explains what can be learned from the commonality that exists among shrines. ("In these circumambulations, the pilgrim imitates the flight of the stars and planets, which orbit the celestial pole, disappearing and reappearing in a harmonic order we on earth find both beautiful and eternal. So the pilgrim enacts the answer to his longing for immortality.") This section also briefly describes the geography and climate of Lourdes, information that makes it both unique and instructive.

The third section is important in establishing both the physical layout of the shrine and in making clear the link between the shrine and the physically infirm.

6. Do you trust Munro's statements of fact? Her description of the shrine? Her interpretation of its meaning? Can you disagree with her interpretation and still believe that she has upheld the contract of quality? Explain.

The question is intended to stimulate discussion about the author's reliability in regard to fact and the relationship between factuality and opinion.

7. Do you believe that the Lourdes shrine would have less religious significance if it were set in a sunny and warm climate amid flat, fertile farmland? Would it have a different literary significance to Munro? Why, or why not?

From a literary standpoint, the scene reinforces the action. One of the most famous examples of scene is the opening of Thomas Hardy's Return of the Native, the heath at the moment between daylight and darkness setting the mood. In other words, authors exploit scenes. (See also the discussion of the opening of In Cold Blood, pages 116-17.) Since Lourdes is a holy place, the setting would probably be largely irrelevant to the pilgrims as is the setting of the Church of the Holy Sepulcher to the pilgrims who go there every Christmas.

8. According to the author, what is the primary difference between Hindu and Western religious thought? How does this difference relate to the significance of Lourdes?

Munro explains, "Hindu religious practice helps you overlook immediate pain and dwell instead on vast metaphysical abstractions. Western religious thought focuses on the narrower, more piercing mystery of human consciousness in an inhuman world." The point is that Lourdes is primarily dedicated to individual human suffering and only secondarily to cosmic mysteries. In other words, though God is the background, the focus is on the individual. Analogically, according to Munro, Christianity is a closeup of an individual, whereas Hinduism is a panorama.

9. What historical incident four years before the occurrence of Saint Bernadette's vision helped to establish the importance of such a miracle?

Four years prior to Bernadette's vision, the Pope had proclaimed the dogma of the Immaculate Conception of the Virgin. That is, Mary, mother of Jesus, was said to have been conceived herself without original sin. According to the author, this was a controversial view within the Catholic Church's ranks but was a popularly held belief among the laity. This vision helped to reinforce the newly established doctrine.

10. Lourdes is identified as a site at which the Virgin Mary appeared nine times, but how it has become associated with the cure of bodily ills remains unclear. What do you think the connection between the appearance and the pilgrimage reveals about the beliefs of the Catholic congregation? According to the article, do they completely agree with those of the Vatican?

The Vatican is reticent concerning the miracles that have been reported, but, obviously, thousands of pilgrims have no reservations. As Munro says, "Even if the cures are dubious or short-lasting, the patients return home, sometimes to institutions that are their lifelong homes, lifted in mind and heart by the experience."

11. Why do you think that the author only incidentally alludes to the great tourist industry which has sprung up around Lourdes?

Possible reasons are that (a) Lourdes tourism is not directly related to the author's purpose and (b) stressing the tourism would diminish the effect of the essay's handling of religious belief.

12. Briefly state the main point of the essay.

Munro explains the psychological and historical reasons for pilgrimages. She has visited Lourdes and wants to account for the effect that the experience has had on her.

Page 406

"Oranges and Sweet Sister Boy"
Judy Ruiz

1. Point out instances in which the author purposefully fails to provide enough information with which to immediately comprehend the exposition. Do you believe

that the author is successful in what she is trying to do? Why, or why not? At several such times, the author provides the necessary information many paragraphs after the initial reference is made. Why do you think the author does this? Would you have written it differently? Explain.

The essay opens with a scene in which the brother informs the author that he has undergone the sex change operation. Ruiz writes, "I am sleeping, hard, when the telephone rings. It's my brother, and he's calling to say that he is now my sister." The reader's confusion with this statement is meant to mirror Ruiz's own disorientation after being wakened with the news. Other points of confusion: Who is the woman in a white suit and the man in a blue uniform on the Texas Zephyr? (Later we learn that the couple are Ruiz's parents.) Who is the lady with hoop earrings as big as dessert plates standing in front of the Alamo? (Subsequently we learn that the woman is Ruiz herself.)

2. Point out examples in which the author juxtaposes two disparate ideas or occurrences without stating what relation they have to each other. What relations does the author imply with each of these juxtapositions?

Paragraph 9 is typical. What is the relationship between oranges, the course called "Women and Modern Literature," and the brother who is now a sister? In particular, the relationship of oranges to the theme of the essay is important, for, after all, Ruiz uses oranges in the title. The answer to this question relates closely to the answer to question 6.

3. It is surprising that the author refers so frequently to her parents when she focuses the exposition elsewhere. Do you believe that these details are relevant? Why, or why not?

She feels that her androgyny was inherited; her mother did not teach her skills of womanhood; and the father beat her and her brother. All of these facts make the author and her brother feel less than whole as adults.

4. What autobiographical details can you glean from the essay? What biographical details are provided about the brother? What do your answers tell you about the focus of the story?

5. Explain what significance the author's tattoo holds for her.

The tattoo is a representation of Yin and Yang. In Chinese philosophy, they are the two principles which affect, among other things, people's destinies. The Yin is the dark, negative, female principle, and the Yang is the bright, positive, masculine principle. For Ruiz, the symbol represents the androgynous nature which she believes is a trait particular to her family.

Her brother is the most obvious example of this tendency to exhibit both masculine and feminine traits, but the author also enumerates the tendency among other family members, including herself. The author had taken to wearing extremely feminine clothing in order to mask her masculine traits. Her father would dress in drag on Halloween and is said to have made a beautiful woman. Finally, the author's daughter is as muscular as a man, and her sons are beautiful rather than handsome.

The representation of Yin and Yang shows the two principles to be in perfect opposition to each other, visually implying some form of harmony, and yet the androgynous trait within Ruiz's family creates a great deal of turmoil. Her brother was unhappy as a man and suffered terribly, while Ruiz is not comfortable with her own sexuality and has fantasies of using a gun to "blow the woman out of her" to relieve her discomfort.

6. Explain what oranges mean to the author. Do they have more than one meaning for her? Cite passages from the selection to support your opinion.

Ruiz uses oranges to symbolize several different things, but the primary quality of the fruit which the author is concerned with is its "mildly intrusive nature." Ruiz first mentions oranges early in the essay when she is awakened by the news that her brother has had the operation. Still groggy, the author thinks that if the brother had yet to undergo the operation she could make him reconsider taking such a drastic step, making him "touch base with reality" by giving him an orange, which is something solid, tangible, and acidic. Oranges are used in much the same way by the author as she instructs a class of socially and intellectually impaired students about metaphor.

Oranges become associated in the essay with sexuality. The author's hands are still orangey after peeling the fruit in class when her professor begins talking about Emily Dickinson's brother having sex with the poet's best friend and about Walt Whitman's attraction to boys.

Nonetheless, oranges are also used to reveal Ruiz's incomplete mastery of her own life and of social graces. She contrasts her own tastes in food (a double cheeseburger and fries) with those of her friend LuAnn (in-season fruit and cottage cheese) and, at the same time, mentions that while she had juice oranges, which are messy to eat, LuAnn had selected the appropriate type and had neatly peeled the fruit in one strip. Earlier, Ruiz had mentioned that the only fruit her mother had brought into the household was canned.

7. The author writes, "Perhaps better than all else, I understand obsession. It is of the mind. And it is language-bound. Sex is of the body. It has no words." The author's brother, however, is proof that this is a false dichotomy. Explain. What other evidence is presented in rebuttal to this belief?

Ruiz quotes John Money, the person who collaborated in performing the first sex change operations, concerning the relation of the brain to language and sexuality. He speculates that the brain's great adaptability and malleability, necessary to construct and employ language, is also the reason that human sexuality is so varied. The fact that Ruiz, by her own account, is a paranoid schizophrenic affects her sexuality and is further evidence that mind and body are inextricably related.

Page 415

"Late Night Thoughts on Listening to Mahler's Ninth Symphony"
Lewis Thomas

1. How has the Atomic Age changed Thomas?

The author had previously been reconciled to death because he saw it as simply part of a cycle that included renewal and the earth's ecosystem as an organism continually replenished. With the advent of the nuclear age, the possibility that there won't be renewal became a probability, making Thomas less unable to accept death as a natural part of things. This realization also seems to have soured his pleasure in all sorts of human endeavors, not just in Mahler's composition. One could assume that the following applies in part to Thomas, as well as to a younger generation: "If I were sixteen or seventeen years old and had to listen to that, or read things like that, I would want to give up listening and reading. I would begin thinking up new kinds of sounds, different from any music heard before, and I would be twisting and turning to rid myself of human language."

2. What sorts of readers is Thomas writing for? What is the evidence for your conclusion?

Because of the essay's philosophical bent and its detailed discussion of Mahler's Ninth, it is obvious that Thomas is writing to a fairly educated audience. However, the audience is not presumed to have prior knowledge of the symphony or a great deal of background information about atomic war strategies. Thomas is speaking to generalists as well as those who have specialized knowledge concerning nuclear strategies. Thomas's description of the symphony provides enough detail for the reader to understand the point without knowing the music: "the long passages on all the strings at the end, as close as music can come to expressing silence itself. . . . the easy sadness expressed with such gentleness and delicacy by that repeated phrase on faded strings, over and over again. . . . a short passage near the very end of the Mahler in which the almost vanishing violins, all engaged in a sustained backward glance, are edged aside for a few bars by the cellos. Those lower notes pick up fragments from the first movement, as though prepared to begin everything all over again, and then the cellos subside and disappear, like an exhalation." Likewise, the information supplied to the reader about nuclear weapons is sufficient. A reference to the MX is followed by a serviceable definition: "these missiles, each capable of creating artificial suns to vaporize a hundred Hiroshimas." The spokesman for the nation's nuclear strategy is paraphrased by Thomas without any of the jargon or dizzying facts that are normally thrown at television viewers and that were also probably wielded as the expert spoke. The policy of mutually assured destruction (MAD) is paraphrased in everyday language. It is also a probability that Thomas is not directly addressing the sixteen- and seventeen-year-olds to whom he refers. First, this type of essay and the themes expressed are not those that most teenagers are particularly interested in. In addition, Thomas doesn't address this group directly in his essay, which he would likely do if he were thinking of them in particular as his readers.

3. Lewis Thomas is a physician and cancer researcher who has authored hundreds of scientific papers. What do you think is his purpose in writing essays such as "Late Night Thoughts"?

Probably most authors, when asked why they write, will, in part, explain that they write for themselves. Self expression is undoubtedly part of Thomas's motivation. The title and subsequent essay imply that Thomas, probably alone and undisturbed late at night, with his mind wandering while listening to the Ninth, had something like a revelation and wanted to put those thoughts down on paper. Composing, however, is a communicative activity, and assuredly Thomas wished to let readers know of his thoughts. The theme of nuclear destruction is pervasive in our culture, to the point that many avoid essays about this topic. However, this constant repetition and the colorless talk of people such as the man on television make the concept of destruction so abstract that it is important to bring one's emotions to bear on the subject and to understand on that level what the abstract discourse really is talking about. This is what happened to Thomas. His purpose is probably less to teach us about the perils of nuclear weapons, which most people understand on an intellectual basis already, than to appeal to readers on an emotional basis. In terms used by this book in the fourth chapter, Thomas wants less to argue than to persuade.

4. Does the essay supply enough detail for a reader unfamiliar with Mahler's Ninth Symphony to understand Thomas's point? Explain.

5. In this essay, is Lewis Thomas logical or illogical? Is the question of logic relevant? Explain your answer.

Logic is less powerful in persuasion than argument. Persuasion is concerned with end results regardless of the means used. On the other hand, pure argumentation is very much concerned about the appropriate method or means of arriving at a conclusion. Thomas does make what most people would regard as illogical statements, such as "I would begin thinking up new kinds of sounds, different from any music heard before, and I would be twisting and turning to rid myself of human language." Of course, Thomas is not working on the literal level with such a statement and really bypasses the issue of logic. Much of this essay is reportorial, communicating to the reader what the author's thought and, more importantly, what his feelings are about the subject. Therefore, although Thomas makes intuitive connections in his thoughts (the music as a reflection of death, the earth as an organism unto itself), he makes no claim that such thoughts are true or should even be accepted by others. All he wants is to let the reader understand how he has come to reawaken in himself the horrors of nuclear war.

6. Thomas draws his information about nuclear bombs and atomic war from various sources. Are these sources reliable? Is reliability (or lack thereof) of sources a major concern in this essay?

Thomas doesn't call into question the facts presented by either the report MX Basing or the man on television. In fact, it is Thomas's assumption that this information is accurate, which elicits in him the horror of today's predicament. Thomas might, however, question the motives of each or the goal towards which they are striving. In one sense, then, Thomas probably regards them as reliable while in another as unreliable. Finally, however, the reliability is not of great concern to Thomas because he is not discussing the factuality of these reports, but, rather, their effect on him.

7. At any point in the essay are you confused because you lack the requisite world knowledge? At any point do you lack knowledge of specific references but feel that your lack of knowledge does not impede your understanding of the essay? Explain.

8. "The realization that humankind can annihilate itself is depressing." Does this statement express the main point of the essay adequately? Explain.

While it does reflect the essay's general lines of thought, the statement is not an adequate reflection of the intensity of feeling that Thomas communicates in his essay. "Make hay while the sun shines" or "Carpe diem" inadequately states the theme of "To His Coy Mistress," and the above sentence robs the essay of its resonance.

9. The essay was written almost ten years ago. Has the situation described by Thomas changed appreciably? How so, or why not?

Page 419

"Nature"
Ralph Waldo Emerson

1. Several times in the essay, Emerson compares two scenes: nature and the civilized world. What does the author imply with this comparison? (The poem with which the essay begins might help you arrive at an answer.)

Emerson begins his essay by comparing humankind in the country with humankind in the city. Nature acts as a medicine or healing source for the person whose senses have been crimped by the city. Later, Emerson notes that the impulse in humankind's search for the picturesque is the same impulse as that which rejects false society. Although this distinction between Nature and the civilized world is useful in making certain points about natural beauty and our need for it, Emerson finally writes that such distinctions are false: "We talk of deviations from natural life, as if artificial life were not also natural." As if to prove his point, the author compares the disappointment we feel with works of art which approximate perfection with our intuition that behind the beauty of Nature lies an even greater perfection that cannot be grasped.

The idea that Nature and civilization cannot be separated is expressed in Emerson's belief that universal laws extend themselves throughout the universe and that Nature <u>and</u> humans are the precipitates of thought and idea. That Emerson makes a distinction between the two in the first place is an indication that he makes value judgments even when Nature infuses everything. People should strive for perfection even though it is impossible to achieve, and Nature serves as the guidepost for our attempts.

2. In regard to manner, Emerson states that most writings about nature are euphuistic. Look up the definition of <u>euphuistic</u> in a dictionary. In what ways do you think that Emerson's own essay is euphuistic? In what ways not? Did Emerson intend the essay to be euphuistic?

The term <u>euphuism</u> comes from the title of John Lily's <u>Euphues</u>, which had a mannered and elaborate style. The term originally referred to writing which modeled itself directly on Lily's style but is currently taken to mean any affected and refined prose. According to the <u>Random House Dictionary of the English Language</u>, Lily used long series of antitheses, frequent similes relating to fabulous natural history, and alliteration.

Parts of Emerson's essay meet this definition:

> These enchantments are medicinal, they sober and heal us. These are plain pleasures, kindly and native to us. We come to our own, and make friends with matter, which the ambitious chatter of the schools would persuade us to despise. We never can part with it; the mind loves its old home: as water to our thirst, so is the rock, the ground, to our eyes and hands and feet. It is firm water; it is cold flame; what health, what affinity!

> He hears the echoes of a horn in a hill country, in the Mountains, for example, which converts the mountains into an Aeolian harp--and this supernatural <u>tiralira</u> restores to him the Dorian mythology, Apollo, Diana, and all divine hunters and huntresses. Can a musical note be so lofty, so haughtily beautiful!

Emerson is aware of his own tendency towards euphuism:

> [W]hether we are too clumsy for so subtle a topic, or from whatever cause, as soon as men begin to write on nature, they fall into euphuism. Frivolity is a most unfit tribute to Pan, who ought to be represented in the mythology as the most continent of gods.

In this excerpt, Emerson does not specifically exclude himself from the offenders of style and purposefully makes reference to the Greek god Pan so as to maintain a euphuistic style while discussing euphuism. His awareness of this tendency is in accordance with his discussion that art is but a mere approximation of the beauty of Nature.

3. Given Emerson's views of the world and of reality, do you think that he would regard the reader of this essay as a miner who digs information and concepts out of the text or as a detective who constructs the meaning of the text in his or her own mind?

Emerson writes, "Man carries the world in his head. . . . Because the history of nature is charactered in his brain, therefore is he the prophet and discoverer of her secrets." With this view that man carries all knowledge of the world within himself, Emerson would most probably think that the reader is more like the detective who constructs the meaning from the text since the meaning would reside within the individual as he or she divined it.

4. Kenneth Burke, a highly influential theorist about language and literature, explains two kinds of structure for texts, syllogistic progression and qualitative progression:

> Syllogistic progression is the form of a perfectly conducted argument, advancing step by step. It is the form of a mystery story, where everything falls together. . . . It is the form of a demonstration in Euclid. To go from A to E through stages B, C, and D is to obtain such form. We call it syllogistic because, given certain things, certain things must follow, the premises forcing the conclusion. . . .
>
> Qualitative progression . . . is subtler. Instead of one incident in the plot preparing us for some other possible incident of plot (as Macbeth's murder of Duncan prepares us for the dying of Macbeth), the presence of one quality prepares us for the introduction of another (the grotesque seriousness of the murder scene preparing us for the grotesque buffoonery of the porter scene). . . (Counter-Statement 124-25).

Explain why you think form in "Nature" is either syllogistic or qualitative. Give evidence from the text to support your opinion.

The essay is not "logically" structured--which is not to say that it is illogical. Rather, one idea or image suggests another, and the essay progresses almost by free association.

5. Emerson talks about two basic laws of nature: motion/change and identity/rest. Does the first law logically contradict the second? Why, or why not? Does one law take precedence over the other?

6. Does Emerson believe in the scientific method? Explain.

"Common sense knows its own, and recognizes the fact at first sight in chemical experiment. The common sense of Franklin, Dalton, Davy and Black is the same common sense which made the arrangements which now it discovers." Almost in the same breath, Emerson explains that the universe is orderly and that the common sense of scientists "prophesied" the laws of nature. Emerson would probably not view the scientific method as preeminent, since it is merely one way in which the individual begins to understand the laws of nature, but as a productive method of consciously arriving at these laws, Emerson would endorse the procedure.   The scientists mentioned are presumably [Benjamin] Franklin (verified the presence of electricity in lightning), [John] Dalton (revived the atomic theory of matter), [Sir Humphry] Davy (used electrochemical methods to isolate elements and hypothesized that chemical attraction was electric in nature), and [Joseph] Black (developed the theories of latent and specific heat and was instrumental in establishing chemistry as an exact science).

Evidence of a more circumstantial nature is contained in Emerson's unquestioning acceptance of the major scientific discoveries of the day. He makes reference to such immensely slow geological processes as rock formation and erosion; he clearly accepts evolution as fact; and at some length he discusses the important scientific principle that the laws of nature are consistent throughout the universe.

7. Does Emerson view nature as perfect or not? Explain.

Emerson regards Nature as wonderful, as almost divine, but he implies that it is imperfect. Every act of Nature contains excess in order to ensure that the desired outcome will occur ("We aim above the mark to hit the mark"). The profuse generation of seeds required to propagate the species and the excess fear instilled in animals that they might survive danger are two examples.

Emerson also states that Nature is only an approximation of perfection (" . . . there is through nature something mocking. . . . All promise outruns the performance"). Such failures to achieve perfection are apparent not only in man's own attempts but also in the landscapes that man admires but senses to be less beautiful than they should be.

In the final part of the essay, Emerson tells us that man does not have the ability to fully understand Nature ("To the intelligent, nature converts itself into a vast promise, and will not be rashly explained. Her secret is untold").

8.   The last paragraph of the essay pretty well summarizes Emerson's philosophy. In your own words, state that philosophy. Explain why you either agree or disagree with it.

9. Emerson attempts to give the reader a feeling for the ineffable qualities of nature. Cite examples of this from the text.

10. For a man who is obviously smitten by nature, Emerson makes many surprising statements in this essay--for example, the passage in which the author tells us to "be men instead of woodchucks." Cite other examples in which Emerson surprises the reader. Explain why you think these surprises strengthen or weaken the text.

11. Find three instances in which Emerson illustrates a difficult and abstract concept with concrete examples.

The excess in man is wonderfully illustrated by the youthful diarist who puts down his thoughts in his most ardent and passionate manner. The words, however, fail to convey the conviction and emotion behind them when read by a friend. Other examples provided by Emerson for clarification:

The beauty of Nature as revealed by Indian summer.
The penetration of Nature's beauty with one stroke of the oar as Emerson
    paddles on the river.

Page 433

"Sounding"
Mark Twain

1. If "Sounding" is typical of the whole of <u>Life on the Mississippi</u>, the book from which the chapter is taken, would you say that Mark Twain idealizes the time and place, the "steamboat era" on the Mississippi? Here is another version of that scene:

These florid palaces [the steamboats], garishly painted and gilded, pine smoke belching from their stacks, seized America in the bulk and set it afloat on the rivers. It was not altogether an America of spiritual loveliness, nor were the boats wholly instruments of creative fulfillment. The trade of steamboating was carried on in a competition which was typical of the age and far worse than anything the pioneering railroads achieved. It was an American commerce, without conscience, responsibility, or control. The financial returns it offered were so great that, whatever happened to boats, crews, or passengers, owners might count on profits. The proverbial frequency of disasters rested on snags, groundings, and lack of skill to some extent, but more than all else on fraudulent jerry-building and inferior material. The soundly built boat was the exception, a product of occasional pride or responsibility; the average boat was assembled from inferior timber and machinery, thrown together with the least possible expense, and hurried out to snare her portion of the unimaginable profits before her seams opened or her boiler heads blew off. Once launched, she entered a competition ruthless and inconceivably corrupt. No device for the fraudulent capture of freight and fares was overlooked. Everything that chicanery, sabotage, bribery, and malfeasance could devise was part of the commonplace mechanism of the trade.
            --Bernard DeVoto, <u>Mark Twain's America</u>. Boston: Houghton Mifflin,
            1967. 108-109.)

Twain's understandable pride in having been a cub on a steamboat and his extreme youth while he was employed on the river colored his perception of "life on the Mississippi." The glamor of the occupation never wore off for Twain even when it rubbed against the abrasive facts set forth by DeVoto. The only admission made by

Twain that the river trade was less than perfect is contained within his lead sentence explaining the process of sounding. "Sounding is done in this way: The boat ties up at the shore, just above the shoal crossing; the pilot not on watch takes his 'cub' or steersman and a picked crew of men (sometimes an officer also), and goes out in the yawl--provided the boat has not that rare and sumptuous luxury, a regularly devised 'sounding-boat.' . . ." Otherwise, Twain writes of his experiences in the same manner as that of young boys who dream of running off with the circus.

2. From the standpoint of purpose, explain why, in your opinion, Mark Twain's view of the steamboat era differs from that of Bernard DeVoto. In your opinion, why did Mark Twain write "Sounding"? What evidence do you have for your opinion?

Twain was well known for his cynicism, yet he idealized river boating, or at least his own encounters with the profession. Twain's pride in his successful employment on the river is one of the major reasons that his view differs from that expressed by DeVoto. (He was a riverboat pilot by the age of twenty-two, for example.) His elegant explanation of the technical aspects of sounding reveals this pride in all of the details as does his fussy footnote explaining, and perhaps justifying, his use of the "larboard," as if he were afraid that his use of the term might imply that he lacked expertise.

The length of time that passed before Twain wrote of these events ("Sounding" was written more than thirty years after the fact) was also probably responsible for his softened outlook. Because Twain was successful at such a challenging trade, the reflective and much older writer could look back on the experience as a great achievement. Naturally, everything associated with his success also benefits from the reflective glow.

"Sounding" was published in 1883 after the great age of the steamboats. By then, railroads had taken over as the transportation arteries of the United States, and the paddlewheel had been supplanted by the screw propeller. It is very possible that Twain felt that it was of importance to document an era whose time had come and gone. Life on the Mississippi contains a wealth of anecdotal information in addition to the ordered and detailed explanations such as Twain's discussion of sounding.

It is also relevant to note that Twain had been a reporter earlier in his life and had previously published books about other adventures which he had lived through. (Innocents Abroad recounts his trip to the Mediterranean and Holy Land, and Roughing It is concerned with his adventures in Nevada and California as a prospector and reporter.) Anyone, but especially an experienced reporter, would recognize the great story that a steamboat pilot would be able to tell.

3. Consider "Sounding" from the standpoint of relation. Is the story about Tom G. relevant or irrelevant in regard to Mark Twain's purpose? Explain.

A reporter always looks for the human interest in any story, and Twain, the former newspaper reporter, provides it when he discusses the rivalry between himself and Tom G. This tale provides the selection's humor, a quality for which Twain is, of course, famous, and it includes high drama as well in the account of the accidental collision.

In anecdotal fashion, the story about Tom G. also provides solid information about steamboating that would interest the historian.   The romantic lure of steamboating is expressed as eloquently by the anecdote concerning the competition between Tom G. and Twain to go sounding as it would be by a documentarian with a flair for explanation.   (It is adventurous, dangerous, gaudy, man-of-war-like, and exhilarating, providing an audience for one's deeds, in Twain's own words.)   The anecdote also stresses the danger of riverboating in remarkable fashion, which is very relevant information to any discussion about this subject.

4.   In regard to manner, explain some of the techniques that Twain uses to make his explanation clear.

The most important factor in the clarity of Twain's explanation is his care in describing sounding in great detail.   Another writer might shorten the explanation in order to get to the story of Tom G. at the expense of clarity.

5.   Does Twain provide you with enough information to understand the reason for sounding and how it is carried out?   Explain.

The reason for sounding is explained in the first sentence of the selection: "When the river is very low, and one's steamboat is 'drawing all the water' there is in the channel--or a few inches more, as was often the case in the old times--one must be painfully circumspect in his piloting."

6.   With regard to manner, in what part of the selection might the reader take Twain's statements with a grain of salt?   Why?

The rivalry between Tom G. and Twain is the basis for many comments that are not to be taken literally.   " . . . he [Tom G.] always had a way of embroidering. However, virtue is its own reward, so I was a barely perceptible trifle ahead in the contest [a funny, backhanded compliment to himself]. . . . I could have done it easy enough [dive directly under the paddle wheel in order to avoid being killed by the steamboat]. . . . That girl couldn't seem to have enough of that pitiful 'hero' the rest of the trip; but little I cared; I loathed her, anyway."

7.   What are the most obvious and accessible sources for information about Mississippi steamboating before the Civil War?   (To answer this question, you might want to preview the discussion of using the library on pages 577-83).

Obvious sources would be a general reference encyclopedia, a general history of transportation, a general history of the United States, or a timeline of the United States.

Page 439

"The Slow Pacific Swell"
Yvor Winters

1. What was the sea like when Winters as a young child watched it from a hill? What was the sea like when Winters rounded Cape Flattery on a boat? What is the sea like in the final stanza?

When Winters was a child, the sea was an undifferentiated shape of blue--soft and unthreatening.   When Winters rounded Flattery, the sea was rough and menacing, drenching the deck. In the final stanza, the sea is but a sound, with no physical reality.

2. What do these three scenes mean? What do they symbolize, or stand for?

Each of the scenes relates to a stage in a person's life.   In the first stanza, the narrator is a small child for whom experience is calm and undifferentiated; the sky is unbroken and presumably blue against the soft blue of the ocean; the wind streamers do not seem to stir. In the second stanza, the narrator is in turmoil on a rolling sea. Finally, the serene and aging poet, now a landsman, longs to experience the power and surge of the sea, the tempestuousness of earlier days.

3. Since Winters chose to write a poem, he was not free to use any words that might pop into his mind, because he needed to maintain his meter (iambic pentameter) and rhyme (for example, hill-still, ground-sound, sand-land).   One might say that to a certain extent, language controlled Winters. In what ways does language always control writers, whether or not they are composing poetry?

Both meter and rhyme dictated, in part, the choice of words.

To a certain extent, vocabulary determines our concept of the world.   For example, acquiring the word idealism as part of one's vocabulary enables one to consider the possibility that all reality is mental. Conversely, there can be no such thing as a condominium until the word (and its definition) come into being, for a condominium is not a physical structure but an agreement about ownership and maintenance of that structure.

Language is rule-governed.   The very fact that we can consciously or unconsciously break the rules demonstrates their existence. For more thoughts, reconsider the discussion of reading in the first chapter of this book and the explanation of the cooperative principle in the third chapter.

4. The language available to writers sometimes limits their possibilities for expression. Explain how language also very frequently creates new possibilities and gives writers unexpected insights.

The answers to this question might, of course, occupy an entire semester. However, here are some of the ideas that students should discover.

Writers usually have some more or less clearly defined goal. For example, the following is a mere parody of creativity in language. Smith's flight on Trans El Monte International Airways arrives three hours late; the food on the airplane has been worse than horrible, the flight attendants have been rude, and Smith's luggage has gone astray. Ragingly angry, he writes cathartically, to vent his frustration. And, miracle of miracles, he finds that he has composed a letter of complaint to the airline.

Actually Smith had a purpose when he began to write: he intended a letter of complaint. However, he could not predict exactly how that letter would take shape, for in the process of composing, one word suggests another, one idea prompts a related notion, the writer's mood determines whether or not the statement will be ironic, and so on.

As W. Ross Winterowd wrote in "A Philosophy of Composition" (Rhetoric Review, Spring 1991):

> Composition is **doing**, symbolic action, not finding or making.
>
> In moments of dissolute idleness, I sometimes use writing to fill (or kill) time, to find or make something. A while ago, on a Friday evening when Norma and I had been deserted by family and friends, I lay on our bed, listening to Big Band music and idly scratching away with a ballpoint. What came out pleased me, and I share this writing with you now:
>
> Parsnip
>
> Ah, parsnip, pallid winter root,
> Thou symbol, yes, thou very fruit
> Of fallow field and frozen ways,
> I alone will sing thy praise
> Before I whack thee quite in two
> And pop thee in this evening's stew.
> Oh, vegetable melancholic,
> When people dine and drink and frolic,
> Thou liest in the basement bin,
> A beetle bumbling blind therein.
> Thou suffer'st yet the vilest taunts:
> You're never served in restaurants.

However, most of the time when I write--poems, stories, letters, memoranda, scholarly papers--I know what I want the finished text to do, though I almost never know exactly how I will accomplish my purpose. (Thank goodness, I'm almost never surprised to find that my writing more or less does what I wanted it to do!) It is hard for me to imagine that very much writing of any kind begins in the ways implied and explained by the Romantics. . . .

As a teacher of writing, my first question to a student about his or her text is this: "What do you want this piece of writing to do?" That question generates a dialogue that allows both me and my student to read and critique the text as a piece of real-world discourse. It allows us to treat the text rhetorically.

5. In regard to purpose, why do you think Winters wrote the poem?

Students will undoubtedly (we think) talk about self-expression through writing. They might overlook the idea that Winters (like most writers) takes pleasure in the craft. Just as a silversmith enjoys creating a well-wrought coffee urn, so a poet enjoys creating a well-wrought poem.

6. State the main point of the poem.

A minimal statement: The main point of "The Slow Pacific Swell" is that peoples' outlook on the world changes as they age.

7. Using this poem as your specific example, explain why you, as a reader, do or do not enjoy poetry.

4. Thinking Critically about Argument and Persuasion

Background and Sources

Rhetorical argumentation falls between the austere elegance of formal logic on the one hand and the blunt reality of empirical evidence on the other. A mathematical equation, a syllogism, or a sorites is either valid or invalid; data are either adequate or inadequate. Argument takes place in that vast human area where arithmetic or formal logic and data or other empirical evidence fail.

Though <u>The Uses of Argument</u>, by Stephen Toulmin, provides the "technical," methodological basis for this chapter, Kenneth Burke was very much present in our minds as we planned and wrote.

In its most dramatic outline, here is the Burkean revolution in rhetoric. Whereas Aristotle stressed <u>persuasion</u>, Burke took <u>identification</u> as the basis of rhetoric. Aristotle said, "So let Rhetoric be defined as the faculty [power] of discovering in the particular case what are the available means of persuasion." The image is that of a rhetor working his or her will upon the reader or hearer. Kenneth Burke said, "You persuade a man only insofar as you can talk his language by speech, gesture, tonality, order, image, attitude, idea, <u>identifying</u> your ways with his. . . . True, the rhetorician may have to change an audience's opinions in one respect; but he can succeed only insofar as he yields to that audience's opinions in other respects" (<u>Rhetoric</u> 55-56). The image is that of a dialogue, the participants cooperating to achieve understanding and knowledge.

This is, of course, a perilous view of rhetoric, for by its terms, no one can "win," and, in a sense, everyone loses. Suppose for instance that I, as missionary of <u>the</u> true church, with absolute faith in my belief, come to convert you, that is, to bring the truth to you. Ideally, since I have the truth, you will attend to my message and (unless you are invincibly ignorant) convert. You may, of course, ask me to clarify or justify points, but you will not put forth your own opinion. You are an empty vessel eager to be filled with the good words. Less than ideally, you will engage me in dialogue (i.e., dialectic), and it will not be genuine dialogue unless I am open to understanding. If I do indeed understand, it can fairly be said that you have converted me just as surely as I might convert you. Furthermore, it is obvious that from the rhetorical viewpoint, there is no absolute Truth, only those halcyon moments when you and I can say that we understand one another.

Clearly, Burke is setting forth not merely a new "technical" rhetoric, but a view of how language brings about (or might bring about) unity rather than division, peace rather than war.

Page 442. Exercise: Thinking about Claims

Each of the following claims involves the evaluative term <u>good</u>, <u>better</u>, or <u>best</u>. What sorts of backing would be needed in order to convince a reader that the claim is valid? Which of the claims might result in an argument?

Example:

<u>Claim</u>: The weather in San Diego is usually good.

<u>Backing</u>: (1) Definition of the term <u>good weather</u>: weather with the following characteristics: no extremes of temperature, little precipitation, and skies that are generally sunny. (2) Data concerning the weather in San Diego: The average temperature is 63.66 degrees F.; high, 98 degrees; low, 38 degrees.   Average precipitation: .69 inches. Clear days in 1985, 146; partly cloudy, 120; cloudy, 99.

1. White Pine State is a good university.

First, of course, the arguer must set forth the criteria by which White Pine State is to be judged. Is it a good university in terms of its national standing and the illustriousness of its graduates? Or is it a good university because students are comfortable there? In other words, the arguer needs to state his or her criteria and then demonstrate the ways in which White Pine State meets the criteria.

2. The Golden Delicious is a good apple.

No argument is possible here. A good apple is one that the eater likes. (In a sense, a good book is one that the reader likes, and good art is what you or I choose to hang on our walls.)

3. Amana manufactures good refrigerators.

The writer would need to specify the qualities of a good refrigerator and then assemble data to demonstrate that Amanas meet those specifications.

4. The Amana is a better refrigerator than the General Electric.

The writer must specify the essential qualities of a refrigerator and then compare the Amana with the General Electric on the basis of those qualities.

5. The Ford Aerostar is a better vehicle than the Chevrolet Astro.

The writer must specify the essential qualities of the type of vehicle (minivan) in question and then compare the Aerostar with the Astro on the basis of those qualities.

6. Truman was a better president than Eisenhower.

What are the qualities of a good president? How do Truman and Eisenhower compare on the basis of those qualities?

7. Picasso was a better artist than Dali.

In our opinion, this is an unarguable proposition, for it depends almost wholly on one's taste. (A statement such as "Picasso was a better artist than Dali" usually means "I like Picasso's work better than Dali's.")   One can undoubtedly prove that (1) Picasso is more widely admired among critics than Dali, (2) Picasso's works sell for higher prices than Dali's, and (3) Picasso's works hang in more of the world's prestigious museums than do Dali's. However, these facts do not prove that Picasso was a better artist than Dali.

8. Colgate is the best toothpaste available.

By what criteria is Colgate to be judged?

9. Stanford is the best university in the United States.

See the discussion of the first proposition above.

10. <u>Moby Dick</u> is the best American novel.

See the discussion of the proposition regarding Picasso and Dali (no. 7, above).

Page 443. Exercise: Arguable Claims

In your opinion, which of the following claims are arguable, and which are not arguable? Using the concepts of <u>definition</u> and <u>uncertainty</u>, explain your judgments. (You may disagree with a claim, yet believe that it is arguable.)

1. Some people oppose abortion.

The claim is unarguable since it is absolutely <u>certain</u> that some people oppose abortion.

2. Any law that limits the rights of citizens to own firearms is a step away from democracy and toward a totalitarian government.

In our view, the claim is arguable, and, in fact, we have heard and read such arguments. That the National Rifle Association, for example, would argue against all gun control and that James and Sarah Brady have mounted a campaign in favor of gun control indicates that the issue lacks certainty.

3. Since it is a common practice in both commercial and scholarly publishing for editors to correct and revise the work submitted to them by authors, it should also be acceptable for a college students to get editorial help with their papers before submitting them to a teacher.

Clearly, the proposition is well defined. Is it uncertain? We feel that the proposition could well generate lively discussion that might lead to some interesting discoveries about writing. For example, the overwhelming majority of books are the result of extensive collaboration between the author or authors and a whole series of editors and proofreaders. If William Buckley, Stephen J. Gould, George Will, Annie Dillard, Maxine Hong Kingston, Sally Bedell Smith . . . get extensive editorial help, should it be "illegal" or unethical for students to enlist editors? (We take no position on this question.)

4. **Because pollution increasingly threatens life on earth, funds should be devoted to cleaning up and preserving the environment.**

The proposition is both <u>certain</u> and <u>undefined</u>. We doubt that anyone (at least anyone we might argue with) would argue against devoting more funds to clean up the environment; however, a lively argument <u>might</u> develop over the source of such funds and priorities in spending them. For example, should the state of California require drivers to use a new clean formula gasoline that will cost ten cents per gallon more than present gas? That is a real issue that is now the subject of argument among citizens, oil companies, politicians, and environmentalists.

5. **The language of the United States has been and is English; therefore, the information on official documents, such as ballots, should be printed only in English.**

The proposition is well defined and is uncertain. It is the topic of ongoing argument throughout the United States.

6. **Every college student should be required either (a) to demonstrate proficiency with computers or (b) to take a course in basic computer science.**

We suggest this proposition as a possible writing assignment. It is the sort of topic that can engage students and that they are prepared to deal with.

7. **No college student should be required to take courses in a foreign language.**

Again, we suggest this proposition as a possible writing assignment.

8. **Government officials should have no sources of income that might create a conflict of interests.**

The topic is adequately defined, but we doubt that it lacks uncertainty. The proposition is so widely accepted that virtually no one would argue against it.

9. **A film is pornographic if it offends the average viewer in a community.**

We think this proposition is adequately defined, and (as the Supreme Court, numerous municipal courts, and various interest groups demonstrate), it is certainly <u>uncertain</u>. The proposition could well serve as a writing assignment.

Page 445. Exercise: Structure of Arguments

1. Is the argument about the tennis-playing daughter--even with the backing, evidence, and qualification--convincing? Explain your answer.

The argument is, of course, both faulty and sophomoric. If the reader accepts the backing for the claim, the evidence is, nonetheless, inadequate--and the claim results from the fallacy of post hoc, ergo propter hoc, or false cause (pages 455-56).

2. The linguistic and social activist Noam Chomsky gives an example of an argument that he thinks is grotesque. Explain your reaction to the argument. Keeping in mind the elements of argument just discussed, do you agree with Chomsky that this argument is grotesque? Why, or why not? Does the argument convince you? How so? What counterarguments could you put forth?

> **Suppose you rent a car and I buy a car. Who's going to take better care of it? Well, the answer is that I'm going to take better care of it because I have a capital investment in it. You're not going to take care of it at all. If you hear a rattle, you're just going to take it back to Hertz and let somebody else worry about it. If I hear a rattle, I'm going to take it to the garage because I don't want to get in trouble later on. In general, I'm going to take better care of the car I own than you're going to take of the car you rent. Suppose I own a person and you rent a person. Who's going to take better care of that person? Well, parity of argument, I'm going to take better care of that person than you are. Consequently, it follows that slavery is much more moral than capitalism. Slavery is a system in which you own people and therefore take care of them. Capitalism, which has a free labor market, is a system in which you rent people. If you own capital, you rent people and then you don't care about them at all. You use them up, throw them away, get new people. So the free market in labor is totally immoral, whereas slavery is quite moral. (Olson and Faigley, 17-18)**

Note that the exercise on "Analyzing an Argument" (Samuel Johnson's argument for freeing a slave, pages 446-47) is, in effect, a critique of the faulty argument in the present exercise.

The argument is, of course, riddled with fallacies, the most obvious of which is the false analogy, equating human beings with automobiles. Equivocation (p. 455) allows rent to become synonymous with hire. The term rent normally applies only to objects; thus, to use rent as a term for acquiring human services turns human beings into things.

Page 446. Exercise: Analyzing an Argument

To study the anatomy of an argument, we need a specimen to work on; asking important questions about a hypothetical argument is like studying literature without reading actual poems and stories. Here is a classic argument. Samuel Johnson, the great eighteenth-century man of letters who compiled the first modern

dictionary, wrote an argument for freeing a slave, Joseph Knight, who had been kidnapped as a child and sold to a Scottish gentleman. Knight's lawyer used Johnson's argument, and the court did indeed set Knight free. Read the argument carefully, and then apply the three questions: (1) Is the backing adequate? (2) Is the evidence adequate? (3) What are the qualifications? In your opinion, is the argument convincing or not? Explain. (The sentences are numbered for your convenience in referring to them.)

[1] It must be agreed that in most ages many countries have had part of their inhabitants in a state of slavery; yet it may be doubted whether slavery can ever be supposed the natural condition of man. [2] It is impossible not to conceive that men in their original state were equal; and very difficult to image how one would be subjected to another except by violent compulsion. [3] An individual may, indeed, forfeit his liberty by a crime; but he cannot by that crime forfeit the liberty of his children. [4] What is true of a criminal seems true likewise of a captive. [5] A man may accept life from a conquering enemy on condition of perpetual servitude; but it is very doubtful whether he can entail that servitude on his descendants; for no man can stipulate without commission for another. [6] The condition which he himself accepts, his son or grandson perhaps would have rejected. [7] If we should admit, what perhaps with more reason may be denied, that there are certain relations between man and man which may make slavery necessary and just, yet it can never be proved that he who is now suing for his freedom ever stood in any of these relations. [8] He is certainly subject by no law, but that of violence, to his present master; who pretends no claim to his obedience, but that he bought him from a merchant of slaves, whose right to sell him never was examined. [9] It is said that, according to the constitutions of Jamaica, he was legally enslaved; these constitutions are merely positive; and apparently injurious to the rights of mankind, because whoever is exposed to sale is condemned to slavery without appeal; by whatever fraud or violence he might originally have been brought into the merchant's power. [10] In our own time Princes have been sold, by wretches to whose care they were entrusted, that they might have an European education; but when once they were brought to a market in the plantations, little would avail either their dignity or their wrongs. [11] The laws of Jamaica afford a Negro no redress. [12] His colour is considered as sufficient testimony against him. [13] It is to be lamented that moral right should ever give way to political convenience. [14] But if temptations of interest are sometimes too strong for human virtue, let us at least retain a virtue where there is no temptation to quit it. [15] In the present case there is apparent right on one side, and no convenience on the other. [16] Inhabitants of this island can neither gain riches nor power by taking away the liberty of any part of the human species. [17] The sum of the argument is this: The rights of nature must be some way forfeited before they can be justly taken away: That the defendant has by any act forfeited the rights of nature we require to be proved; and if no proof of such forfeiture can be given, we doubt not but the justice of the court will declare him free.

The claim is this [17]: "The rights of nature must be some way forfeited before they can be justly taken away." Virtually the whole argument consists of backing: sentences 1-16. The evidence is taken for granted: that Joseph Knight was a slave. In the judicial proceedings, evidence may, indeed, have been produced: bills of sale, copies of Jamaican law, and so forth.

Johnson argues on the basis of natural law: "[I]t may be doubted whether slavery can ever be supposed the natural condition of man [1]. It is impossible not to conceive that men in their original state were equal; and very difficult to image how one would be subjected to another except by violent compulsion [2]." If the addressee (reader or hearer) does not accept this premise, then, of course, the argument fails--as does the argument in the Declaration of Independence, which holds as a self-evident truth that all men are created equal.

Page 449. Exercise: Argument Log

During one twenty-four hour period, keep a record of the arguments that you read and hear. Note the claim and the backing and evidence. If the argument is written (in a newspaper or magazine), perhaps you can cut it out and have it available for discussion. If you hear the argument (on radio or television, for instance), write down as many details as possible. Advertisements, the newspaper's editorial page, and candidates' speeches are good sources for arguments.

Once you have compiled your log of arguments, analyze them, asking these questions about each one:

1. Who, actually, is the arguer? (A TV announcer in an ad is not the arguer; the sponsor of the ad is.) How does the nature of the arguer influence your judgment?

2. Where did the argument appear? (On public television? On the editorial page of the newspaper? In an advertisement for a product? In a bull session with your friends?) What influence do place and time (scene) have on the argument?

3. What is the purpose of the argument? What does the arguer say the purpose is? In your opinion, is that the real purpose? Explain.

The questions are from the Pentad and are one way of demonstrating that the present chapter relates closely to others, particularly Chapter 2, "Thinking Critically about Narratives."

Page 450. Exercise: Ad Hominem

Find examples of ad hominem fallacies and the arguments they are responding to. Determine whether the arguments have an implied assumption which the fallacy addresses or whether the fallacy has no relevance whatsoever. Almost certainly, you can find examples in your daily newspaper and in popular magazines. (Political cartoons are often ad hominem attacks.)

For example, from the November 21, 1991, Los Angeles Times: "[Mario] Cuomo compared [President] Bush to the captain of the Titanic and [Vice President Dan]

Quayle to his cabin boy, and he scorned them for allegedly attempting to blame the ship's sinking on its seamen.

"Cuomo further twitted: 'Good, Danny, get him another warm milk.'"

Page 451. Exercise: Ambiguity

1. List three words that have strong connotations, and then discuss how differences in opinion could result from using these words to characterize situations. For example, people who support the right-to-life position often call physicians who perform abortions "murderers," but those who hold the pro-choice position would not use that word in this context. You can find specific examples in such magazines as <u>Time</u> and <u>Newsweek</u> and, of course, in the newspaper.

(a) "Abortion" can be either murder or a woman's right to control her own body. (b) "Gay," used by the homosexual community, is either neutral or favorable, as in "Gay Pride"; used by some conservatives, the term connotes deviation and even sin. (c) A "myth," as in Plato's "myth of the cave," is, on the one hand, a story that conveys a truth; on the other, the term means falsehood or claim without backing, as in "the myth of fairness in taxation."

2. Explain the ambiguity of terms in the following selection. In your opinion, did the author use the ambiguous terms purposely? If so, why did he use them?

Toys ' Я Cussed

While many women still pay homage to Barbie at places like Evelyn Burkhalter's Barbie Hall of Fame, others have a beef with America's best-known doll. Many critics feel that the toy fills young women with unrealistic expectations, leading them to a life of vapid consumerism, endless exercise, eating disorders and worse. In short, Barbie kills.

Listed below, some of the cultural viruses that lie dormant in other seemingly innocent toys, such as:

<u>Mr. Potato Head</u> Playing with Mr. Potato Head encourages young people to believe that parts of their bodies, especially facial features, are disposable. The ultimate example of the dangers of prolonged exposure to Mr. Potato Head: Michael Jackson.

<u>Etch a Sketch</u> Touted as a creative toy, the only thing this magnetic box "etches" into a child's mind is an insatiable desire for a constant stream of new images. There is a direct correlation between the introduction of Etch a Sketch in the sixties and the proliferation of MTV in the eighties.

<u>Pickup Sticks</u> Teaches children to "pick up" things. And what do kids usually pick up? Foul language. Facts of life from street corners. Annoying, disfiguring diseases. Members of the opposite sex. Members of the same sex. Bad morals. Crazy notions. Wild dances. And after picking up all this, they must then pick up the pieces of their shattered lives.

Erector Sets Erector, erection--who do they think they're fooling? Leaves us with men who can perform only with use of intricate machinery.

Pop-Up Books Same as above. Substitute magazines for machinery (Rahlman, 20).

Students might assume that terms used figuratively (e.g., "cultural virus") are ambiguous since they have both a literal and a metaphoric application, but in context, figurative language is no more inherently ambiguous than literal language (if there is any such thing). Here is a list of the obviously (and intentionally) ambiguous terms in the selection: "etches" (imprints in minds), "pick up" (learn, adopt as a way of life), "erector" (correlated with "erection"), "perform" (the sexual function), "intricate machinery" (aids to sexual function), "pop-up" (equated with "erection"), "magazines" (substituted for "machinery," i.e., pornography).

3. In the Gorgias, a Platonic dialogue, Socrates presents the following argument. Is it valid? If not, why not?

SOCRATES: Well now, a man who has learned building is a builder, is he not?
GORGIAS: Yes.
SOCRATES: And he who has learned music, a musician?
GORGIAS: Yes.
SOCRATES: Then he who has learned medicine is a medical man, and so on
    with the rest on the same principle; anyone who has learned a certain art
    has the qualification acquired by his particular knowledge?
GORGIAS: Certainly.
SOCRATES: And so, on this principle, he who has learned what is just is just?
GORGIAS: Absolutely, I presume.

The fallacy here is a complicated bit of word-play. In the first place, "building/builder," "music/musician," and "medicine/medical man" are nouns denoting bodies of knowledge and practitioners, but "just" is an adjective and therefore does not denote a body of knowledge or an art. One can say that a person who knows and practices the art of building is a builder, just as one who knows and practices the art of music is a musician. One who knows and practices what is just is not, however, a justice, but a just person.

Page 456. Exercise: Fallacies

Explain the problems with the following arguments, and name the fallacies that they illustrate.

1. I never should have loaned my car to my son. He drove it for one day, and the next day the transmission went bad.

False cause (post hoc, ergo propter hoc). The argument does not establish a causative connection between the events.

2. Having received a D on a term paper, a student tries to convince the professor to raise the grade: "My father just left my mother, and my older brother is now in jail for drunk driving. When Mother sees this grade, it will be more than she can bear, considering her other problems."

Ad misericordiam (appeal to pity). The argument ignores the real question--the quality of the paper--and argues on the basis of the student's personal problems. Even if successful because the professor is humane and caring, the argument, nonetheless, is fallacious.

3. Some dogs have fleas. My dog has fleas. Therefore, my dog is some dog.

Equivocation. The meaning of some shifts from a quantifier (some, but not all) to an attributive adjective. Paraphrasing the argument makes its fallacy obvious: Some dogs have fleas. My dog has fleas. Therefore, my dog is a wonderful dog.

4. Every qualified citizen should serve two years in the United States military. We must defend the stately marble temple of democracy.

Reification. "Democracy" becomes a building, to be defended by armed force, whereas defending democracy as a system of government calls for actions such as voting, obeying the laws, paying taxes, and so forth.

5. The governor has proposed that air pollution standards be tightened within the next two years. However, everyone knows that the governor is under the control of the Sierra Club and other environmental groups, so no one takes him seriously.

Ad hominem. The issue of air pollution standards is independent of the governor's character or political affiliations.

6. To learn Chinese well enough to read The People's Daily, one must learn about 2,500 characters. Since each of these characters is easy to learn, it is easy to learn to read Chinese.

Composition. Though it may be easy to learn one item in a set, learning thousands of items in the same set will probably be very difficult.

7. Blacksmiths are gradually disappearing. Herb is a blacksmith. Therefore, Herb is gradually disappearing.

Equivocation. In the first sentence, "disappearing" means "becoming fewer and fewer in number." As applied to one blacksmith, however, that meaning is impossible, forcing the humorous interpretation: Herb is gradually becoming more and more imperceptible.

8. The printouts on my computer are garbled, so there must be something wrong with the new disks that I bought yesterday.

False cause (<u>post hoc, ergo propter hoc</u>). The disks may or may not be the cause of the garbled printouts, but simply because the garble came after purchase of the disks does not establish a causal connection.

9.   No one can prove conclusively that mental telepathy is impossible. Therefore, it must be the case that my friend sent me a telepathic message from Germany; otherwise, how would I have known that he drank beer and ate sausage in Munich?

<u>Ad ignorantium</u> (arguing on the basis of ignorance).   Lack of proof is an inadequate basis for a conclusion. No one has ever proved that there is no life in outer space; therefore, extraterrestrial life must exist. There is no proof that Jones is innocent; therefore, she must be guilty.

10. A father was advising his son about the future. "If you don't go to college and prepare for a career, you'll wind up with a routine, dull job that you'll hate."

Accident. The hidden premise is that only by going to college can one avoid dull, routine jobs. Though a college education does create options, many people without college educations have successful, exciting careers.

11. I believe in the Golden Rule, which says, "Do unto others as you would have them do unto you." Since I would want to give a classmate the correct answers during a final examination, my classmates should give me the correct answers.

Accident. The generalization set forth in the Golden Rule may apply in many cases, but not in every case.

12.   Nature improves animal species by eliminating the less fit members. Therefore, we should eliminate unfit people in American society.

This argument is a <u>non sequitur</u> ("it does not follow") because of equivocation and accident. In the first sentence, "animal" applies to nonhuman species; but in the conclusion, it applies to human beings as well. Furthermore, the first sentence implies that elimination of the unfit is a natural process; the conclusion strongly implies that "we" should employ euthanasia or eugenics, which are not natural processes.

13. Only man is rational. No woman is a man. Therefore, no woman is rational.

Equivocation. In the first sentence, "man" means "human beings." In the second sentence, it means "male human beings."

14. "Who did you pass on the road," the King went on, holding his hand out to the Messenger for some hay.

"Nobody," said the Messenger.

"Quite right," said the King, "this lady saw him too. So of course Nobody walks slower than you."

"I do my best," the Messenger said in a sullen tone. "I'm sure nobody walks much faster than I do."

"He can't do that," said the King, "or else he'd have been here first" (Lewis Carroll, <u>Through the Looking Glass</u>).

Ambiguity. This is the old Abbott and Costello routine: "Who's on first?"

15. Since Susan is a resident of Beverly Hills, she must be wealthy.

Accident. Most residents of Beverly Hills may (or may not) be wealthy, but the norm may not apply in an individual case.

16. "God exists." "How do you know?" "Because the Bible says so." "How do you know the Bible is true?" "Because it's the word of God."

Circular reasoning. And how do you know it's the word of God? Because the Bible says it is.

17. Was it through stupidity or calculated malice that the registrar botched up the class schedule this semester?

Complex question. As the query is phrased, the answerer must choose between stupidity and malice, with no other possibility, except not answering.

Works Cited

Burke, Kenneth. <u>A Rhetoric of Motives</u>. Berkeley: U of California P, 1969.
Toulmin, Stephen. <u>The Uses of Argument</u>. London: Cambridge UP, 1958.

Page 459

"Ethics and Animals"
Steven Zak

1. Two terms are important in this argument: "virtue thought" and "rights thought." (a) Define each. (b) Explain the distinctions between the two. (c) Explain why these distinctions are important to the argument.

Virtue thought holds to "the argument that cruelty is demeaning to human character" and rights thought is "in favor of the idea that the lives of animals have intrinsic value."

The two differ in that the focus of virtue thought is on the humans who interact with animals while rights thought is concerned with the well-being of the animals themselves. Virtue thought condemns cruelty to animals because such actions demean the human race. Whether someone is demeaned or not, whether or not an action against an animal has scientific value, is not the concern of rights thought. Regardless of the reason, rights thought condemns inflicting pain on animals.

Towards the end of the essay, the author points out an instance in which virtue thought would not have protected an animal but rights thought would have. The author's discussion of this case points out the importance in distinguishing the two ideas. A Maryland Court of Appeals ruled that a researcher should not be punished for conducting an experiment in which monkeys' hands were mutilated because it was not the researcher's intent that such should occur. According to the author, virtue rights can be measured in two ways: by the predictable effects an action will have on animals and by the usefulness to society of the action. The author states that the latter criterion was used by the courts to uphold the right of the researcher to conduct the work with the monkeys.

2. Why does Zak disagree with virtue thought? What backing does he have for his position?

Zak criticizes virtue thought because it does not guarantee that animals will not suffer. The discussion of the Maryland Court of Appeals case involving the monkeys used in a research project is an example of the failure of virtue thought to prevent the suffering of animals.

3. Zak states his basic claim in the last paragraph of the argument: "Barriers against the exploitation of animals ought to be erected in the law, because law not only enforces morality but defines it." How firm a position do you think Zak takes on this claim? Do you believe that one must accept this claim without qualification in order for the argument to succeed?

Zak seems to be an absolutist in his desire to protect animals through enactment of laws. If he does believe that the law defines morality (and there is nothing in the article to contradict this), if morality is a complex issue which requires a good deal of thought and discussion to understand, and if the article itself has shown how intricate and complex any discussion of morality can be, then the laws enacted to define this morality must be many and varied. Most probably, then, Zak is adamant about adopting laws to protect animals.

The author's statement that the law defines morality is the exact opposite of what he argues. In the article, Zak presents an argument for rights thought as the moral basis for human relationship to the animal kingdom and hence as the basis for laws to control animal experimentation. The twist in the statement is probably not a careless error, however. The statement seems to be directed at the great majority of people, who have not considered these issues. Zak believes that changes in the law will have to precede changes in their actions.

The conclusion to "Ethics and Animals" makes it clear that Zak doesn't think that his beliefs will be readily accepted and codified in law. He asks his readers to "suppose, just suppose, that the AWA were replaced by an animal-rights act, which would prohibit the use by human beings of any animals to their detriment." The "just suppose" is a rhetorical tactic used to cut off vehement disagreement at the outset of the discussion, so Zak makes known his belief that the law will not change radically. He is, however, moderately optimistic; he notes that a 1988 study by the National Research Council found that alternative techniques could reduce the number of animals used in research. He doesn't seem to hold to an all-or-nothing philosophy, but wishes to make as much headway as possible toward the reduction of animal testing.

4. Explain why the following sentences define the argument that Zak develops in "Ethics and Animals": "The researchers' position is that their use of animals is necessary to advance human health care and that liberation actions waste precious resources and impede the progress of science and medicine. The animal rights advocates' position is that animal research is an ethical travesty that justifies extraordinary, and even illegal, measures" (par. 2).

Students should be able to explain how virtue thought is the basis for the researchers' position and how rights thought defines the animal rights advocates' argument. In addition, they should also be able to paraphrase some of the arguments made for each case.

5. What sort of backing does Zak provide for his claim? Is the backing convincing?

6. On the basis of manner, would you say that the argument is as readable as possible? If you feel it is unclear, explain its shortcomings. If you feel it is clearly stated and developed, point out some of the ways in which Zak helps the reader.

The author frequently reasons by <u>analogy</u>:

The rights of marginal human beings who lack many of the same human qualities as animals are compared with the rights of those animals.

The dilemma of thinking about animals' rights when the animal world is so diverse is compared with the fact that we do confront the problem of developing an ethics for dissimilar members of the human race ("men and women, citizens and aliens, the autonomous and the helpless, the fully developed and the merely potential, such as children and fetuses").

The idea that animals deserve little consideration because they do not belong to the family of man is compared with the obligations which people have to their families and community, which take precedence over obligations to outsiders.

The argument that animals deserve little consideration because they do not have strong claims to our attention as a result of their great distance from the family of man is countered with the analogy that we have obligations to certain humans who nonetheless are outside of our community (e.g. future populations).

Utilitarianism as an argument for using animals in experiments is countered by showing how repugnant the concept could be if someone advocated using aboriginal people for experiments designed to create cars that better withstand crashes.

Viewing an animal in an experiment as merely an instrument is like forcing a person to donate a kidney.

The analogies are very useful in changing the perspective with which one views the issues concerned with animals' rights. The analogies clarify some very complicated ethical questions.

7. From the standpoint of relation, do you think that paragraph 19, which outlines the history of human relationship with animals, is relevant? Explain why the paragraph is or is not relevant.

8. Do you have any questions about the quality of the argument? Explain. (Does the information in the argument seem reliable? Why, or why not?)

9. Explain why the argument centers on the problem of viewing animals either as agencies or agents. What are the different consequences of these views in the scene of modern medical research?

If animals are agencies, humans can use them like other instruments--test tubes, computers, dummies--without ethical considerations. If animals are agents, they have rights, and using animals for scientific research involves ethical and moral considerations.

10. From the standpoint of quantity, is the evidence sufficient to support the claim? (That is, does the evidence convince you that there is a basis for argument?)

Page 471

"Free the Hacker Two"
Eric Corley

1. Is the argument logical? Does it contain fallacies? Explain.

Corley reasons largely by analogy, which, from a strictly logical standpoint, is not valid--although it can be a very powerful way to explain an issue. Among Corley's analogies are these:

Mitnick's disruption of Kristy McNichol's phone lines with wire clippers rather than with a computer.

Mitnick's entry into the North American Air Defense Command Center through an open door rather than via computer.

"Like the authors who rose to defend Salman Rushdie from the long arm of hysteria, we must rise to defend those endangered by the hacker witch-hunts."

An attempt to counter-argue via analogy might read like this:

A person who circumvents the lock system on my doors in order to gain entry into my house without my permission is breaking the law regardless of whether that person takes anything from the premises or not. Why should we not regard the same person as breaking and entering when he or she uses a computer to circumvent the security system and gain access to a data base or computer program, regardless of whether anything was copied?

Authors, musicians, and artists are protected by the law from unauthorized reproduction of their work. The United States recognizes the right to retain one's intellectual property as much as it recognizes the right of citizens to retain their physical, private property. Why, then, shouldn't we also recognize computer data, derived from the intellectual labor of specialists, as property which cannot be copied without express permission? The same argument could also apply to those who copy computer programs without permission.

The Soviet Union punished Mathias Rust for invading Soviet air space and landing his airplane in Red Square, despite what it taught the general in command of defense; hackers who enter into secure computer systems should also be punished.

The main problem in reasoning from analogy is that there is never a perfect congruence between the actual argument and the hypothetical used to advance the argument. The less fit between the two, the less valid is the argument by analogy.

Corley probably commits a fallacy of ambiguity when he writes, "The newspapers accused Zinn of stealing software, but all he did was _copy_ some programs." His emphasis on the word _copy_ means that he is using the word in a neutral sense, like "_copy_ a recipe for my neighbor" or "_copy_ the phone number on a match book." How can you steal what you leave behind, after all? However, copyright laws provide an exacting answer to such a question. Copying in this particular instance is not a trivial matter.

Corley argues that there is special pleading on the part of the government and prosecution. He argues that simply because computers are involved in these transgressions, the authorities are asking that extreme punishments be handed down.

2. Is the following an accurate structural analysis of Corley's argument?

<u>Claim</u>: **Hackers should not be punished. (Hacking should be decriminalized.)**
<u>Evidence</u>: **Both Kevin Mitnick and Herbert Zinn, Jr., have been prosecuted for hacking.**
<u>Backing</u>: **Similar crimes that do not involve computers either go unpunished or incur light penalties.**
<u>Qualification</u>: **None.**

Explain why you think that the structural analysis is or is not accurate.

This is the essence of Corley's argument, although it leaves out the great weight that his argument gives to explaining that the use of computers in any breaking or entering makes people unreasonably vindictive in passing judgment.

3. Is the evidence for the claim adequate and appropriate?

Given the backing for Corley's argument, the evidence is certainly appropriate. For the length of the article and the publication in which it appeared, it is adequate because any prosecution of hackers would concern Corley.

What the argument doesn't make clear is whether the severity of these prosecutions are anomalies or not. For the average non-hacker, this would be an important issue because the general applicability of Corley's argument would depend on such information. In this case, then, the evidence, while still appropriate, is insufficient for the average reader.

4. Is the backing adequate and appropriate?

Whether one agrees or disagrees with Corley's argument, the backing is appropriate. That is, it relates directly to both the claim and the evidence. However, whether it is adequate is subject to debate because it is questionable as to whether the punishments for noncomputer transgressions are as light as Corley makes them out to be. Corley writes that Mitnick had less success than a murderer in obtaining bail. Although Corley does not mention the fact in his article, Mitnick did indeed have a very difficult time in obtaining bail because the judge thought it likely that he would commit additional crimes while free. Since bail depends on the probability that a person will return to court at the time of the hearing and that he or she will not commit another crime while on bail, it is not the case that a murderer would have an easier time obtaining bail if the judge thought another murder was likely. Furthermore, is it really the case that someone who breaks and enters into the North American Defense Command Center would simply be "thrown off the grounds or, at worst, arrested for trespassing and held overnight"?

5. State the gist of Corley's argument.

The gist of Corley's argument is that people are irrational when they are called to judge actions committed by a computer hacker.

6. The argument first appeared in <u>2600</u>, the "hacker quarterly," and was reprinted in the September 1989 issue of <u>Harper's</u>. Does your knowledge of these sources affect your judgment of the argument?

The fact that the argument was written for a hacker's magazine should put the reader on his or her guard against any biases the author might reveal. Although the publication would not necessarily prejudice the reader, it should warn the reader that some of the arguments against hacking might be glossed over.

<u>Harper's</u> reprints articles, memos, and advertising which discuss the issues of the day. Oftentimes, it is the attitude revealed by the article, rather than the article itself, which provides the reason for publication, and many of <u>Harper's</u> reprints are ironic. As a result, the reader should be on guard because the reader-writer contract is often broken with the reprints.

7. Is the argument adequate from the standpoint of quality? Explain.

Corley's estimates of the severity of punishments for such actions as entering into North American Air Defense Command without permission or for maliciously cutting the telephone wires of a celebrity are suspect. Otherwise, there is no reason to dispute the facts as presented by Corley.

8. Do you agree with Corley's views on intellectual property (such as computer programs)? Do you think he would consider unauthorized appropriation of a personal computer (hardware) more or less serious than the appropriation of a computer program (software)?

Corley seems to have some disdain for intellectual property since he does not equate the copying of programs with theft. Corley gives one the impression that hacking is all just a game and that those who prosecute hackers are vindictive killjoys. He doesn't consider the fact that the theft of computer programs possibly deprives another of real income or that the necessary construction of computer security costs real time, money, and effort. On the other hand, the theft of Corley's modem or monitor would undoubtedly outrage him.

9. Explain why you agree or disagree with Corley's argument that the punishments meted out to the two hackers were unduly severe because computers were involved.

Corley's argument has some valid points. Because there are two ways to prevent crime, things which are new and misunderstood, such as personal computers, often seem to aggravate the seriousness of a crime. One can enact laws and make sure that punishment will be meted out to the offenders, or one can construct security measures which prevent a crime from taking place. What Corley points out in his argument is that since the security measures are not currently as sophisticated as they need to be, society is legislating harshly against hacking in order to prevent its abuses. As a result, probably some computer hacking is too severely punished.

Page 474

"Profits vs. Injury"
Bill Brubaker

1. Could Brubaker be accused of the fallacy of hasty generalization? Explain your judgment.

Brubaker does not compare the number of injuries in boxing with those of other dangerous sports, such as mountain climbing, auto racing, and skin diving, nor does he attempt to determine if changes in the boxing rules would reduce the risk of injury to the point where critics would approve the sport.   Therefore, he does seem to reason that because some injuries and deaths occur as a result of the sport, the sport itself should not continue.   In addition, Brubaker doesn't seem persuaded that the sport's regulations would change enough to make it substantially safer, although this conclusion is based on anecdotal information about several boxers who did not report their injuries.

2. Does Brubaker make effective use of statistics in his argument? Explain.

The statement, "By some accounts, more than 500 boxers have died of ring-related injuries over that last 80 years" is a very effective use of statistics, misleading though it might be. (The author doesn't explain whether or not the statistic refers to worldwide competition and does not make any comparison to other dangerous spectator sports.) Otherwise, the evidence presented in the article is either anecdotal or the testimony of experts.

3. Is either of the following an adequate statement of Brubaker's claim?

a. Boxing should be outlawed.
b. Boxing should be more closely regulated.

If neither is adequate, give an adequate statement of the claim.

The title of the article, rewritten as a statement, appears to be the author's claim: The human toll of boxing outweighs its merits as a sport. The claim is much more ambivalent than (a) above because, although Brubaker might very well believe that boxing should be outlawed, he probably does not believe that outlawing it is possible. Brubaker would surely agree with (b) as well.   One could make a fairly good argument for the second choice as Brubaker's claim. He writes in the article, "But aggressiveness is not the overriding problem in boxing: It's the determination of many fighters to compete when they are medically impaired and the inability of some trainers, managers, promoters and regulating organizations to stop them." However, that claim might be too specific for the article, which takes a larger view of the boxing issue than that. For example, the final anecdote about James Jones has nothing to do with medical impairment but simply the dangers of the sport.

4. Is the following an accurate and adequate analysis of the argument?

Claim: (a) Boxing should be outlawed, or (b) boxing should be more closely regulated.
Evidence: The many cases of boxing mayhem cited in the argument.
Backing: The cases of bad regulation cited in the argument.
Qualification: None.

The previous question considered a more accurate claim for Brubaker's argument. The answer to this question, therefore, should address the problem of whether or not the evidence and backing, as expressed above, are accurate summaries of those parts of Brubaker's argument. We believe that they are. One might also add slightly more backing and state that mayhem can occur in this sport no matter what precautions are taken.

5. From the standpoint of quantity, is the evidence sufficient to be convincing?

6. From the standpoint of quality, is the evidence reliable?

7. From the standpoint of quantity, is the backing sufficient?

8. From the standpoint of quality, is the backing sufficient?

9. In your opinion, is Brubaker biased or unbiased? Explain.

10. What is your own opinion about boxing? Explain why this argument did or did not alter your opinion in any way.

Page 482

"On Boxing"
Joyce Carol Oates

1. In some ways, Oates refuses to make an argument on boxing's behalf. At the beginning of this essay she writes,

> How can you enjoy so brutal a sport, people sometimes ask me.
> Or pointedly don't ask.
> And it's too complex to answer. In any case I don't "enjoy" boxing in the usual sense of the word, and never have; boxing isn't invariably "brutal"; and I don't think of it as a "sport."

Later, she repeats herself by stating, "I have no difficulty justifying boxing as a sport because I have never thought of it as a sport." In a strictly logical sense, does Oates's refusal to consider boxing a sport obviate the requirement to justify its existence?

Regardless of whether or not boxing is considered a sport, its existence must be justified. Oates makes a very clever move at the start of her essay by setting the argument for or against boxing strictly in terms of its existence as a sport. She then sidesteps the entire parameters of the argument by stating that she does not regard boxing as a sport. This question is designed to make apparent this tactical move and to point out that sidestepping the issue of sport does not free Oates from the requirement of justifying boxing.

2. Do you believe that Oates really _is_ trying to justify boxing even though she attempts to define away the argument? Why, or why not?

Oates is very interested in justifying boxing's existence. She uses her considerable skills as an author to interest the reader by making the sport high drama. One section of the essay begins, "Each boxing match is a story--a unique and highly condensed drama without words." The drama is carried out on a psychological level, as well, and begins with the ceremonial ringing of the bell. The essay also notes that the sport meets Aristotle's definition of tragic drama in that it is serious, complete, and of a certain magnitude. She also emphasizes those aspects of boxing which make it unique. The one element which makes boxing so unlike any other sport is that its participants must constantly perform acts that are counterintuitive. The boxer is trained to "have heart," that is, to absorb punishment beyond what the body's own language says it should endure. As Oates writes, "The boxer must somehow learn, by what effort of will nonboxers surely cannot guess, to inhibit his own instinct for survival. . . ." Her emphasis on Time as an important element of the sport is well taken, for although Time is an opponent in all other sports, in no other is Time packaged into so many parcels, each three minute round a countdown with each of the opponents tailoring strategy to the remaining seconds in each of the rounds. Finally, the introduction of the idea of a shadow self points out another unique aspect of boxing, for there are few sports that involve only two competitors, and among those that do (tennis being the only major spectator sport which comes to mind), only in boxing do the competitors come within such proximity of each other, with action bringing forth an immediate reaction from the "shadow self."

3. In another part of the essay not included in this selection, Oates notes,

In December 1984 the American Medical Association passed a resolution calling for the abolition of boxing on the principle that while other sports involved as much, or even more, risk to life and health--the most dangerous sports being football, auto racing, hang gliding, mountain climbing, and ice hockey, with boxing in about seventh place--boxing is the only sport in which the objective is to cause injury. . . . To say that the rate of death and injury in the ring is not extraordinary set beside the rates of other sports is to misread the nature of the criticism brought to bear against boxing (and not against other sports). Clearly, boxing's very image is repulsive to many people because it cannot be assimilated into what we wish to know about civilized man.

Do you think that this argument is more persuasive than that of the selection in calling for the maintenance of boxing as a "sport" or profession? Why, or why not?

This argument for boxing--that it points out aspects of human nature many would just as soon forget--gets to the main controversy surrounding the sport, not attempting to sidestep the issue as in Oates's refusal to regard boxing as a sport.

4. At least one implication of this passage is that boxing should not be banned because other, more dangerous sports are not banned. What would a logician have to say about the validity of this argument?

This argument begs the question of whether or not boxing should be banned. (Other drivers on the freeway who were speeding didn't get tickets, so why should I get one?)

5. Do you think that the purpose of this essay is to present an argument? To persuade? Why, or why not?

The question is intended to motivate discussion about the distinctions among explanation, argument, and persuasion. Oates certainly is attempting to explain her fascination with boxing. If this explanation succeeds, has she convinced the reader that boxing is a legitimate sport?

6. Do you think Oates would be willing to attend boxing matches in which the opponents wore protective head gear like that which is worn during sparring? Would Brubaker? Explain.

Since the elemental brutality of boxing fascinates Oates, she perhaps would be uninterested in the sport if participants wore protective gear. However, Brubaker's argument is not against boxing _per se_, but against the way in which the sport is currently conducted. Brubaker presumably would enjoy boxing if the fighters wore protective gear.

7. What did Flannery O'Connor mean when she wrote, "If the Host is only a symbol, I'd say the hell with it"? What is Oates's point in quoting O'Connor? Do you see boxing as metaphorical?

The Host is, of course, the consecrated wafer of the Roman Catholic Eucharist, a bloodless reenactment of the crucifixion. According to the doctrine of transubstantiation, the Eucharistic wine becomes the actual blood of Christ, and bread--the Host--becomes His body. O'Connor is saying that she believes in transubstantiation; if the Eucharist is only symbolic, she is uninterested. And that is what Oates says about boxing: the individual matches are not--or at least not only--symbolic of something else, but "each boxing match is a story--a unique and highly condensed drama without words."

8. Oates makes a surprising claim for a writer when she states that boxing is not a metaphor for anything else. Do you agree with her? Is she herself consistent in this assertion? Why, or why not?

Oates, of course, contradicts herself, as the following quotations, among others, indicate:

> In the boxing ring there are two principal players, overseen by a shadowy third. The ceremonial ringing of the bell is a summoning to full wakefulness for both boxers and spectators. It sets in motion, too, the authority of Time. (par. 7)

> Every talent must unfold itself in fighting. So Nietzsche speaks of the Hellenic past, the history of the "contest"--athletic and otherwise--by which Greek youths were educated into Greek citizenry. (par. 9)

9. It would be difficult to state that the essay has one particular gist, for it develops several ideas. Do you feel that the writing is disjointed as a result? What are some of the points developed in the essay?

Life is like boxing, but boxing is unique.

Boxing is a story without words--high drama. It is a tragedy in the Aristotelian sense.

Boxing is "obliquely akin to those severe religions in which the individual is both 'free' and 'determined'--in one sense possessed of a will tantamount to God's, in another totally helpless."

10. The essay violates the reader-writer contract concerning relation in that the subsections do not relate to each other except in the broadest terms. Does this make the entire piece more difficult to understand? Does each subsection violate or uphold the contract regarding relationship?

The following is from The Rhetoric of the "Other" Literature, by W. Ross Winterowd (Southern Illinois UP, 1990):

> The lyric in prose gains its coherence from what Burke called qualitative progression, in which "the presence of one quality prepares us for the introduction of another" (Counter-Statement 124), not from the syllogistic progression that structures "Natural Selection and the Human Brain."
>
>   In "Form, Authority, and the Critical Essay," Keith Fort serendipitously and convincingly explained what should have been, but was not, the obvious: available forms determine attitudes. If, for instance, the only form available to students for their responses to literature is the conventional expository essay, with its clear-cut topic and its treeable structure, then the attitude expressed must affirm the discursiveness of literature. The prose lyric breaks out of the "syllogistic," lincar, Western form and in so doing frees itself of the strictures of discursiveness.
>
>   The essential difference between the coherence of the discursive essay and that of the presentational essay can be expressed metaphorically. In its

superstructure, the well formed discursive essay is a branching tree diagram or organizational chart with the topic, enthymeme, or macroproposition (van Dijk 42) at the top. In an image adapted from Kintsch ("Psychological Processes" 7-8), the form of a presentational essay is that of a galaxy, with dense clusters of bright stars related as subsystems within the whole as it spirals through the universe.

The prevailing dogma is that a clear-cut topic (in the scientistic language of van Dijk, a "macroproposition") is essential to coherence, but Witte and Faigley give a more useful view of coherence as "those underlying semantic relations that allow a text to be understood and used . . . conditions governed by the writer's purpose, the audience's knowledge and expectations, and the information to be conveyed" (202). In effect, <u>any text will be coherent if the reader takes it to be so,</u> and a case in point is <u>The Waste Land,</u> which Cleanth Brooks analyzed as a perfectly coherent whole <u>(Modern Poetry and the Tradition</u> 138-159) and Graham Hough likened to a painting with "pointillist technique in one part . . . and the glazes of the high renaissance in another" <u>(Reflections on a Literary Revolution</u> 38).

One of Wolfgang Iser's points . . . is that readers must fill "gaps" in the text and thus are actively involved in constructing, not merely recovering, the meaning.

11. Oates is a respected author and essayist, but she is not generally known as an expert on boxing. (She implies that she saw films of two infamous fights for the first time only in preparation for writing this essay.)   Does this undermine her authority in writing about boxing? Explain why or why not, and cite passages from the text to support your view.

The essential point is this: Oates is not writing as an expert. She is an intelligent observer. All writers--including students--can be intelligent observers of almost any subject.

Page 491

"Piltdown Revisited"
Stephen Jay Gould

1. Briefly explain the four reasons that Gould advances for the success of the Piltdown hoax.

"The imposition of strong hope upon dubious evidence": There has always been rivalry between the cultures separated by the English Channel. In the field of paleoanthropology, the many remains of Cro-Magnons and Neanderthals found on French soil and the dearth of finds within Great Britain intensified the rivalry. The implications extended beyond the scientific field because they implied that France had a much longer history of human settlement (both Cro-Magnons and Neanderthals are classified as <u>Homo sapiens</u>) and culture.

"Reduction of anomaly by fit with cultural biases": Scientific thought valued mankind's supreme intelligence within the animal world and used it to define our "humanness." Investigators then used circular logic to deduce that intelligence makes a human a human; therefore, if Cro-Magnons and Neanderthals were human, they must have been intelligent.

In addition, the Piltdown hoax was aided by racism, for it appeared that white people could trace their ancestry to Piltdown while other races would have to trace their origins back to Peking man, with its smaller brain. The implication was that the whites became "humans" much earlier than people of other colors. A further implication was that white man of today are superior because the evolution of the species would have continued at the same pace after the time of Piltdown.

"Reduction of anomaly by matching fact to expectation": Paleoanthropologists often have to view specimens as much with the eye of the art historian as that of the scientist. In trying to determine whether Piltdown man possessed apish or human characteristics, the scientists resemble art experts evaluating an old master in order to confirm its pedigree. Does the brushwork definitively prove that Rembrandt painted the portrait rather than one of his students who modeled his style after that of his mentor? In such cases, the natural bias of evaluators tends to blind them to the traits that contradict their opinions.

"Prevention of discovery by practice": Most of the experts who worked on the Piltdown mystery were not permitted to examine the actual remains. Instead, they were allowed only the use of replicas, which do not reproduce all of the nuances of trait, no matter how well done.

2.   Summarize the data that supported the authenticity of the Piltdown remains. What was the first incontrovertible evidence that Piltdown man was a fraud? Once it was known that Piltdown was inauthentic, what other evidence that the fossils were not real became readily apparent?

The bones were deeply stained, indicating that they had been in the earth for a great deal of time. In addition, the materials found along with Piltdown man, flint which had been chipped and shaped and ancient mammalian remains, indicated that Piltdown was ancient. The teeth were apish but worn down in a manner more characteristic of human than ape. The same association of tooth and cranium was found at another site as well, establishing irrefutably the connection between the two.

Once Piltdown was shown to be a hoax, the scientists noticed that the teeth had been crudely abraded rather than worn down in the manner of a living beast who had ground the teeth together. In addition, the bones had not absorbed sufficient fluorine to have lain in the soil for as long as an authentic discovery must have. Finally, the abraded tooth was too young to have been worn down to such an extent. The three conclusive pieces of data that moved Kenneth Oakley to conclude that Piltdown man was a hoax were his determination that the bone had been stained artificially, the flints had been shaped with modern instruments, and the other animal remains had been imported.

3. Summarize the structure of Dawson's argument in favor of the authenticity of Piltdown man. (Claim? Evidence? Backing? Qualification?)

<u>Claim</u>: Piltdown man is the oldest hominid in Great Britain.

<u>Evidence</u>: Deep stained bones; large, humanlike cranium; apish jaw and tooth abraded in a human manner; parallel discoveries of the same bones at different sites.

<u>Backing</u>: Man's ancestors exhibited both simian and human traits; the brain of our ancestors developed at a faster rate than other physical features because intelligence is the evolutionary result which differentiates us from the rest of the animal kingdom; bones and remains lying in the same strata of earth are from the same time period; bones found together at two different sites must be associated with each other in some manner other than by simply that of chance; the longer bones remain in the earth the more stained they become; humans and apes wear down their teeth in different manners.

<u>Qualification</u>: None.

4. Summarize the structure of Gould's argument.

Gould develops several arguments, the most important of which concerns the reasons that such a hoax should have been accepted by the scientific community; the second concerns the identity of the Piltdown perpetrator(s).

The argument concerning the reasons for acceptance could be outlined thus:

<u>Claim</u>: "Science [is] a human activity, motivated by hope, cultural prejudice, and the pursuit of glory. . . ."

<u>Backing</u>: The backing consists of the four reasons for acceptance as outlined in the answer to Question 1 (imposition of strong hope upon dubious evidence; reduction of anomaly to fit with cultural biases; reduction of anomaly by matching fact to expectation; prevention of discovery by practice).

<u>Evidence</u>: Prior to Piltdown, England had no information about its ancestors other than some dubious remains; French anthropologists loved to harp on the disparity between the richness of the French findings and the lack of English remains; Piltdown appeared to pre-date the French discoveries by a great span of time (evidence for the backing "imposition of strong hope upon dubious evidence"). In 1913, anthropologists favored "brain primacy"; works advancing the notion of white supremacy throughout antiquity appeared (evidence for the backing "reduction of anomaly to fit with cultural biases"). The evidence for "reduction of anomaly by matching fact to expectation" consists of quotes and paraphrases about the apish nature of the skull and the human features of the teeth and their position within the jaw. "Piltdown's keepers severely restricted access to the original bones" and an anecdote about Gould's own attempt to

study the Piltdown bones provide evidence for his claim concerning the "prevention of discovery by practice."

Qualification: In discussing how human error must intrude upon the perception of reality, Gould writes, "Somehow, I am not distressed that the human order must veil all our interactions with the universe, for the veil is translucent, however strong its texture." That is, humans can overcome their biases and failures of perceptions.

The second claim concerning the perpetrator(s) actually consists of two arguments. The first concludes that Dawson was involved. The second presents the case for a co-conspirator.

Claim: Charles Dawson perpetrated the Piltdown hoax.

Backing: Dawson's personality was that of a person who would be willing to concoct the hoax; the replication of old bone could have been done by an amateur; the discovery of the skull with the apish tooth at two different sites is not coincidence.

Evidence: Dawson was highly motivated, overenthusiastic, and probably unscrupulous; the abrasion of the teeth was not very well done; Dawson (it is implied) was the only person present at the second finding.

Qualification: Gould mentions other candidates and the reasons for suspecting them, instead.

The second argument concerns the possibility of a conspiracy and the identity of the second person.

Claim: Father Teilhard de Chardin was a co-conspirator.

Backing: The discovery of the second tooth and skull fragments must have occurred in 1915, but Teilhard's recollection that he was at the site of the second discovery when Dawson told him of the discovery cannot be true. (There is the implied backing that Teilhard could not have entirely made up this fundamental recollection of such an important event in his life if he was not one of the perpetrators.)

Evidence: There is no reason to believe that the announcement would not have been made immediately after the discovery if Piltdown were real; Teilhard could not have been at the discovery site with Dawson any time after the discovery because Teilhard was at the French front in World War I at the time of the discovery, and Dawson died soon thereafter, nor could Dawson have told Teilhard of the finds for the very same reasons.

5. In your opinion, was Teilhard de Chardin aware of the hoax? Give the backing for your claim.

The answer to this question will depend on whether or not the students believe that Teilhard, when reflecting back across forty years, could have scrambled or fabricated such basic and important facts as having learned directly from Dawson about the second finds and discussing these events at the site of the discovery.

6. What level of world knowledge outside the field of paleontology does Gould presume that his readers possess? Does a reader require at least some knowledge of paleontology in order to appreciate the essay? Explain.

Gould does not expect the reader to know any technical information. The significance of the fluorine tests, for example, is explained without burdening the reader with any of the scientific details, such as why bone absorbs fluorine or how the level of fluorine correlates with the length of time the bone is in the ground. However, the reader is expected to know some basic scientific principles. These include the assumption that materials buried in the same stratum of rock or soil are of roughly the same age, a general idea of how paleontologists go about their business of reconstructing bone fragments, and some understanding of the evolutionary history of the hominids.

7. The essay seems to have two main points. What are they? Do you think that multiple gists necessarily make a piece of writing more confusing? Explain.

The main points are (a) the fallibility of scientists in spite of the apparently objective nature of their work and (b) the ability of even a person of great repute to become involved in duplicity. The two emphases are complementary since they both point to human shortcomings.

8. Why does Gould believe Dawson and Teilhard perpetrated the hoax? Were you interested in the reasons that Gould advances for their actions? Why, or why not? Were the purposes credible?

The reasons for Gould's belief are outlined above, and readers should be interested in the motives of Dawson and Teilhard, for without the element of motive, the article becomes a slightly dry, deductive puzzle. With the inclusion of motive, the essay becomes a real mystery, almost a whodunit. For example, Gould had earlier written that Dawson was an overenthusiastic amateur who very well could have conceived the hoax or agreed to it in order to spite the professionals; and Teilhard, a Frenchman, might have wanted to taunt the British with France's superiority in the field of paleoanthropology. However, these motives do not make sense unless the hoax is then exposed, to the embarrassment of the professionals and the British, in particular. Since this never did occur, except through further scientific enquiry forty years after the event, Gould also states reasons for the silence. For each person, Gould guesses that the events simply got out of hand because of the magnitude of the reception that greeted the findings. Revelations made at a later time were impossible for Dawson, since he died soon after the second find, and Teilhard may have feared that a full disclosure would harm his promising career.

9. What cultural and intellectual ideas of the time led the experts to believe in Piltdown man?

See the answers to Questions 1, 2, and 8.

10. According to Gould, what should be the relationship between facts and theory?

11. Gould gives one example in which the scientists actually changed a "fact" in their rush to believe in the Piltdown man. What fact was changed?

See paragraph 27.

12. Although several scientists were very close to discovering the full truth of the case, it appears from the information supplied by Gould that not one of the authorities who suspected the hoax ever attempted to duplicate it himself. Why do you think that is so?

Page 504

"The Creation of Patriarchy"
Gerda Lerner

1. Lerner writes,

> It was only after men had learned how to enslave the women of groups who could be defined as strangers, that they learned how to enslave men of those groups and, later, subordinates from within their own societies.
>   Thus, the enslavement of women, combining both racism and sexism, preceded the formation of classes and class oppression.

Does this argument have any backing or reservations? (You will want to reread quite a few of the succeeding paragraphs to answer this question fully.)

Backing for the argument includes an account of Mesopotamian societies (par. 5) and the disadvantage that sex creates for women (par. 7-11).

2. The following pairs of sentences seem to be contradictory. Do you believe that they are, indeed, contradictory? (You might benefit from rereading the text in which these sentences appear.) How would you rewrite these sentences so that they would be clearer?

> Thus, the enslavement of women, combining both racism and sexism, preceded the formation of classes and class oppression. . . . Class is not a separate construct from gender; rather class is expressed in generic terms. (par 4)

The sentences are from paragraph 4. Paragraph 3 explains the reasoning behind the claim.

The product of this commodification of women--bride price, sale price, and children--was appropriated by men. . . . But it is not women who are reified and commodified, it is women's sexuality and reproductive capacity which is so treated. (par. 6-7)

In other words, women are valued as sexual objects and as reproductive organisms, not as human beings.

Women, no matter how exploited and abused, retained their power to act and to choose to the same, often very limited extent, as men of their group. But women <u>always and to this day</u> lived in a relatively greater state of unfreedom than did men. (par. 7)

Women were trapped in ways that men were not. Men could be enslaved and exploited as workers, but women were not only slaves, they were unwilling sex partners and child bearers.

   3. What qualifications does Lerner make to her claim that "the vast majority of single women are, by definition, marginal and dependent on the protection of male kin"? (par. 14)

Convents and other enclaves have provided havens for women in some historical eras.

   4. According to Lerner, how is the cooperation of women within the patriarchal system ensured?

   Cooperation is assured through education in which the appropriate roles for women are expressed in the "values, customs, laws, and social roles. They also, and very importantly, were expressed in leading metaphors, which became part of the cultural construct and explanatory system" (par. 2).
   Later in the essay, Lerner succinctly itemizes other ways in which cooperation is achieved: "educational deprivation; the denial to women of knowledge of their history; the dividing of women, one from the other, by defining 'respectability' and 'deviance' according to women's sexual activities; by restraints and outright coercion; by discrimination in access to economic resources and political power; and by awarding class privileges to conforming women." The most powerful of these controls, at least up to this point, is the economic control exerted by males. By controlling the means of production, men could force women to conform out of necessity and not just voluntarily through indoctrination. In earlier times, the cooperation was also ensured by securing women as slaves and using physical force.

5. Do you believe that Lerner would agree with the statement that women are an oppressed class? Explain.

The key word in this question is <u>class</u>. Lerner writes, "Class and racial privileges serve to undercut the ability of women to see themselves as part of a coherent group, which, in fact, they are not, since women uniquely of all oppressed groups occur in all strata of the society." That is, since women are found in all classes, they find it difficult to relate to all other women as a group. Lerner, therefore, would not agree that women form a class unto themselves. Earlier in the essay she writes that "At any given moment in history, each 'class' is constituted of two distinct classes--men and women." What she is saying in this sentence is that each socioeconomic class is composed of two distinct subclasses, the first subclass consisting of men, the second of women.

6. The title of this essay could just as easily be "The Liberation from Patriarchy." Explain.

Only the first few paragraphs are concerned with the origination of patriarchy. The majority of the essay is actually concerned with a historical interpretation of fully formed patriarchy. In the conclusion, which is quite lengthy, Lerner raises a call to step outside of patriarchal thought in order to create a new society.

7. Lerner makes a startling pronouncement when she writes that women entered history in the nineteenth century. How does Lerner define history? Is this definition different from that which you normally use? If women's history is such a recent phenomenon, how can women ever have the rich history which Lerner's essay calls for?

Lerner defines history as "recording, defining, and interpreting the past." An important aspect of her definition is her requirement that history evaluate the past by defining and interpreting, not simply recording. There has been relatively little record of women's actions in the past, although Lerner disputes the notion that information about women is as scarce as appearances imply. The problem is that this record has not, as yet, been made into history; that is, the raw material has been recorded, but it has not been defined or interpreted.

The term <u>history</u> is frequently used synonymously with <u>written record</u>. That is, people's use of the term omits the analytic dimension of the definition. This difference in the definitions is why Lerner's statement is so surprising.

Lerner herself only begins to answer the question of reconstructing a rich history for women. She does state that "Two decades of Women's History scholarship have disproven this fallacy [that women have no past, history, or religion of their own] by unearthing an unending list of sources and uncovering and interpreting the hidden history of women. . . . We are only beginning to understand its implications." She expresses optimism, but her own argument about men's control of the symbols and value systems of society should serve as a qualification to such hope.

8. In terms of manner, this essay is written almost in terms of a manifesto, such as the Declaration of Independence, rather than as a carefully constructed argument. Explain.

The essay presents many claims and backing but virtually no evidence for such claims. The third paragraph of the essay is a case in point.

Claim: "The sexuality of women . . . was commodified even prior to the creation of Western civilization."

Backing: "The development of agriculture in the Neolithic period fostered the intertribal 'exchange of women,' not only as a means of avoiding incessant warfare by the cementing of marriage alliances but also because societies with more women could produce more children."

Evidence: None.

Claim: "Men-as-a-group had rights in women which women-as-a-group did not have in men."

Backing: "Women were exchanged or bought in marriages for the benefit of their families; later, they were conquered or bought in slavery. . . ."

Evidence: None.

Claim: "In every known society it was women of conquered tribes who were first enslaved, whereas men were killed."

Backing: "It was only after men had learned how to enslave the women of groups who could be defined as strangers, that they learned how to enslave men of those groups. . . ."

Evidence: None. However, it must be noted that the selection is the final chapter of a very thick book that discusses its subject in detail.

Page 521

"A Game of Chicken"
Franklin E. Zimring and Gordon Hawkins

1.   Is the following argument logical or illogical?   Explain.   If capital punishment deters potential murderers, then painful forms of execution should be more effective than those that are relatively painless.   Thus, advocates of capital punishment should also advocate methods of execution such as death by fire at the stake.

The argument is fairly logical, although not strictly so, in its conclusion. The premise, that capital punishment deters potential murderers, assumes only that the threat of death is preventative and does not address the issue of pain at all. Nothing in the argument supports the implication that the fear of pain is preventative, as well. The argument, therefore, is not internally consistent.

In the real world, the argument is also problematic. Very probably the vast majority of people who are in favor of the death penalty want the punishment to be administered in the least painful way. That is, they impose a moral dimension on the punishment even though it involves the taking of a human life. The fact that it could prevent murders would not convince most adherents of the death penalty to agree with burning at the stake, for this method of execution would offend their moral sense. What this demonstrates is that consistent or valid arguments must also be considered from the standpoint of context (or scene).

2.   In the final three paragraphs, the authors briefly allude to possible qualifications to their claim. What are these?

The authors state that the untenable situation which the United States currently faces would disappear if those who decide the questions posed by capital punishment were allowed to make decisions privately. While such a statement implies that the public officials are privately opposed to the death penalty, the authors then write, "We cannot say that those who hold power on such matters would abolish the death penalty." The first statement qualifies the authors' claim, and the second statement qualifies the qualification, almost negating it.

3. Which of the following two statements is a truncated argument? Explain.
a. There is a steady increase in the death row population.
b. There is an untenable increase in the death row population.

The first sentence is merely a statement of fact, verifiable with available data. The second statement is arguable. Should the death row population be increasing as much as it is?

4. The argument for the death penalty appears simple enough: an eye for an eye, a tooth for a tooth. What backing can you give for this proposition? Is the basis for the backing primarily moral or pragmatic?

5. How do the following data influence your judgment of the quality of this argument? (a) Franklin E. Zimring is professor of law and director of the Earl Warren Legal Institute at the University of California, Berkeley. Gordon Hawkins is a senior fellow of the Earl Warren Legal Institute. He was formerly director of the Sydney University Institute of Criminology. (b) The book from which the selection is taken was published by Cambridge University Press.

Both the authors' vitae and the publisher should assure the reader that any facts presented are correct. The reader, for example, wouldn't question the statement, "Eleven persons were executed in the United States between 1977 and the end of 1983."

The bulk of the essay, however, is concerned with interpretation, not facts. As a result, the reader should be critical of opinions and conclusions because the authors are probably opposed to the death penalty. After all, the University of California at Berkeley is known as a stronghold for liberals, and Earl Warren, after whom the legal institute is named, was the most important liberal Supreme Court chief justice of this century.

6. What elements of scene are important in this argument?

The essay is concerned with the results of the Gregg versus Georgia decision handed down by the Supreme Court in 1976, in which state capital punishment laws were approved. A major aspect of scene, therefore, is the United States since 1976. In a more abstract view, the scene is the legal and political world of our nation as opposed, for example, to the moral realm of society's values (which the essay does not discuss).

7. In regard to manner, did you find this selection easy to understand or difficult? Explain. Did the authors' failure to relate their "game of chicken" metaphor to actual cases make the argument more difficult to understand?

As noted in question 5, the failure to specify the participants in the game of chicken makes the article unnecessarily difficult. In other respects, however, the essay is quite clear in style and explanations of ideas. Sections are given subheads, and the authors make good use of examples, statistics, and even a diagram to make their points understandable.

8. Does this selection advance an argument against capital punishment? If not, what is the claim?

The article does not argue against the death penalty per se but against the discrepancy between public policy as stated in the law and the rhetoric of public debate and the failure to adhere strictly to that policy. Zimring and Hawkins claim that our society is reluctant to enforce the death penalty in spite of public support for capital punishment.

9. Who are the two drivers in the game of chicken?

Zimring and Hawkins never identify the two players in the game of chicken (except through context). The final section with the subheading "An Apt Analogy" is the clearest explanation of who the players are. The authors view the participants collectively. One group is the citizenry of the United States. The other consists of the "key actors in the American government," especially the politicians elected by the citizenry. The politicians, afraid of going against the perceived will of the people, campaign as supporters of the death penalty and enact laws that promote it. Judges, beholden as they are to both the electorate and the politicians who appoint many of them, are in much the same position as the politicians.

The reader should have little trouble in understanding that the judiciary and the political wing of government comprise one group of players in the game, but the second group, the citizenry, is less clear. The analogy presumes each player is fearful of the consequences of either chickening out or of not flinching, yet Zimring and Hawkins do not make clear their presumption that the citizens are fearful of the outcome if they do not flinch. He does state that most would be horrified if the executions of those sentenced were carried out. Zimring's analogy breaks down when one considers the citizenry's fear of backing down from the collision.

10. What are the reasons for the pileup of convicts on death row?

Zimring begins his explanation with the assumption that very few people would actually support the execution of the large number of convicts who have been sentenced to death. He writes, "Those who support the concept of capital punishment do not necessarily want any executions, and would be horrified by the kind of perpetual bloodbath that would ensue were the criminal law to keep its promises literally." Therefore, there isn't a groundswell of public opinion pushing for more expeditious executions to alleviate both the backlog and the ever-increasing number of newly sentenced.

The relatively large number of convicts sentenced to death, creating the backlog in the first place, is the result of several factors. First of all, Zimring cites two types of passing the buck which help to ease the conscience of those who condemn a person to death. Because the legal system has a large number of review bodies which must consider a sentence before it is enacted, the responsibility in sentencing a person to death is spread out among the "local prosecutors; the local judiciary, with or without a jury; state appellate courts; federal courts; the U.S. Supreme Court; and executive clemency review processes. . . ." Those involved at the lower levels of this review process tend to rationalize that their decision will be reviewed by those in higher offices or positions, and therefore any decision is less important than would be the approval granted at higher levels.

At the higher levels of the review process, the buck passes in the opposite direction. These offices tend to look at the number of other, lower levels of review which have sanctioned the death sentence and become reluctant to overturn what has already been apparently decided at many other levels.

Federalizing the death penalty takes away the power of citizens at the local level to deter this punishment. At the same time, the ability to institute the death penalty resides at the state and not the federal level. According to Zimring and Hawkins, because the state government is traditionally more bound to the immediate and local concerns of its citizens, there are probably more death sentences than there would be if the federal government administered the law.

The above explanations go a long way towards accounting for increases in death sentences but don't explain why the number of executions has not increased. Zimring and Hawkins believe that many who support the penalty are more ambivalent about carrying it out. The ambivalence ranges from that of average citizens to that of the politicians they vote in.

In addition, the authors probably assume that the reader has some knowledge of the proceedings which must occur before the convicted are executed. Alluding to the complexity of the review process, they write, "In the 1980s no death sentences can be enforced without decisions by local prosecutors; the local judiciary, with or without a jury; state appellate courts; federal courts; the U.S. Supreme Court; and executive clemency review processes, frequently including the governor of the executing jurisdiction." The authors do not elaborate on this process or explain the length of time required to conduct it, but they probably assume that the reader has some knowledge of the length of the appeal process.

Page 533

"The Naturalist and the Supernaturalist"
C. S. Lewis

1. What is Lewis's claim?

Lewis's claim is stated in the concluding sentence of the essay ("Our first choice, therefore, must be between Naturalism and Supernaturalism"). It is also addressed in the first paragraph of the essay, although the question posed, seemingly the actual claim, is never answered: "Some people believe that nothing exists except Nature; I call these people Naturalists. Others think that, besides Nature, there exists something else: I call them Supernaturalists. Our first question, therefore, is whether the Naturalists or the Supernaturalists are right."

2. He gives no evidence for the claim. Does he need evidence? Explain why or why not.

Lewis does not require any evidence for his claim because it is a tautological proposition. That is to say, it does not exclude any of the logical possibilities. One must agree that either something does or does not exist outside of nature.

The fact that Lewis does not have to provide evidence as to the truth of his claim does not relieve him of the obligation to convince the reader that the claim has relevance. It is rare that a proposition of the form "Either A or not A" would be enlightening in and of itself. Instead, the implications of the tautology are what is of interest. Lewis understands this fact. "The Naturalist and the Supernaturalist" is an essay written to explain the ramifications of the claim rather than to prove it. For example, Lewis points out that "no thoroughgoing Naturalist believes in free will: for free will would mean that human beings have the power of independent action, the power of doing something more or other than what was involved by the total series of events. And any such separate power of originating events is what the Naturalist denies." In addition, the author notes the other following implications: Naturalism is democratic and Supernaturalism is monarchical; "the difference between Naturalism and Supernaturalism is not exactly the same as the difference between belief in a God and disbelief"; "it by no means follows from Supernaturalism that Miracles of any sort do in fact occur."

Though the point may be a quibble, nonetheless, Lewis's claim does not contain absolutely all possibilities and is therefore not strictly a tautology. There is the possibility that multiple closed Natures exist without benefit of a "Primary Thing." Such a situation is akin to the Naturalist position in that nothing from the outside has influence on the system nor does there exist a primum mobile. Because Lewis's comments on the Naturalists' position also apply to this situation, the possibility of existence is not damaging to Lewis's essay nor does it create a need for evidence not previously required when regarded as a tautology.

3. What is his backing for the claim?

The backing is simply the body of the essay itself: Lewis's argument.

4. Point out instances in which Lewis uses analogy to support or clarify his point. Are these analogies successful?

The opening quote from Giant-Land is an excellent illustration of the difficulty in contemplating alternate worlds. It also offers a gentle rebuke to the skeptic who would immediately rule out the possibility of other Natures without considering the argument.

Lewis compares the Naturalist position to democracy and that of the Supernaturalist to monarchy. The analogy is excellent. It illustrates how the Naturalists and Supernaturalists view the relation of events and physical presences within a system. In addition, it provides an interesting speculation that there exists a relation between the type of government within a society and the view of ultimate reality held by people in that society.

The relation of multiple Natures to each other is compared to that of various novels written by the same author. The analogy is useful in showing that the elements of each system are bound by that system and cannot normally influence the other existing systems. In addition, it points out that these multiple systems are related to each other and might share common traits because they are the products of a common Supernatural force.

5. Are you a naturalist or a supernaturalist? Present some backing for your position. (Does any empirical evidence--facts and figures--relate to your claim?)

The argument between naturalists and supernaturalists is, finally, based on personal belief and faith more than on empirical or logical reasons. Lewis does employ logical reasoning to explain why the two beliefs are unresolvable. The only manner in which the supernatural position can be established is in a supernatural intercession of Nature, which Lewis has defined as a miracle. However, inexplicable events might be misidentified as miracles when, in fact, they are simply the results of the complete system of Nature within which we live. On the other hand, Lewis points out that the absence of miracles does not disprove the Supernatural position. "God (the primary thing) may never in fact interfere with the natural system He has created."

6. Lewis starts by defining <u>miracle</u>, <u>naturalist</u>, and <u>supernaturalist</u>. Why are these definitions crucial for the argument? (What happens to the argument if the reader does not accept the definitions?)

As noted earlier, Lewis's essay explores the definitions of <u>naturalist</u> and <u>supernaturalist</u>. These definitions are crucial to the argument because they comprise the largest part of the essay. In one sense, the reader cannot disagree with the author because Lewis presents a stipulative definition for each of these terms. That is, he tells the reader up front that he will define <u>naturalist</u>, <u>supernaturalist</u>, and <u>miracle</u> in a particular way. Nonetheless, a stipulative definition has relevance only if it has some commonality with the standard or typical definition used by the general readership.

7. In regard to manner, most readers would say that C. S. Lewis is a remarkably clear writer, making complex ideas relatively easy to understand. What are some of the ways in which Lewis makes his argument easy to follow?

It has already been pointed out in question 4 that Lewis uses analogies to clarify his ideas. Lewis is careful to define the terms used in his essay so that ambiguity doesn't cloud the issue. The very first paragraph defines the terms <u>Miracle</u>, <u>Naturalists</u>, and <u>Supernaturalists</u>.

The author elaborates on the definitions by comparing and contrasting the two philosophies. For example, he points out that the two positions both agree that there exists a basic "Fact" so elemental that it cannot itself be defined, since it is the axiom upon which all explanations rely. In addition, Naturalism and Supernaturalism both admit to the existence of what we could call God.

The differences are also carefully drawn. The basic "Fact" of Naturalism is the entire closed system itself, and that of Supernaturalism is the existence of a primary thing which exists independent of the entire system. The God of Naturalism is a cosmic consciousness which arises from and depends completely on the entire system, while the God of Supernaturalism, as noted above, is separate from the system.

Lewis also stands conventional philosophy on its head by declaring that it is the Naturalist, not the Supernaturalist, who does not believe in free will. It had been argued that Supernaturalists did not believe in free will because of their belief that God controlled the destiny of the beings within Nature. Not so, claims Lewis. The author argues that an independent God does not have to interfere in the system at all. On the other hand, because each event and element within the Naturalist's system is so interlocked, nothing occurs on its own but is the result of the sum of all events prior to the event as well as the relationship between all other things within the system.

8. What conclusions can you draw about Lewis (the agent) on the basis of the work (his act).

Lewis is obviously a theist, and he is probably a political conservative. (Though he seems to be neutral in the argument, even naive readers can assume that the book from which this essay is taken is an argument in favor of theism. When he says that

Supernaturalism is like a monarchy, he does not apologize or qualify. We would expect a liberal or left-winger to qualify the analogy.) He is also deeply learned. An interesting question: Can one draw these conclusions merely on the basis of the essay? After all, the general nature of Lewis's biography is widely known, and the headnote to the selection contains evidence.

9. What influence do you think scene has had on Lewis's thinking? Recall that for more than a quarter of a century he was a tutor at Oxford and that he was an infantry officer in World War I. What would be a reliable source to consult for more information about the scenes of Lewis's life (i.e., his biography)?

For information about Lewis's biography: <u>Dictionary of National Biography</u> or a general encyclopedia.

10. How was Lewis's novel <u>The Screwtape Letters</u> received when it first came out? What source would you consult to learn what critics thought of the book?

Students could check <u>Book Review Digest</u> and general indices. The first step, of course, would be to find the date of the novel (1942).

11. Why is the definition of <u>miracle</u> with which Lewis begins his argument important to the argument?

Lewis's definition of <u>miracle</u> contains the essence of his argument. If miracles can occur, then the supernatural exists, and if the supernatural does not exist, then miracles cannot take place. The absence of miracles does not definitively prove the Naturalist's position. Things might exist outside of our own "nature" and not be able to enter into our system.

Page 540

"A Modest Proposal"
Jonathan Swift

1. Briefly outline Swift's argument: claim, backing, evidence, qualification.

<u>Claim</u>: The use of children as food would benefit society.

<u>Backing 1</u>: ˜The many children currently living in poverty are a drain on society.

<u>Evidence 1</u> (that the many children currently living in poverty are a drain on society): These children prevent their mothers from working, they beg on the streets rather than plying a trade, and grow up to become thieves, members of a foreign army, or indentured servants.

<u>Backing 2</u>: The plan to use children as food would prevent voluntary abortions and the murdering of bastard children by their mothers.

Evidence 2 (that such a plan would prevent voluntary abortions and the murdering of bastard children by their mothers): Because the author suspects that these abortions and murders are a way of avoiding additional child expenses, the prospect of a future sale of the child would provide an economic incentive for keeping the child alive up to that point.

Backing 3: The meat of children is "a most delicious, nourishing, and wholesome food."

Evidence 3 (that the meat of children is "a most delicious, nourishing, and wholesome food"): The author's very knowing American acquaintance has affirmed this fact.

Backing 4: Squires would learn to be good landlords.

Evidence 4 (that squires would learn to be good landlords): Landlords "have best title to the children" because they have already half devoured the parents. [The author implies that since the landlord has a special interest in the child, special care will be given to the child and his or her parents.]

Backing 5: The number of Papists would be reduced.

Evidence 5 (that the number of Papists would be reduced): Because there are a disproportionate number of Catholic children living in poverty, their use as food would help to reduce their numbers disproportionately.

Backing 6: A child's skin would make fine gloves or boots.

Evidence 6 (that a child's skin would make fine gloves or boots): None.

Backing 7: The parents would gain from the sale of their children.

Evidence 7 (that the parents would gain from the sale of their children): They would now be able to pay their rent and would be rid of the cost of maintaining children after the first year.

Backing 8: The sale of children would generate new profits.

Evidence 8 (that the sale of children would generate new profits): The "new dish introduced to the tables of all gentlemen of fortune in the kingdom who have any refinement in taste" is assumed to be a popular treat.

Backing 9: The profits generated from the sale of children would circulate within the home country.

Evidence 9 (that the profits generated from the sale of children would circulate within the home country): The goods are entirely of the home country's growth and manufacture.

Backing 10: "[T]his food would likewise bring great custom to taverns."

Evidence 10 (that "this food would likewise bring great custom to taverns"): "[T]he vintners will certainly be so prudent as to procure the best receipts for dressing it to perfection, and consequently have their houses frequented by all the fine gentlemen, who justly value themselves upon their knowledge in good eating. . . . "

Backing 11: The sale of children for food would be a great inducement to marriage.

Evidence 11 (that the sale of children for food would be a great inducement to marriage): None.

Backing 12: The sale of children for food "would increase the care and tenderness of mothers toward their children."

Evidence 12 (that the sale of children for food "would increase the care and tenderness of mothers toward their children"): The mothers would be assured of profit rather than expense from their children.

Backing 13: There would be "an honest emulation among the married women."

Evidence 13 (that there would be "an honest emulation among the married women"): The married women would compete in bringing the fattest child to market.

Backing 14: Men would become fond of their wives during pregnancy.

Evidence 14 (that men would become fond of their wives during pregnancy): None stated outright. The reader can infer, however, that such fondness arises from a profit motive.

Backing 15: Men would not beat or kick their pregnant wives as is currently too frequent a practice.

Evidence 15 (that men would not beat or kick their pregnant wives): The men would fear a miscarriage presumably because it would mean a loss of income.

2. Swift ends his ironic tour de force by assuring the reader,

> **I profess, in the sincerity of my heart, that I have not the least personal interest in endeavoring to promote this necessary work, having no other motive than the public good of my country, by advancing our trade, providing for infants, relieving the poor, and giving some pleasure to the rich. I have no children by which I can propose to get a single penny; the youngest being nine years old, and my wife past childbearing.**

What would be the purpose and effect of such a testimonial in an argument that was not ironic? What is its ironic effect?

Swift's conclusion avers that his argument is not a case of special pleading but is for the good of all. It is consistent in tone and content with the rest of the essay and therefore is horrific if taken literally and scathing in its attack if seen as ironic.

3. Why would a skillful arguer start with premises on which everyone could agree before introducing the controversial claim? Explain how Swift captures his readers' sympathy and agreement before he jolts them with his claim.

Any person who wishes to be persuasive must first establish that he or she is reasonable in character in order to win the sympathy of the audience. In addition, the arguer wants the audience conditioned to agree with the argument as it proceeds. The greater the tendency for the audience to reflexively concur with the claim, backing, or evidence in an argument, the less critical the audience becomes.

Swift begins his modest proposal with an appeal to pity. He cites the terrible situation of children born to poverty who are condemned to begging on the streets. Swift then writes, ." . . whoever could find out a fair, cheap, and easy method of making these children sound, useful members of the commonwealth would deserve so well of the public as to have his statue setup for a preserver of the nation." Modern-day readers would be more wary of this statement than contemporaries of Swift. It implies that children should be put to use, which goes against our society's basic philosophy that childhood should be unencumbered by major responsibilities other than obtaining an education. In 1729, however, children in the lower classes worked in various capacities in order to help in the financial support of the family. Therefore, Swift's utilitarian pronouncement would not be questioned by many readers of the time but would, rather, be endorsed.

Swift informs the reader that he has contemplated the problem for many years. He also states that he has maturely considered the solutions proposed by other people and found them in error based on his own calculations. These statements, of course, serve to bolster the credibility of the author.

Swift employs bogus statistics in his argument to lend "scientific" support to his proposal. By his calculations, the child born to poverty becomes an extreme economic burden after the first year, and it is at this point in a child's life that Swift proposes a solution. The need for a solution is supported by additional statistics. Based on the population of Ireland, Swift calculates the number of breeders, and from that number those who are able to support their own children. From the remaining number, the author determines the number of children born to poverty after making allowances for miscarriages and accidental deaths. The apparent ease with these numbers and calculations leads the reader to trust the rational nature of the author and to agree that the number of children born to poverty is too great for previously proposed remedies by others to be possible.

4. What means does Swift use to satirize scientific thought? What else is the subject of his attacks?

The introductory part of the essay is rich in the use of such scientific tools as statistical evidence and rational deduction, as noted in the discussion of question 3. It is fascinating to note that Swift's essay was written almost seventy years before Thomas Malthus's revolutionary study of population, <u>An Essay on the Principle of Population</u>, which concludes that the world's population grows faster than the ability to support it, with famine and poverty as the inevitable outcome. The similarity between such a conclusion and Swift's outline of the problem of poverty is eerily similar and indicative of how incisive is Swift's satire.

The discussion of children born into poverty is purposefully devoid of humanistic terminology. Mothers are referred to as dams, and women who are able to conceive are called breeders. In addition, Swift makes use of the term <u>solar year</u> as if it lends more scientific weight to his calculations and pronouncements.

Swift uses his essay to satirize intolerance and prejudice, particularly as it is directed against the people of Ireland. Catholics are singled out for scorn both because of the number born to each family (because, according to Swift, fish is a prolific diet) and because of their allegiance to the Pope. He notes that the poor children of that kingdom are probationers in the art of theft as if it were axiomatic that a poor person must be dishonest. The aged and infirm are said to be encumbrances, and Jews are murderers.

5. In regard to manner, Swift uses irony to advance his argument. What are the advantages and the disadvantages of this device? Might some readers fail to perceive the irony and thus conclude that Swift was a monster?

Swift's use of irony avoids two major pitfalls. First, there is no mistaking the author's intent in this case as there might be with a less outrageous ironic proposal. Should readers misunderstand the author's intent because the ironic stance is subtle, they cannot be persuaded by the author to adopt his or her own point of view.

Secondly, irony is oftentimes used when an author does not wish to reveal his or her true beliefs or in circumstances in which an author does not possess strong beliefs or opinions about a subject. This is certainly not the case with Swift. The reader is assured of Swift's moral outrage at the poverty seen in his land and his disgust with prejudice in its various guises.

By adopting the opposition's stance and using exaggeration to make it appear foolish, the ironist has a very effective rhetorical tactic for criticizing the opposition. In addition, it is a way of holding the reader's attention through discussions of difficult subject matter such as that of poverty.

Irony is also very hard to rebut. Because irony sidesteps the use of logical argumentation, one cannot easily use facts, deductions, and proofs to counter. Moreover, any use of irony in a counterargument falls flat since that tactic has already been used by the opposition.

6. How would the concept of world knowledge help explain why some readers might fail to perceive Swift's irony and read the essay as a literal argument for butchering and consuming children?

If readers know nothing about Swift and his other writings, about the history of the British Empire, about the Anglican religion, about human values, about literary techniques, about the way the world works . . .

7. State the ironic gist of the essay. State the literal gist.

The ironic gist of the essay is that poverty in Ireland is intolerable.

The literal gist is also the essay's claim: the use of children as food would benefit society.

8. Why does Swift talk of "a child just dropped from its dam" rather than of "a newborn child" and of "breeders" rather than "mothers"? Check the meanings of <u>drop</u> and <u>dam</u>. (What source would you use to find what those terms meant in the eighteenth century?)

As noted in the discussion of question 4, this terminology dehumanizes the subjects and treats them as objects of study rather than as a group of human beings with feelings and emotions. This is a parody of the manner in which scientists and other rationalists write and speak when discussing the subject of their study.

A good college dictionary of the English language should provide the appropriate definitions for these terms as used in the eighteenth century, although the reader might have to use the context of the essay to determine which definition is applicable. Students should also become familiar with the <u>Oxford English Dictionary</u>.

9. Swift uses statistics to back his argument. Do you think that his statistics were accurate? Does their accuracy matter? Explain.

The accuracy of the statistics is irrelevant to the point which Swift wants to make. However, the satire would be all the more effective if the statistics were accurate. For example, Swift gives considerable attention to determining the number of children annually born to poverty and to the problem of providing for them. If the numbers were totally inaccurate, the essay would not resemble the reasoned calculations of scientists and economists, which is what Swift is aiming for.

Page 548

"Civil Disobedience"
Henry David Thoreau

1. Explain why the following statement is either logical or illogical: "The authority of government, even such as I am willing to submit to,--for I will cheerfully obey those who know and can do better than I, and in many things even those who neither know nor can do so well,--is still an impure one: to be strictly just, it must have the sanction and the consent of the governed. It can have no right over my person and my property but what I concede to it." (par. 37)

Thoreau's statement would probably be viewed as a fallacy of division (what is true for the whole is true for the parts). A democratic government must have the consent of the majority but not the totality. Any one individual within the group might disagree with the government. The fallacy of division is compounded by the fallacy of ambiguity. Most people would agree that the verb <u>consent</u>, when used in the context above, refers to only the majority of the governed, but Thoreau subsequently uses the verb concede in the singular, raising this question: Does governmental authority come from the consent of the majority or the concession of the individual?

2. What is Thoreau's claim?

The claim: through civil disobedience, one must oppose any demand of the government on the individual if such a demand contradicts one's beliefs. The gist of the essay is the backing for the claim.

3. In many ways, Thoreau argues for radical self-centeredness. What backing does he provide for such a position? Explain why you agree or disagree with him.

As the headnote points out, Thoreau's close friend and mentor was Ralph Waldo Emerson, and a leitmotif in Emerson's works is self-reliance: "To believe your own thought, to believe that what is true for you is true for all men--that is genius. Speak your latent conviction, and it shall be the universal sense" ("Self-Reliance" 145). "The soul active sees absolute truth and utters truth, or creates" ("The American Scholar" 50).

4. Thoreau uses metaphors to characterize obedience to and action by the government. How do these metaphors add to the persuasiveness of the argument?

Among the metaphors used by Thoreau:

"It [the government] is a sort of wooden gun to the people themselves. . . ."

"[T]he people must have some complicated machinery or other, and hear its din, to satisfy that idea of government which they have. . . ." and elsewhere, "[A]ll machines have their friction; and possibly this does enough good to counterbalance the evil."

"The mass of men serve the State thus, not as men mainly, but as machines, with their bodies."

Quoting Cyril Tourneur, "'A drab of state, a cloth-o'-silver slut, / To have her train borne up, and her soul trail in the dirt.'"

"I saw the State was half-witted, that it was timid as a lone woman with her silver spoons, and that it did not know its friends from its foes. . . ." [This is, by the way, an example of reification, portraying the state as a half-witted woman alone with her silver spoons.]

"[The seat of the county government was seen] in the light of the middle ages, and our Concord was turned into a Rhine stream, and visions of knights and castles passed before me."

"A State which bore this kind of fruit, and suffered it to drop off as fast as it ripened, would prepare the way for a still more perfect and glorious State. . . ."

Although the last metaphor is at least benign, if not positive, the majority are pejorative. Even in comparing government to machinery, seemingly an innocent enough act and certainly an understandable turn of phrase made as it was within the period of the Industrial Revolution, Thoreau's use is probably meant to be negative. In his conclusion that the State must recognize the greater right of the citizen and must respect as neighbors those individuals who choose to live aloof from it, Thoreau's conception of ideal State is organic, not mechanical. Earlier in the essay it is completely clear that Thoreau's reference to man's servitude to the State as machinery is meant to condemn such actions, and the later reference to the State probably carries this same connotation.

5. Near the beginning of his essay, Thoreau says, "That government is best which governs not at all" (par. 1). Then he mounts a withering assault on the United States federal government, accusing it of becoming a standing government against Mexico, asserting that the government has never furthered any enterprise, does not keep the nation free, does not educate, and so on. Finally, however, he states, "I ask for, not at once no government, but at once a better government" (par. 3). Most people would agree with the final statement. Do you think that most would also agree that the government which governs not at all is best? Explain.

Most people, other than members of the Libertarian Party, would, of course, disagree with the first statement. In addition, most people reading "Civil Disobedience" at the time of its initial publication would disagree with all other statements listed above except, perhaps, for the last. Importantly, Thoreau has a major qualification to his pronouncement that the best government is one which does not govern and that is "when men are prepared for it. . . ." An excellent question is the reason for this change in the essay, from a battery of provocative declarations to a statement whose reasonableness would win the agreement of most readers. Is this a deliberate rhetorical tactic on Thoreau's part in order partially to win over the reader? After the list of grievances, the reader, having been put on the defensive, must be relieved to discover a point to agree with.

6. Characterize Thoreau's tone. Is he calm and reasonable, or strident and impatient? Which of the following are most like "Civil Disobedience" in tone: "Hackers in Jail," "Profits Vs. Injury," "A Game of Chicken," "The Natural and the Supernatural," or "Ethics and Animals"? If you were to write your own version of "Civil Disobedience," would you change the tone? In what way or ways?

"Civil Disobedience" might well be closest to "Hackers in Jail" in its tone, which is strident and unyielding. The primary characteristic of the other selections is that although they all convey a definite opinion about the subject being discussed, they provide a well-reasoned, temperate discussion.

7. "Civil Disobedience" influenced Mahatma Gandhi and Martin Luther King, Jr., as well as other international figures. Explain why, in your opinion, it has had such an impact. (It will be useful to think in terms of agent, scene, and purpose.)

This question should encourage students to use standard reference sources, such as encyclopedias and dictionaries of biography.

8. Would Thoreau agree with the adage that "if you are not a part of the solution, then you must be part of the problem"? Explain.

Such passages as the following answer the question: "But, to speak practically and as a citizen, unlike those who call themselves no-government men, I ask for, not at once no government, but _at once_ a better government. Let every man make known what kind of government would command his respect, and that will be one step toward obtaining it" (par. 4).

9. In Thoreau's view, what is the moral authority by which a democracy exists? What moral authority should a state abide by?

"Can there not be a government in which majorities do not virtually decide right and wrong, but conscience?--in which majorities decide only those questions to which the rule of expediency is applicable? Must the citizen ever for a moment, or in the least degree, resign his conscience to the legislator? Why has every man a conscience, then? I think that we should be men first, and subjects afterward. It is not desirable to cultivate a respect for the law, so much as for the right. The only obligation which I have a right to assume, is to do at any time what I think right. It is truly enough said, that a corporation has no conscience; but a corporation of conscientious men is a corporation with a conscience" (par. 4).

10. Evaluate the essay from the standpoint of quantity. Could Thoreau have deleted parts? If so, which ones?

11. What circumstances of scene generated the purpose for the argument?

Thoreau was against the Mexican War (1846-48), and he opposed slavery. He was deeply troubled by the literal and figurative mechanization of the Industrial Revolution, which was just beginning. (Refer to the metaphors in Question 4.)

12. State the gist of the argument. Explain why you think it either does or does not concern civil disobedience.

The essay is Emersonian in its concern for individual responsibility and freedom. Civil disobedience is one aspect of these themes.

13. In regard to relation, evaluate Thoreau's account of his night in prison. Is the narrative relevant to his argument?

14. According to Thoreau, two specific problems undercut the authority of the government. What are these problems? Do you agree with Thoreau's conclusions about these problems? (What source would you consult to find background on the problems?)

"Action from principle,--the perception and the performance of right,--changes things and relations; it is essentially revolutionary, and does not consist wholly with any thing which was" (par. 15).

Withdrawing support from the government; refusing to pay taxes. See, for example, paragraphs 17 and 20.

Page 567

"The Loneliness of the Military Historian"
Margaret Atwood

1. The narrator states that "it's no use asking me for a final statement." Why does she write this? Do you believe that the poem itself has a final statement--that is, a claim--to make? If so, what is it? If not, explain why not.

Santayana wrote, "Those who are ignorant of history are condemned to repeat it." One of history's great claims as a discipline is that we can learn from the past. The narrator in Atwood's poem, however, begs off on any request for a summary statement because "for every year of peace there have been four hundred years of war." That is, no one has learned from the past, and it is implied that we will continue to wage war in the future. This could be construed to be the narrator's claim, although it is merely implied and not stated.

2. Atwood cites a statistic: "for every year of peace there have been four hundred years of war." Do you believe this statistic to be true or false? Does the author intend it to be taken literally? Why, or why not? What backing or qualification do you think Atwood would present to reinforce her argument?

The statistic has a rhetorical purpose. However, it would not be surprising to find that this statistic is close to the truth, and certainly Atwood doesn't intend the statistic to be hyperbole. To be taken literally, the statistic would need several important qualifications. At the least, the argument would have to be limited to the period of recorded history. Secondly, the statistic would have to be qualified: for every year that there has not been a war recorded anywhere in the world there are four hundred years in which there has been a war recorded somewhere. That is, it would have to qualify peace as existing everywhere and war as existing somewhere but not everywhere.

3. What do you think that the poem is meant to persuade the reader to believe in or take action with? Do you think that it is effective in its purpose? Why, or why not?

Atwood wishes to persuade the reader that war is not a glorious pursuit which rewards those who are noble or brave. The poem successfully makes such a point by discussing wars in dispassionate terms.

4. The narrator states that "women should not contemplate war," yet that is her very profession. Does the narrator see this as a contradiction? Why, or why not? (Remember, the "speaker" in the poem is a fictional character, not Margaret Atwood.)

There isn't a contradiction between the narrator's profession and her agreement that women should not contemplate war. The narrator looks to women in times of war as the source of emotional appeals (marching for peace, inspiring bravery, moral cheerleading). She believes that these functions are of value and does not disparage them, but sees a higher truth in war, arrived at dispassionately: war itself does not generally have a purpose. As the narrator admits, "Wars happen because the ones who start them think they can win."

5.   This poem has many examples of wild, graphic scenes of horror counterbalanced by a dispassionate analysis or staid imagery.   Give several examples of this. Why do you think the author uses this technique?

The juxtapositions in the poem include: dresses of sensible cut/a prophetess's mane; Vikings out for a few months of killing and Arabs with their sharp scimitars/the lack of monsters despite the propaganda; men who burst like paper bags of guts/the lack of potatoes as the reason for defeat; battlefields liquid with pulped men's bodies/grassy nests where nothing hatches. The author first describes a commonly held vision of war and then contradicts such a viewpoint with the professional air of a military historian.

6. Do you think that the military historian is avoided because of the subject of her profession or her attitude toward it? Explain.

Part of the repugnance people display toward this military historian probably has to do with the fact that she is female. The historian herself admits that, in general, "women should not contemplate war." Her profession runs contrary to the image that most people believe females should conform to. In addition, military historians are expected to speak passionately of the bravery or cowardliness of the men involved in battle and to elevate the stature of killing to that of patriotic duty. The narrator, however, refuses to speak of the glories of war. As a result, she is an unwelcome reminder that the pursuit of war is not something which anyone should be proud of.

7. The tone of the poem is dispassionate. Does this tone contradict or agree with the intention of the piece?

The tone of the poem is consistent with the intent of the author. The author includes scenes of graphic horror but seems resigned to the fact that such horrors, which have become part of our lives (four hundred years of war for every year of peace), can no longer shock people. The intention is to persuade through cool reasoning, which is the tone established by the narrator.

8. Do you feel that it would be more productive to view the poem as a narrative or as exposition? Do you base your answer on the fact that the text is a poem, on the subject matter, or on some other factor? Explain.

Page 571

"The Declaration of Independence"

1. The following is a list of some of the background knowledge that a reader needs for a full understanding of the Declaration of Independence:
   a. the philosophy of John Locke
   b. the concept of Laws of Nature, as it was held in the eighteenth century
   c. the Divine Right of Kings
   d. the Continental Congress
   e. the biography and philosophy of Thomas Jefferson
In how many of these areas of knowledge are you proficient? What sources would you consult to learn about those with which you are insufficiently familiar?

A general encyclopedia--such as the Americana--would provide sufficient background information.

2. Can the Declaration of Independence mean exactly the same to you as it did to a contemporary of Jefferson attending the Continental Congress? Explain.

This question should take students back to the first chapter of The Critical Reader, Thinker, and Writer. Is the reader like a miner, digging buried meaning out, or like a detective, (re)constructing meaning? (The miner and detective analogies, like all analogies, will take one only so far.)
The question invites (lures) one to raise the questions of (in)determinate meaning and deconstruction.

3. In what sense might it be said that the Declaration of Independence is a holy document, like the Bible and the Koran?

Americans venerate the document, investing it with almost religious value. They take elaborate measures to preserve the original draft, in the Smithsonian. Latter Day Saints believe that the document was inspired by God.

4. What are the consequences for the argument in the Declaration if we deny the self-evident truths? Is it, for instance, a self-evident truth that all men are created equal? Explain.

If we deny the self-evidence of the premises, the argument crumbles. All arguments must begin on the basis of agreement. For example, if Smith supports socialized medicine and Jones is unalterably opposed, no argument can proceed from Smith's premise that socialized medicine is essential to the well-being of the nation.

However, an argument can develop from the following premise: <u>Health care in the United States must be improved</u>.

5. What is a declaration? How does a declaration differ from a statement and an appeal?   (What source would you consult for information regarding this question?)

A declaration is what language philosophers would call a "declaration" or a "performative sentence"--a speech act in which the saying is the doing. For example, when a judge (in the right context) says, "I hereby sentence you to thirty days in county jail," the saying is the doing. Pronouncing the sentence is imposing the sentence. "I hereby christen this ship the Bottoms Up." "I (hereby) promise I'll be on time." "I (hereby) vow my allegiance to the cause." But notice that in the following, the saying is not the doing: "I (hereby) walk down the street." "I (hereby) believe that Fred is telling the truth." "I (hereby) am as hungry as a wolf."

To find information about the question, students would need some ingenuity. First, they might check a general encyclopedia under <u>language</u>, and they might, further, look in the card catalog, where they would undoubtedly find the subcategory <u>speech acts</u> under <u>language</u>.

6. In regard to the previous question, which of the following statements seems strange to you?
   a. I hereby declare that I am free.
   b. I hereby hope that I am free.
   c. I hereby vow that I am free.
   d. I hereby guess that I am free.
Explain this strangeness.

See the answer to the previous question. Hoping and guessing are not declarations. Remove the <u>hereby</u>, and the sentences are not anomalous: I hope that I am free; I guess that I am free.

Page 575

"To His Coy Mistress"
Andrew Marvell

1. Point out the gaps in the logic of this argument.

<u>Claim</u>: "[Life is very short, so] Now let us sport us while we may. . . ."

<u>Backing</u>: "[A]t my back I always hear / Time's winged chariot hurrying near. . . ."

<u>Evidence</u>:   [Y]onder all before us lie
                  Deserts of vast eternity
                  Thy beauty shall no more be found,
                  Nor in thy marble vault shall sound

> My echoing song; then worms shall try
> That long preserved virginity,
> And your quaint honor turn to dust,
> And into ashes all my lust.
> The grave's a fine and private place,
> But none, I think, do there embrace.

Gaps: Love and desire are influenced by beauty and youthful vigor. Time adversely affects beauty and youthful vigor.

2. In what way or ways is the argument unfair?

Marvell defines beauty and attraction as a variable of time, which isn't necessarily the case. He also places high value on the achievement of desire, which is not necessarily shared by his mistress. Therefore, the argument is set in terms to which both parties do not necessarily agree. From another angle, the speaker in the poem views his mistress as an agency, an object to be manipulated and used, not as an agent.

3. If the arguer expects his coy mistress to "fall for" the argument, what must his opinion of her be?

The arguer apparently has little respect for the intelligence of the woman. One can visualize her becoming more and more wide-eyed as he tells her about the grave and how the worms crawl in, the worms crawl out, the worms crawl over your nose and snout.

4. Is the argument comic or serious? Or in tone is it a mixture of the comic and the serious? Explain.

Marvell's gently mocking humor comes through in the couplet, "The grave's a fine and private place, / But none, I think, do there embrace." The hyperbole expressed in Marvell's allotments of time in which to praise the various aspects of the mistress is also tinged with humor. However, the reader is in no doubt that the narrator's basic premise, to "sport us while we may," is to be taken seriously. The tone of the poem perfectly expresses an amoral young man's playful but earnest beseechings to his mistress. (In the last half of the twentieth century, the poem is an archetypical expression of sexism.)

5. Would it be valid to say that this is a bad poem because it is based on fallacious logic and unfair argument? Explain.

The poem's power comes not only, perhaps not even primarily, from the strength of the argument expressed but from the manner in which it is expressed. Does its language sound pleasing to the ear? Does the language successfully express the sentiments of the narrator? Does the language elevate an idea, a sentiment, an emotion? Because the poem's purpose is not to present an argument but rather to portray a lover's ruses, fallacious or unfair argumentation is part of the author's intention. Without the specious logic, the poem would lose its tone and humor.

6. Is the poem, like "A Modest Proposal," ironic? Explain.

The poem can be taken as irony, in which case, it becomes Marvell's criticism of the sexual ethos of his time.

7. Assess the poem on the basis of the writer-reader contract (quality, quantity, manner, relation).

8. Interpret the poem from the standpoint of the _agent_ (the speaker in the poem). What do we learn about the agent when we consider the _act_ itself (the argument), the _purpose_ of the act, and the _agency_ (the poem in which the argument is embodied)?

Index to the Readings by Author